Sound Design
for the Stage

Sound Design
for the Stage

Gareth Fry

THE CROWOOD PRESS

First published in 2019 by
The Crowood Press Ltd
Ramsbury, Marlborough
Wiltshire SN8 2HR

www.crowood.com

British Library Cataloguing-in-Publication Data
A catalogue record for this book is available from the British Library.

ISBN 978 1 78500 553 4

Photograph previous page: a Shure SM58 vocal microphone – a simple, robust design icon.

Typeset and designed by D & N Publishing, Baydon, Wiltshire

Printed and bound in India by Parksons Graphics

CONTENTS

DEDICATION AND ACKNOWLEDGEMENTS

This book is dedicated to my amazing family: Laura, Phoebe and Lewis.

There are many people who taught me, or from whom I learnt, as I found my way into this career. I can't hope to name all of them, but Tom Vinelott, Simon Whitehorn, Ross Brown, Peter Barnett, Paul Groothuis and Chris Shutt all deserve my thanks.

Thanks to Max Pappenheim, Harry Johnson and Pete Malkin for reading this over and pointing out my mistakes. And thanks to Crowood for their patience!

All product names, trademarks and registered trademarks are the property of their respective owners. All company, product and service names used in this book are for identification purposes only. Use of these names, trademarks and brands does not imply endorsement.

Figure 53® and QLab® are registered trademarks of Figure 53, LLC. Gareth Fry is not affiliated with Figure 53, LLC, and this text has not been reviewed nor has it been approved by Figure 53, LLC.

All photos are by Gareth Fry, except where credited, or are product photos courtesy of the manufacturers.

INTRODUCTION

Many of the books I've bought with similarly vague titles such as *Sound Design for the Stage* are sat, mostly unread, on my bookshelf. They tend to focus on the physics of loudspeakers and microphones, on recording sound effects, and how to mark up a script. But they rarely discuss how the industry works, how to get work, how to discuss ideas with a director, or how you might generate the concept for your sound design in the first place.

This book places emphasis on the practical process of creating the sound design for a show, in close collaboration with the director, writer and performers. We will discuss aspects of acoustics, vocal intelligibility and sound systems along the way, but we will focus more on the psychological and artistic effects of the decisions we might make.

Theatre happens at many different scales. I started off in pub fringe venues with just a cassette player and two knackered HiFi speakers. Since then I've worked on pretty much every scale of show, up to Broadway and the Olympic Games. The level of resources may differ radically, but the thought processes are often very similar, because we are still telling a story. The story can be a narrative story or it can be a musical story. It can be told with words or it can be told with movement. It may not be linear and it may not be discernible to the audience, but it's rare that we put a bunch of random things on stage in a random order. We use technology to tell these stories – but let's think about technology as our paintbrushes, and focus more on what we might want to paint.

I'm also going to talk about when things went wrong, or didn't go to plan, and how I gracefully got myself out of trouble – or, in some cases, didn't.

I am writing this book with the emergent sound designer or director in mind. Perhaps you are a student, or a graduate, or have come straight into theatre by some other route.

A lot of the information that follows is going to be my personal opinion, my ethos, and my own particular experiences, rather than objective facts. Your version of 'good' sound design is probably different to mine, so feel free to disagree with me entirely and find your own way.

Let's start by looking at how the industry works, how a creative team is assembled, what is expected of a sound designer, and how they get work.

1

HOW TO BECOME
A SOUND DESIGNER

WHAT IS A SOUND DESIGNER?

The job title 'sound designer' means different things in different industries. In theatre it is an all-encompassing role, which essentially means you are responsible for all audible aspects of a production. That is, of course, incredibly vague, and deliberately so, because what those 'aspects' are varies massively from show to show, depending on the story you're telling (if there is one), the venue, the budget available, and a huge number of other factors.

It can involve sound effects recording, music production, sound system design, live music reinforcement and amplification, vocal reinforcement and amplification, room acoustics, creating multi-channel sound effects and soundscapes, amongst other things. Each of these is a huge topics in itself, so we'll touch on them briefly and pragmatically, so we don't get weighed down by an excess of information.

On some shows you may do only a couple of those elements, on others you may be involved in all of them. Of course, no one is an expert in all those fields. Many of us have specialisms in certain aspects, and we often work with others to bolster any skills gaps we might have. Sound design involves working in a creative team, with directors, writers, designers, performers and musicians, collaborating together to make something hopefully awesome!

One of the lovely aspects about theatre sound design is that often we have complete control of the end-to-end process. That is to say, we control the recording process, the mixing process, the sound system it is played back over, and the venue it is played back in. This is in contrast to, for example, sound design for cinema, where you have control over the recording and mix of the sound design, but you have no control on how good the cinema sound system is, or indeed whether an audience member will hear it in a cinema or through a tiny speaker on their mobile phone.

Theatre is reasonably unique in giving us this end-to-end control, which opens up a lot of creative possibilities. For example, we can, if we want, put lots of sub-bass speakers underneath the audience's seating. Or we can pan sounds around hundreds of different speakers in the auditorium. The limits tend to come from the architecture, the budget or our imagination!

THE SOUND DESIGNER'S PATH TO EMPLOYMENT

It is difficult to look at becoming a sound designer in terms similar to traditional careers, which may offer formal career paths with structured opportunities for professional development and advancement, and regular hours.

Like many careers in the arts, and increasingly in many industries, there isn't an official path into it or through it. Everyone is making it up as they go along, and basically it's up to you. This can be either terrifying or liberating, depending on your perspective. This lack of structure makes many 'arts' jobs feel like an insecure choice of career, but many people make a living doing good, interesting work. Like many freelance careers, the early years trying to get a footing can be challenging.

Sound design jobs are very rarely advertised, and this is down to two factors: how sound designers are employed, and how the creative team for a show is assembled. The 'creative team' typically refers to the director, the set, costume, lighting, sound and video designers, the composer, the movement director and suchlike. Each person is typically the creative lead for their department, with the director at the top.

For a good part of the twentieth century the sound design for a show was done by a combination of the director, stage manager and a member of the electrics (lighting) department – there simply weren't sound engineers working in theatre, or anywhere else for that matter. As technology advanced, expectations rose, and the role grew more complex, and so sound departments started to appear. The sound design was created by a member of the sound department, alongside their other duties.

This was quite typical until the mid-1990s: by then, directors increasingly wanted to work with specific sound designers rather than whoever was available in the venue. Many sound designers responded to this by going freelance, and so in-house designers are much less common in the UK and USA now than they used to be. If you are interested in a more complete history, David Collison's *The Sound of Theatre* is a great resource.

While in the UK most full-time sound designers are freelance, there are also those who work for a venue and may perform a range of duties as well as sound design. Many people like the variety of different job roles that working in-house brings, and obviously a guaranteed regular wage can suit some people's personal circumstances more than the variable income typical of freelance employment. In the Appendix you can read an interview with the Royal Court's Head of Sound, David McSeveney, talking about why he enjoys working this way, amongst other topics. When an in-house person designs a show for their venue they will often, though not always, be paid an extra fee, and someone may be brought in to cover their normal duties if they are not able to do both.

Some other sound designers work for companies, most often sound equipment hire companies, who might offer a complete package: all the sound equipment and all the staff necessary for a show, including the sound designer. These companies may also do dry hire, where they just supply the equipment without staff.

The designer benefits from a guaranteed income, and will be able to specify and budget for equipment from a stock they are very familiar with, plus have the full support of that companies infrastructure at their disposal. You can read an interview in the Appendix with Ian Dickinson, who talks about the benefits of working for Autograph Sound, a UK based company.

Also featured in the Appendix are interviews with Melanie Wilson, a freelance sound designer and composer, and Gareth Owen, who runs his own company, Gareth Owen Sound Ltd, talking about what works and their own experiences of sound design.

The USA is similar to the UK in terms of how sound designers are employed. In Europe, larger arts subsidies means there are more subsidized producing houses, many of which perform shows in repertoire (where two or three different shows might perform in the same theatre space each week). This means that the technical rehearsals for a show are typically much longer because they only happen in the mornings and early afternoons around the performance schedule. The longer duration of creating work is less compatible with a freelance existence, so in-house designers are still common.

ASSEMBLING A CREATIVE TEAM

The way creative teams are assembled is a big factor in why it can be difficult to get work as a sound designer. To explain this, it is necessary to explain briefly how a typical show might be produced.

Typically, an artistic director or a producer (the two people who choose what a theatre or theatre company will perform) will have an idea of a show that they want to put on in a certain slot in their calendar. Maybe that will be a specific play or a piece they have in mind, or an author they have commissioned. Perhaps there is a particular theme they want to explore, or a certain director or choreographer whom they want to come and make a show of their own choosing, or an actor whom they want to star in a show. Maybe they aim to programme a certain number of different types of show in each season.

They might then look for a director to develop and direct that show (though sometimes a director will come to a producer with a play they want to direct). In the dance world, it may be the choreographer who is the creative lead on the project, and it is likely they will do many of the things I shall discuss when referring to the director, going forward from here.

The director will often then develop a concept for that show. They may have creative team members with whom they work regularly, and with whom they want to work again. Or they may have someone new whose work they've seen or heard, with whom they'd like to work. Failing that, the producer or venue may have a list of creative team members they've worked with before to recommend to the director. Once the director and producer have identified the individuals they'd like to have on the creative team, those designers are contacted by the producer's staff to see if they are free to work on the show: this is known as the availability checking period.

An availability check may happen long in advance of a show starting rehearsals – for example, an opera availability check might be anywhere between a year to three years before it is due to open. Plays typically are not scheduled as far in advance, so 'AV' checks may happen six to nine months before rehearsals begin, though it's not unusual to get an enquiry just before rehearsals begin. The latter can often happen when the director is closer to the start of the project and identifies more specific needs that perhaps hadn't been apparent in the planning stages – for instance, they hadn't been planning to employ a sound designer but now they need one! However,

the latter scenario is increasingly rare as sound designers are becoming a standard part of the creative team.

Some theatres and producers run planning – or 'parameters' – meetings far in advance of rehearsals beginning, to ascertain what resources, scheduling and budget a show will need. All these timelines can be affected by how the project is funded, and how much or little time there is between funding being confirmed and rehearsals beginning.

An availability check usually comes in the following form: 'We are planning a show, it will begin rehearsals on … Fit-up will start on … First preview is on … Press night is on …'. Sometimes they may tell you the name of the show, the writer and the director, sometimes not, depending on whether the show has been announced to the public. Availability checks often contain confidential information that isn't in the public domain, so it is important to keep them confidential.

Sound designers typically work with many different directors, so it's not uncommon for the director's first choice to be unavailable, in which case the producers then move on to AV checking another candidate. This is another reason why you might get an availability check close to rehearsals beginning – they've spent time going through other candidates before getting to you.

Once a designer has been identified as available, more details of the project will be revealed, and a fee can be negotiated. Some venues may have 'fixed' fees, particularly subsidized ones. Some designers may not be able to make the project work for the fee offered, and so the producer will move on again in their search.

This process may vary if the venue concerned has an in-house designer, or if the producer is looking to work with a complete service company. But you will have deduced the following from the above:

- Directors often have sound designers they work with regularly, and bring with them from show to show
- Directors often have people in mind with whom they'd like to try working, based on other work

they've been to see, or designers they've heard about

- Producers often maintain lists of designers to suggest to directors. These may be designers they've worked with before, or well-known designers. Equally, they may well have a 'black list' of people they've had bad experiences with in the past. Black lists are illegal so may not actually exist on paper, but certainly if a producer has had a bad experience with someone previously, they'll wish to dissuade a director from working with them (without blocking them outright)

Whilst there is much common sense in this method of employing a creative team, it does make the industry difficult to access when you are starting out. It is the typical Catch 22 of employment: you need experience to get work, but you need to get work to gain experience. This is one of the reasons why the industry is not as diverse in terms of gender, class or ethnic background as it should be. The UK theatre industry is predominantly inhabited by white male middle-class people, and so white male middle-class people find it easier to access the industry. This is something that must change, which we'll discuss later.

In the UK there is a large theatre industry, both in London and across the country. This vibrancy means there are often plenty of jobs to go round, at a variety of pay scales. Producers and directors are often looking for new people to work with, just because they want someone new to work with, or because the usual candidates aren't available, or won't/can't work for the available money. This means that opportunities do open up for those emerging into the industry.

THE SOUND DESIGNER'S BACKGROUND

As I consider the current crop of sound designers, I see a range of people who have come into the industry by a variety of paths:

- Some have trained at drama school, or attended specialist sound courses
- Some have been doing theatre sound for youth groups or amateur dramatic societies since their youth and have moved into professional sound (and to be clear here, I generally define 'professional' as meaning that you are earning part of your living from doing it, rather than doing it as a hobby)
- Some have worked in various roles in the theatre sound industry
- Some have moved across from other sound industries, either being trained in, or working in, studio recording, live sound (bands, concerts, church sound), film sound, radio, and so on
- Some have come in from a music background, starting out as a composer or musician, and then gained more interest in the sound world beyond that

Some people have started off with a degree, but many have started out with little or no training and have learned everything on the job. Many prefer to play with the technology and see what it can do. Some people even read the manuals. All of these paths are equally valid.

Beyond their backgrounds, some designers have then specialized in certain types of work. Those specialisms might be certain types of musicals, plays, dance, opera, devised work, site-specific work, and so on. This diversity of backgrounds and specialisms means that individual designers are often sought out for specific projects – it is what makes them stand out from the crowd. Of course, what makes you more employable in one sector can make you less employable in another, and designers can become 'typecast', based on their body of work.

WHAT DO EMPLOYERS LOOK FOR IN A SOUND DESIGNER?

It's important to know what your potential employers want from you, namely the director, and the producer and the production manager.

The Director

For the director you occupy two roles, one as the sound designer, and one as a creative team member. It's easy to concentrate on the former (covered in detail later) and forget about the latter, so we'll consider that now.

You are there to be on the director's side, to bounce ideas around – not just sound, but more generally, whether this or that scene is working, or not, and why. You have a responsibility to support them creating the show, and to do this you have to look at the show from the director's point of view.

To do this you have to build up a line of communication with them, to be able to discuss the show dramatically, artistically and, of course, sonically. You need to develop your taste, your opinion, of what is 'good' and what is 'bad' because you will be asked for your opinion, or there will be times when it will be useful to express it and justify it. What for you is 'good acting'? Everyone has different notions of what is good and bad, and for you to be a useful team member you should work to develop your taste, and question why you like or connect to something. You can do this by visiting plenty of shows, films, exhibitions, and so on. Go with a friend who likes different things, so you can reflect, discuss and argue about it – being able to strongly and reasonably justify your subjective response, whilst acceding that other strong subjective responses are also valid, will become very useful.

Your taste and opinions will evolve the more you watch and listen. Why does one thing work and not another? What is the crucial missing ingredient(s) in a failure? It's useful to analyse what you would like to have been better, and if there was a route, to do it better. But equally it's important to be sympathetic that only so much can be achieved by a team in the time and circumstances available, and with the money, and resources, available for the creation of any piece of work. Can you spot where compromises were made, and why?

Watch some shows that you wouldn't normally go to watch, things you think you'll dislike. What can you take away from them? There is virtually nothing you can't watch without learning some aspect of storytelling, right or wrong. Once you have a notion of what makes a piece of work good or bad, then you can start to talk about whether the sound design is good or bad. There are times when a sound design can be objectively bad outside the context of the aesthetic of a show – bad feedback or an inability to hear any dialogue are usually strong indicators. Does 'good' equate to 'appropriate'?

Keep in mind that what *you* think is good is an entirely subjective opinion. What *you* consider bad, someone else may think is brilliant. Life would be very boring if we all liked the same things.

By watching and listening to a great deal of work you are also building up a set of reference points that you can utilize so as to find ways to talk to a director, to find common ground to talk about the piece, and about sound – for example: 'We could do a similar thing to…'. You need to be able to reference other work as a means to describe what you want to achieve.

It's also important to understand the different ways that directors direct shows. Directors have different styles, both in the process they employ and the style of work they direct. Some directors specialize (or have become typecast) in certain types of work. Watch different directors' shows to seek to understand what they are trying to achieve and the techniques they use to achieve that. Find a director whose work you like, and see all their shows. Watch how they adjust their style to match the piece, and how their style evolves across different works. Watch different productions of the same script to understand how much the creative team brings to a production.

You can only ever create a 'good' sound design for the director if you understand what they are trying to achieve.

The Producer and Production Manager

The producer also has a number of things that he needs from you, but these tend to be more pragmatic. Producers often employ a production manager to co-ordinate the various aspects of a production, notably the schedule and the budget. They need you to do the following:

- To deliver, as far as is reasonably possible, what the director is asking of you, but within the allocated budget, timeframe and the confines of the venue. They may eventually want you to create a touring version of it, too
- To plan the sound system, so it can be budgeted for and costed up, and the installation of it can be co-ordinated with other departments (for example, where the set manufacturer needs to build holes in the set for speakers)
- To assemble, or assist with assembling a team, who are going to keep the show running and deal with any minor technical issues that may arise. To ensure that those people are good members of the company, who can co-operate and collaborate
- To create a sound design that delivers consistently good sound to all sections of the auditorium. Producers don't like having to refund patrons who couldn't hear properly
- To deliver a system that is reliable, that will not break down in such a way as to cause the show to stop, or worse still, be cancelled. A backup show computer may be expensive, but not as much as refunding 800 tickets when the only computer breaks down

Whilst most of the above will be achieved in co-ordination with the production manager, generally we will liaise with the producers to clear the copyright of any music or other copyrighted sounds. Producers tend to handle clearances because these often involve financial and contractual negotiations with the artists or their publishers, and discussions about box office revenue. I will often provide information about the context in which the material is being used, and for how long.

MAKING OURSELVES A POTENTIAL CANDIDATE

In the following section we'll discuss making contact with people, but nowadays the second you make contact with someone they are going to google you, and search for you across social media. And what they find there will probably determine whether they decide to reply to you, or not. You'll be judged on your online presence first, long before you get to meet anyone in person.

It is therefore essential to turn your web and social media presence into a reflection of your business as a sound designer – and to hide away your personal life. Start by making all your social media accounts as private as possible. Delete any posts that could be construed badly by a potential employer or collaborator, whether public or private. Google '(Your name), sound design', as that's what they'll likely search for: is it useful, constructive, positive? And if it isn't, what can you do about it?

If you don't have a website, now is a good time to make one. There are many good, free offerings that don't require programming skills. The point of your website is to provide a point of contact for you when people google you – they can't offer you work if they can't contact you. Beyond that, it's there to encourage them to choose you above someone else, by providing positive information about you and your skills, your background, or any other pertinent information. What are the things that make you stand out, that are unique to you?

Avoid it sounding like a CV with unhelpful personal statements such as 'I'm highly motivated', and whether or not you can use Microsoft Office. And it's better to have no information than to list your school holiday job. Normal Job Centre-type CV tips do not apply here! If it's not directly supporting your cause, don't put it on there. Register a domain name with a company such as 1&1: this will get you a web address such as www.jobloggs. com and an associated email address. Avoid email addresses containing your year of birth.

Have a look at other designers' websites and see what works for you. It can be as simple as a nice big image, your name, phone number and email address, and the words 'Sound Design'. Put your contact details on every page of your website: visitors may have arrived via a search engine and won't necessarily go to the home page first. Avoid using those unattractive contact forms – and don't include a blog that you'll fail to keep up writing after three posts.

Focus your website on the work you're trying to get, but sell yourself in a way that is inclusive to all potential clients, as you are likely to end up doing all sorts of different work along the way to obtaining the work you want. You want to encourage them to contact you, too. If you have specialist skills, whether it be an encyclopaedic knowledge of Serialist music, a proclivity for recording high speed cars or a talent for synth programming, these can attract certain employers to you, so use them as a selling point. Once an employer has been persuaded to take you on because you have the special skills they need for a certain project, then hopefully you can further persuade them that your broader skill set will do for all their projects.

Sound design for theatre is frustratingly difficult to represent online – something that sounds great in a show sounds rubbish removed from the context of the performance. If it doesn't sound good alone, don't put it online. Most sound designers don't put much work online, preferring to let the list of shows and collaborators speak for their reputation. However, sounds that you've made for web trailers or to accompany video design often work well. Add a note that the audio will be best heard over headphones, rather than on an iPhone speaker.

Get a friend to check your website for spelling, mistakes and the tone. The people you want to read your website read scripts for a living – they'll notice your spelling and punctuation errors and judge you! Put a recurring alarm in your calendar to update your website every three months.

Social media can be a great way to advertise your day-to-day activities, which you mightn't put on your website. Careful use of who you connect with, comments, retweets, and so on, can help spread 'Brand You'. But beware the drunken tweet….

Many websites (LinkedIn, Mandy, the Association of Sound Designers) offer the opportunity to write a profile about yourself. However, rather than write something that will quickly be out of date, link to a biog on your website. Look through the profiles of members of the Association of Sound Designers to see how to write a biog.

What is your name? Are you Joe Bloggs or Joseph Bloggs, Jo or Joanne? If you have a name with variations, choose one and stick to it – be clear and consistent with 'Brand You'. If you have a name that is similar to someone out there doing theatre sound, then find a variation to use to distinguish *you*. Avoid nicknames. Your name is your brand, and it is you whom producers and directors will want to bring on to a creative team. Whilst we want to create a business-like look to convey a level of professionalism, a director is rarely going to say that they want JB Services Ltd to come in and design their show – our clients want to employ a specific person because of their specific skills, experience or attitude.

Business cards are worthwhile, though you may only give out one or two a month. They create a better impression than scribbling your email address on a scrap of paper, and can drive a visit to your website to find out more about you. Don't include too much information: your name, job description, phone number, email and website are plenty. Check out magazines such as *Creative Review* for inspiration on more interesting visual designs.

Being able to be found is essential for a freelancer. Register on LinkedIn, Mandy and with the Association of Sound Designers to expand your presence – though LinkedIn is not really used in the theatre world.

MAKING CONTACT

The first step to getting work is about getting someone to appreciate who you are. Person-to-person networking is very important: theatre is a people business. Finding opportunities to meet people isn't always easy, but fortunately most people in the industry are actually quite obliging. If you email them saying that you're an emerging sound designer and love their work/venue, most people will give you fifteen minutes over a cup of coffee to talk.

The work won't find you – you have to find the work, and getting your first job can be trickiest of all. But once you have one show on your CV everything becomes slightly easier.

Emailing someone out of the blue can be quite daunting. Don't think you have to write an essay, though – explain that you are an emerging sound designer, that you are looking for people to collaborate with, then talk briefly about your background, and talk passionately about your interest in their work (research their work). You are more likely to receive a reply to an email personalized to whom you're sending it to, showing that you are aware of their interests, and demonstrating your interests, than to a generic email. People respond to passion, so don't be afraid of stating your interests. The aim of your email is to ask if it would be possible to meet for a coffee, to have a chat.

Who should you be emailing? Rather than emailing the artistic director of the National Theatre (or whoever) and getting rejected, research the associate directors or the associate movement directors on the shows you like. They are probably directors in their own right, at an earlier stage of their career (that is, closer to your stage of your career), and we can assume they like the shows that *you* like, to a certain degree. Tracking down email addresses can sometimes be difficult if they don't have a website or an agent, but most theatre companies have administration offices, whose staff can pass on your email to the relevant person.

Research people working in fringe theatre (not to be confused with the Edinburgh Fringe), who are likely also to be emerging professionals in their own field. They are unlikely to be in a position to get you paid work, but if you can support yourself with a side job, the fringe offers valuable ways to gain experience designing shows, with less pressure to deliver what might be expected of an experienced professional.

Very importantly, whether face to face or online, no one likes someone who is being really pushy in trying to get them to meet them. Remember you are trying to encourage people to employ you, so don't irritate them with spam or scare them with cyber stalking.

An over-a-coffee meeting is an opportunity to demonstrate what a nice person you are, and your enthusiasm to work with them. Use it to ask them about their past work, their interests and passions. Invite them to see your work, if that's possible. Don't push them about any future projects they might have, but be clear that you would be interested in working with them in the future if they have any interesting projects coming up. That can then be their cue to talk about any interesting projects they might have – or not to talk about them, if they don't want to.

Depending on who you are meeting, you might be aiming to work with them in the future. However, if you feel that's unrealistic, perhaps ask if you might come and watch some rehearsals, or some tech rehearsals at some point, to see them at work. There may a discussion of process, of how you like to build up a show, and of how the director likes to work. 'What's your process for making a sound design?' is not an uncommon question from a director when meeting them for the first time. If you're not sure how to answer that question, read the rest of this book!

There are many other ways to get yourself noticed by people, such as attending or getting involved with organizing industry events, exploiting any contacts you may already have, posting your business card out to venues, being a presence on email forums.

Fringe theatres and companies are often looking for sound designers. We'll discuss the economics of fringe shortly, but these enterprises are worth getting in touch with, sending a business card to, and going to 'scratch' performances (which involve experimenting with a half-developed idea).

Scratch performances often involve feedback sessions, and are a very good way to meet the people behind each show, to meet potential collaborators.

Building a freelance career can take a while as you build contacts and design credits, working your way towards more lucrative work. It will take several years to build up to a point where you are able to live purely off sound design work. Having another income stream, theatre related or otherwise, is essential in the early days.

Many sound designers start off as sound operators, technicians, radio mic runners, assistants or associates. A paid position is financially useful whilst you build up your design career, and is a good opportunity to build contacts and get to know the equipment that is commonly used in the industry, as well as to observe other creative teams developing work. Indeed, not everyone wants to design full time, and many people enjoy moving between a variety of sound roles.

If a sound designer is unavailable for a project, they might be asked to recommend someone else, and they will tend to suggest people they know. This is why it is useful to get to know other sound designers, too. This can be via the can-we-go-for-a-coffee route (to see if there is any possibility of associating or assisting with a production, or of just coming along to it), or via industry events such as trade shows, or events organized by professional associations such as the Association of Sound Designers (ASD) or the Theatrical Sound Designers and Composers Association (TSDCA). These events are great for meeting people outside your normal circuit, and for getting your name known, which is often the first step to getting work of any kind via your peers.

Some operating and radio mic running jobs are advertised in trade newspapers and on online job boards. Increasingly these, and other temporary opportunities, are advertised more informally on theatre sound-specific social media. The Audio Cartel group on Facebook is often used by West End theatre sound departments to find new 'deps' – the deputy, an additional staff member who is needed occasionally to cover when sound department members are ill, on leave, or learning to cover each other's jobs, or as staff members move on to other shows. Getting on a show as a dep is a very good way to access the industry. Some jobs aren't advertised at all, as staff members may be approached directly by producers, production managers, sound designers or sound operators who want specific people on their team for their show.

Work placements (work experience) are also a useful way to access various parts of the industry. Employers often choose to employ someone they know in preference to someone they don't know when both have similar skills and experience. Work placements can help you become known.

ATTITUDE

I can't emphasize enough how important your attitude is as to whether you get work. There's no shortage of people with talent and abilities who can do what you can do – indeed, many people come into the industry without previous experience and make a success of it. What makes for success, what shines through everything else, is positivity, the ability to collaborate, the ability to see the world through other people's eyes, to make compromises and concessions, to work together.

We see plenty of examples of difficult and controversial characters succeeding in all walks of life, but it is a lonely path to tread. I've worked with quite a few 'difficult' people, and they are often bitter and lonely, and this often feeds into a destructive circle, ending with no one wanting to employ them. Avoid that path.

Also avoid using slang labels for people, such as 'techies', 'musos', 'turns' and so on. Be respectful and call people by their job titles. Techies rarely like being called 'techies': they are often a highly diverse bunch of people with individual specialist skills.

One of the hardest balancing acts for someone emerging into the industry is appearing confident

ASSOCIATES AND ASSISTANTS

I expect an associate sound designer to be a fairly capable person, who will work either directly with me, or will work in my place if I'm not there. They need to be diplomatic, and capable of talking with directors, producers and operators with a high level of proficiency. They will often have a specific role, such as making sound effects, or a particular task, such as looking after things in my absence, perhaps during some rehearsals or previews.

When a show is successful, it may transfer to another venue, or tour, which may be arranged at relatively short notice and may not fit in with the designer's pre-existing commitments, so it is fairly common for an associate to look after the re-mount, transfer or tour of a show in the designer's place.

An assistant usually holds a more junior, and less well paid, position. They might often be given less critical tasks to do for a show, such as updating paperwork or sourcing low priority sound effects. I wouldn't expect an assistant to fill in for me in my absence, or to deal with directors or producers.

Different sound designers have different skills, and work on different types of show, so they may well require different things of their assistants and associates.

Assistants are increasingly less common, certainly in the UK, and associates have become more common. This is a reflection of the increasing demands that are required of us when putting on a show, in that where an assistant might have sufficed in the past, it is now more likely that a person with the more advanced skills of an associate is needed.

Many associate sound designers are 'early career' sound designers. Being an associate gives you the chance to experience the sound design process (and what you might choose to do differently in the same position) at close quarters, a degree of artistic contribution to the show without the pressures and responsibilities of being the named designer, and offers the opportunity to meet corresponding associate directors, choreographers and so on, who might give you work on other projects.

I have a few people to whom I turn regularly to associate with me, as they know my aesthetic, process, workflow and work politics. I also use my associates for occasional 'spec' work – if I'm struggling to get everything done I may employ an associate for a day or two, rather than across the whole project, often to work on a specific aspect of something.

without being arrogant. Almost every job will be a leap into the unknown, taking on a job and saying 'Yes, I can do that', but not necessarily having done it before, or not knowing how to do it, or if you really can. It's important to take these leaps, because without them you will only ever do what you already know, and will not go anywhere else.

Risk is important. Risk will push your creativity. You can improve the odds of a safe landing through research, preparation, by not overselling speaking to people who've done that before and by asking their advice. Be confident in yourself that you can make it work by being prepared, by knowing when to ask for help, and knowing how to act if it goes wrong (we'll cover that later). Arrogance is thinking you can make the leap without preparing, by refusing help and by deflecting blame when things go wrong.

When those leaps occasionally go wrong it's important to pick yourself up, gather your confidence and carry on. Everyone suffers these setbacks, whether it is a technical or an artistic one. We'll cover dealing with disaster later on.

You'll need a sense of confidence as your career progresses, because you may work in increasingly large scales of theatre, or move into different genres and types of theatre. There will always be leaps into the unknown: that's half the fun of it.

My route into the industry took several years. After graduating I spent a few years working in an office, initially doing data entry. A friend pinned my business card on the notice board in the office of a Fringe theatre, which led to designing a number of tiny Fringe theatre shows for next to no money. These were often equipped with little more than a cassette player and some worn out HiFi speakers. Those shows didn't particularly lead anywhere, but gave me a huge amount of real-world design experience, collaborating with many people, and working fast, and they gave me some design credits.

One of my jobs was operating a play in the West End, which was useful for seeing a professional sound designer at work, and the pro-level equipment in use, and I was able to meet a few directors, associates, production managers and producers. I spent several more years operating shows, and gradually getting designs from the contacts I made on those shows. Eventually the ratio of time that I spent operating or engineering to the time I spent designing shifted to the point where I was designing full time.

I am always doing that which I cannot do, in order that I may learn how to do it.
Vincent Van Gogh

If you only do what you can do, you'll never be better than what you are.
Kung Fu Panda

I am writing ... design the sound for the our p...

Dates are as follows:

REHEARSAL, PRODUCTION AND P

- Rehearsals from:
- Technical rehearsals from:
- First preview:
- Press Night:
- Last performance:

NB Please note the productio... theatre archive but also for s... monitoring. It will not be use... and subject to the Sound De... good faith.

2
FIRST CONTACT

At some point you will be asked if you are available to design a show. On no account say 'yes' – at least not straightaway. Instead take down the details, say it sounds very interesting, but you don't have your diary to hand, and ask if you can get back to them. This gives you the opportunity to research the script, the producer, the venue, the director, what they've done before and their style of work, and whether you really are available to do the show with whatever commitments you already have. Do you know anyone who has worked with any of them? What do they think about the people involved, or know about the project?

In your research you may come across something that makes you think 'Oh, actually, no, I don't want to work on this!' or 'I can't work on this'. Then you can call them back and say, 'I'm so sorry, but the dates don't work for me'. Have a good excuse, one that means you're not available for the tech week. Make it clear that you'd love to work with them in the future, but it won't work on this occasion. Don't burn bridges. This is better than saying 'Yes' immediately, then having to back out the following day with a flimsy excuse because you've discovered a reason not to work on it. Aim to reply within forty-eight hours – don't keep them hanging on. You are much less likely to be availability checked again if you keep them waiting a week for a 'yes' or 'no' answer.

It's important to bear in mind that an availability check isn't an offer of work. The producer will often simultaneously 'AV' check a number of sound designers to offer the director a few to choose from. Don't be offended if an availability check that you respond positively to, doesn't lead to an actual job. This happens no matter how experienced you are – whilst I've been writing this book I've had three availability checks resulting in a 'The director has decided to go in another direction' email.

Sometimes the director will want to meet you before committing to employing you. This is often a sort of job interview, where they want to hear a little about how you work, how you respond to the text, and whether they think they'll like working with you. Sometimes they may have minor test questions for you, such as how you would go about achieving the so-and-so scene in their show.

NEGOTIATING A FEE

Occasionally a fee will be mentioned in the AV check, but more often that information won't be mentioned until they offer you the job.

Sound designers are typically offered a flat fee to cover their work. They are expected to be self-employed freelancers (though some set up a company to operate from). In the UK this means that income tax and National Insurance are not deducted at source, and you are required to pay your own taxes. In contrast, a production sound engineer may be paid per day (though a fee is not uncommon for long periods of employment), and a sound operator would most likely receive a weekly wage on a salaried basis.

You may be asked 'How much do you normally charge?' If they sound like a relatively young person it means they are probably fairly new to producing, truly don't know, but probably don't have a large budget at their disposal. In the UK there is little guidance for producers on what sound

MANAGING YOUR SCHEDULE

Most calendar programs do not allow you to plan your time in the level of detail that you need if you have overlapping projects. I use a spreadsheet that allows me to see the schedule of every project on any given day, and where I will be relative to those projects. I use this spreadsheet to keep track of my business (such as tax deadlines) and family commitments, and regular reminders such as updating my website.

			am	lunch	pm
Monday	25th	bank holiday			
Tuesday	26th		Young Vic 1st day reh's		
Wednesday	27th		Menier rehearsal		
Thursday	28th		Menier rehearsal		
Friday	29th		Menier rehearsal		
Saturday	30th		12noon Menier run thro		
Sunday	31st		day off		ASD social
Monday	1st September		Frantic 1st day reh's		fit-up
Tuesday	2nd		plotting		2pm - TECH STARTS
Wednesday	3rd		tech		Dress
Thursday	4th		tech		
Friday	5th		tech		
Saturday	6th				3.30pm preview
Sunday	7th				1530 preview
Monday	8th				
Tuesday	9th		Young Vic reh's		Young Vic reh's
Wednesday	10th		Young Vic reh's		4 - 6 workshop
Thursday	11th		AT HOME - admin		
Friday	12th		Young Vic reh's		Frantic reh's
Saturday	13th		day off		
Sunday	14th		day off		
Monday	15th		Young Vic reh's		Frantic reh's
Tuesday	16th		Young Vic reh's		Frantic reh's
Wednesday	17th		Young Vic reh's		Frantic reh's
Thursday	18th		Young Vic reh's		Frantic reh's
Friday	19th		Young Vic reh's		Frantic reh's
Saturday	20th				
Sunday	21st		day off		
Monday	22nd		Young Vic reh's		Frantic reh's
Tuesday	23rd		Young Vic reh's		Frantic reh's
Wednesday	24th		Young Vic reh's		Frantic reh's
Thursday	25th		Young Vic reh's		Frantic reh's
Friday	26th		Young Vic reh's		Frantic reh's
Saturday	27th		Young Vic reh's		Frantic reh's
Sunday	28th		day off		
Monday	29th		Hampstead 1st day reh's		
Tuesday	30th		to Plymouth		tech
Wednesday	1st October				tech
Thursday	2nd	David's birthday			tech
Friday	3rd				tech
Saturday	4th				tech
Sunday	5th		to London	day off	
Monday	6th	9.30 pickup			fit-up
Tuesday	7th				2pm tech
Wednesday	8th				2pm tech
Thursday	9th				2pm tech
Friday	10th				2pm tech
Saturday	11th				2pm tech
Sunday	12th				day off
Monday	13th		Hampstead reh's		2pm tech
Tuesday	14th		9am CDT course @ CSSD		2pm tech
Wednesday	15th		9am Abeton Live @ CSSD		2pm tech
Thursday	16th		Hampstead reh's		2pm tech

Spreadsheet of a sound designer's schedule and current projects. This is a particularly busy period, with four projects happening simultaneously.

designers should be paid, so to a degree, everyone is making it up as they go along.

You will soon notice that what you are offered has no bearing on the amount of work they want you to do, or the amount of time it will take to do it. Instead, the fee's amount will often reflect the audience capacity of a theatre. Why? Because, for many producers, the income they receive is related to the number of tickets they can sell. If there are only 100 seats in the theatre, then their

It is important to be realistic about what you can achieve, and not to book yourself up so much that you leave all your clients disappointed with your work. How many shows can you do, whilst giving them all the appropriate thought and planning they need? If you have to pay an associate to cover you whilst you deal with other commitments, at what point is it still profitable to do the show?

eve		Menier Chocolate Factory	Young Vic	Frantic / Hampstead	
		reh (London)	reh Jerwood 1		
		reh	reh		
		reh	reh		
		reh	reh		
		reh	reh		
			reh		
		fit-up	reh Jerwood 1	reh Jerwood	
		tech	reh	reh	
8pm preview		preview	reh	reh	
8pm preview		preview	reh	reh	
8pm preview		preview	reh	reh	
8pm preview		preview	reh		
8pm preview		preview			
			reh Jerwood 1	reh Jerwood	
8pm preview		preview	reh	reh	
7pm press		press	reh	reh	
			reh	reh	
			reh	reh	
			reh		
			reh Jerwood 1	reh Jerwood	
			reh	reh	
			reh	reh	
			reh	reh	
			reh	reh	
			reh		
			reh Jerwood 1	reh Plymouth	
			reh	reh	
			reh	reh	
			reh	reh	
			reh	reh	
			reh		
					Hampstead
Plymouth			reh Jerwood 1	tech	reh
tech			reh	tech	reh
tech			reh	tech	reh
tech			reh	tech	reh
preview			reh	tech	reh
			reh	preview	
			fit-up	preview	reh
			tech	preview	reh
preview			tech	press	reh
preview			tech		reh
			preview		reh
			preview		
preview			preview		reh
preview			preview		reh
preview			preview		reh
press			press		reh

maximum income is going to be tied to that, and hence the budget to make the show and to employ everyone is tied to that. That's not always the case, especially with venues that receive private funding or public subsidies.

Let's take a moment to examine some of the organizations you might work for. In the UK, we have the Arts Council, funded by government, which subsidizes a lot of arts venues and theatre companies. Most of our producing houses, whether a regional studio theatre or the National Theatre, receive most of their income from the Arts Council. Some may produce shows that will transfer into the West End or commercially tour the country. There are many theatre companies that primarily produce touring work, but whose administrative backbone is funded by the Arts Council.

There are also theatre companies that don't receive regular funding, but which apply for funding on a production-by-production basis. Many towns have a subsidized theatre or arts centre, which may produce its own work or have a mix of its own work and shows that tour in for a day or a week. We do also have many theatres that produce work without Arts Council funding, such as London's Old Vic, to the many commercial theatres nationwide. There are many producers and production companies that produce work, at many different scales, without subsidy.

In the USA there is the National Endowment for the Arts, but whereas the Arts Council will spend £622 million in 2018 in the UK, the NEA only has $150 million for the entire USA. Without equivalent subsidies, venues and theatre companies in the USA rely far more on ticket sales, and private donations or corporate sponsorship for their income. There is still a diverse theatre community nonetheless. There are producers making work for Broadway or touring the country. There are large and small theatre companies that create and tour work. There are producing houses and a wealth of regional venues, too. Universities often have well funded and well resourced theatre programmes with numerous small and large-scale venues.

All these organizations have different funding sources and different amounts to spend. Understanding something of the organization you are potentially working for is a critical part in the fee negotiation process.

You will often be negotiating a fee before anyone can know how much work a job will actually involve – that may only become apparent some weeks or months later. It takes experience to estimate how much time a particular show, with a particular director, working in a particular style, in a particular venue, will take. This is important to calculate, not just to negotiate this project, but also so you know how much time you have for any other projects or side-line jobs you have.

Different producers and venues all have different approaches and resources available that determine how long a show will rehearse for, how long the production week(s) will be, and the sound budget available. Typically, commercial shows may have relatively short rehearsal periods, but may have longer preview periods in the theatre. The budget for a commercial show may often be higher because an entire sound system may need to be hired in, whereas a subsidized house may have a small budget because they have a lot of in-house equipment.

Many shows in Europe rehearse using a schedule similar to a UK opera schedule, which might mean you have a short amount of time in the rehearsal room, followed by lots of rehearsals onstage, but only until about 4pm each day when the entire set will be pulled offstage, and that evening's set will be put on ready for one of the many shows in the repertoire to be performed that evening. As you can only work half a day each day, the process can take twice as long. If you are working in an outdoor venue, parts of the tech may happen overnight so that it is dark enough for the lighting to be visible, or there may be curfews in place that dictate when sound can, and cannot, be played.

How much should you be paid for your work? Should it be proportionate to the earning potential of the show? Or related to the amount of time you will spend creating it? Does it diminish the creativity of your work to reduce it to an hourly rate? How can we find a quantity to charge for the creativity, and our intellectual property, within our design? These are not easy questions to answer simply, and no one has come up with a good answer yet.

There are some guides out there on fees for set designers and lighting designers, which can be useful. In the UK, various organizations all publish documents, outlining minimum fees for a variety of design roles. These are often not reflective of what is actually paid, as they are designed to indicate the lowest possible wage someone might receive for the simplest show with the shortest time commitment. They are rarely useful other than to check that you aren't being paid below that minimum. In the USA, USA829 (the union branch that covers sound designers across the USA) have negotiated more realistic minimum wages with the League of Regional Theatres (LORT) and the Broadway League.

Whilst there are plenty of sound design jobs that pay well, getting those jobs often involves building up contacts and experience by working the jobs that don't pay so well. These may be in the smaller, less well funded venues. In my quick rundown of the UK and USA above – sorry, other countries, for not mentioning you! – I excluded a large and important sector: the fringe. Fringe theatres (not to be confused with the Edinburgh Fringe, which is a seasonal entity unto itself) are typically unsubsidized, and have low seating capacities, so often have little income. Some fringe theatres produce work themselves, and some are available to be dry-hired by external producers.

If you are working with a small-scale fringe producer, you may find that they are also in the early stages of their career. There are also well-established fringe theatres, such as The Gate in London, where seating capacities are marginally larger than the typical room-above-a-pub, and there is a small, full-time, paid staff running the venue, producing work, and paying better – though not awesome – fees.

There has been much debate about the fringe circuit in the UK recently, as many people work in small-scale fringe on a 'profit-share' basis, which is to say, they don't get paid unless the show makes a profit, and the majority of them don't make a profit, or enough of one to begin to recompense the time of all involved. If the venue only seats twenty people, and the tickets aren't expensive, that's not going to leave much over once you've paid for the venue hire, and basic production and marketing costs. People don't produce or work in fringe theatre for the money because usually there isn't any to be made.

People work on the fringe for a variety of reasons. For many it is the place they love to work because it has a range and diversity of work that doesn't find a foothold in mainstream theatre. For some it is the place where they can put on the show they've always wanted to put on, or can do something different from what they are known or typecast for. For some it is a place to break into the industry, where they can gain valuable show credits and get people to experience their work, whether as an actor or sound designer. Whilst I firmly believe that everyone should receive the minimum wage for their work, this model isn't viable in the majority of fringe theatres.

The fringe is one of the ways to get into the industry – it is the way I got into it. However, the economics of it do not make it an easy route. There is so little potential for income, that most people have jobs on the side to pay the rent. If we were to force every fringe production to pay the minimum wage, it would simply mean that 80 per cent of fringe productions simply couldn't happen under the current model, and that would deny many people their route into the industry. There are, of course, other solutions that can be explored to make fringe more sustainable, such as subsidizing the theatres – but that's a discussion for a different book.

Is it a Fair Offer?

We have established that it is useful to know who is producing the show, how it is being funded, and where it is being put on, to understand what they can afford to pay you and whether they are making a fair offer.

Whatever the scale of the show, consider your own costs: can you pay your rent and afford to eat? What are the basic costs that you might incur in making the production, for example travel? Are there any additional costs, such as needing to do special location recording sessions to record sound effects, or employing an associate to cover any absences in availability you might have? Each show has to contribute towards your ongoing costs too: the cost of your computer software and hardware, other sound equipment, and the purchase of sound effects.

It is important to negotiate with the producer what they are expecting you to supply out of your fee, and what the production will have to pay for. Typically, I will supply myself and all the sounds needed for a production. If a sound studio will be needed (for example to record a voice-over or some music) then I would expect the production to pay for the hire of that. But I wouldn't expect them to hire a studio for me to sit in to design the sound (not that I do that anyway).

If the production has particular demands – for example, it requires a steam train to be recorded – then we would discuss that need, and I would propose that the costs of hiring a steam train would not come out of my design fee. I would be happy to supply steam train sound effects free of charge, but if the play required something so bespoke as to warrant recording one, then that is a cost I would expect the production to bear. I would likely supply the recording equipment, if I have it, free of charge, otherwise they would have to pay to hire in the specific equipment needed.

If I'm having to travel across town to record something, I wouldn't expect them to pay for travel. However, if I have to travel halfway across the country to the steam train, I would expect them to pay for travel and accommodation, if needed. Typically, if any long-distance travel is required for your work, then you should expect the producer to offer a travel allowance to cover that, and accommodation if they are asking you to work so far away from home that you are not able to commute. A per diem (daily allowance for food) may also be offered, but this is usually only offered for international work. Some countries have laws in place about what companies can and can't pay for in terms of per diems and travel expenses.

I have, on occasion, completely misjudged the income versus the cost to me of doing a production, of meeting my contractual obligations, and have ended up either not making any money from doing a show, or worse still, making a loss. Often this is because I have underestimated the time I need to spend on a project, or have booked in overlapping projects, and have then needed to employ an associate to cover where I couldn't be.

All of these reasons, and many others, is why we don't say 'Yes' to a job offer the second we pick up the phone. We want to have time to do our research – into the producer, the director, the writer, the script, the venue. Having received an offer from the producers, we must decide whether to accept, decline, or to haggle. The first two options are relatively straightforward, and depend on how close, or not, the offer is to what you need it to be, or whether the terms of engagement work for you. Haggling for a better fee is a nerve-racking process, especially for those with old-fashioned 'I don't like to talk about money' sensibilities. It is difficult to know how much flexibility there is to the fee being offered. How have they arrived at that fee? Have they offered you a bit less than they have budgeted for in anticipation of haggling over the fee?

Some venues (often the subsidized ones) have fixed fees with no negotiation. Some claim to have fixed fees but there may be some leeway. Some producers may offer fees relating to how established a sound designer is, or how many times they have worked with them previously. The perceived hierarchy of the creative team (by the producer) of set designer – costume designer – lighting designer – sound designer often places your offer in relation to what they have been offered. There are even still some producers who offer the lighting designer a higher fee, and when questioned, the reply is because the lighting designer has to draw a plan, ignoring the amount of preparation the sound designer has to do, and the amount of resources needed by a sound designer. It is often worthwhile to ask whether what you are being offered is on a par with the lighting designer – it is increasingly the case, but not always. If the reply comes back that you are being paid less, then you can ask them why.

Negotiating Better Terms

If you want to negotiate it is best to do it politely and in a business-like manner – avoid getting personal. The easiest reply to a low offer is to say, 'Is there room for movement on the fee, as this is lower than I'd expected?' If you've talked to the director by this point and they're asking a lot from you, then you can use that to justify why you need more: 'The director has asked me to be in rehearsals more than I normally would. This means I'm going to have to turn down work that I'd otherwise be able to do.'

There is no normal amount of rehearsal attendance that is expected, but I'd say that anything apart from being in rehearsals for the last week or two can easily be argued as extraordinary. The style of work I often do requires me in rehearsals a lot, so this is often a reason I give to seek a fee increase. But I do ensure the director is aware that I'm negotiating this way, so they don't get blindsided by producers questioning them. You can get the director on side with: 'I'd love to be in rehearsals to do what you're asking, but I need the producers to increase what they're paying me, so I can afford to be there.' There is such variety in productions, and how they're made, that standard fees and contracts often don't fit, and there are often perfectly reasonable reasons to negotiate for a higher fee.

Royalties

Some shows, especially those that expect to run for a long while, will also pay a royalty. This is especially the case in the commercial sector. Subsidized theatres almost never offer a royalty, unless one of their shows is transferring into a commercial theatre or going on tour. In subsidized theatre, where income is less tied to ticket sales, it may not be able to calculate a profit, if there is one, so royalties are rarely offered.

One way to think about the royalty is that the fee is to cover your creation of the sound design, and the royalty is the continued use of it. The other way to look at it, and the historical reason for royalties, was so the producer can pay you less in advance (when they have little income), and more later on (when people start buying tickets to come see the show). A royalty may be paid as a fixed weekly sum, or at a percentage of the profit the show makes, typically between 0.4 per cent and 1.5 per cent of the weekly operating profit. This may often start at a lower rate before the show has recouped the costs of putting the show on, moving to a higher rate once it has paid off those costs.

There may be a minimum weekly royalty specified in the offer as well as, or instead of, a percentage royalty, that will be paid out regardless of how much profit the show is making.

The fixed weekly sum is a known quantity that you can plan your life around, to a degree, whereas being in the 'royalty pool' may earn you considerably more money, depending on how much profit the show makes. Unless the show doesn't make a profit…

Regardless of what sort of royalty you negotiate, if a show is running at a loss, the producers may ask you to defer or waive your royalty, so they can reduce the outgoings of the show (so it is making less of a loss) and keep it running longer. This is not uncommon, and obviously means the people employed full-time on the show can keep their jobs longer, but at your expense! Make sure your fee is enough to cover all your costs in case the negotiated royalty never materializes.

Be aware of the 'royalty advance', which appears at first as if you are being offered a larger fee, but is actually them paying you what you might make in the future in royalties, in advance. For example, if they offer you a £5,000 royalty advance,

that means you get £5,000 up front, but it also means that if the show makes a profit, you won't get any royalties until that advance has been 'paid off'. It's a bit like a loan, but one you don't have to pay back if the show doesn't make a profit. If you feel the show isn't likely to make a profit, then it's a good thing. If you feel the show is likely to make a profit, this number just makes your fee look bigger than it really is.

Other Negotiation Items

As well as negotiating a fee and a royalty, we may also be negotiating the travel allowance, per diems, which class of travel we might fly in, the order of the billing on the poster, and many other aspects of the contract.

Another common negotiation item is if there is a period of dates for which you are unavailable, particularly during the 'first call exclusive' period – when you can only be working for them and no one else, which is normally the tech and previews. A 'first call non-exclusive' period is when you can be working for multiple people, but your priority must be this production. If you can't be around for the last two previews and press night because you have another project you were already booked for, you *must* get that period of non-availability (and any others) written into your contract. Directors and producers can have hazy memories of when you said you'd be around, particularly if you only told them over the phone, and have been known to deny any knowledge of what you'd told them.

You might also agree to employ, and pay, an associate sound designer to be there in your absence to look after the show. On larger shows in the UK the producer may pay for the associate sound designer, especially if they are there regardless of when you are also there. On smaller shows, you'll be expected to pay for them out of your fee. In the USA, associate sound designers are far more commonplace.

Some sound designers have agents, in the same way an actor might. Whereas an agent plays a key role in getting auditions for actors, a designer's agent handles availability checks and the negotiating of the contract – they will rarely get you work, simply because that's not how directors and producers seek creative team members. Your agent can argue and haggle on your behalf, being the bad cop, whilst you can remain on good terms with the producer. Agents typically earn 10 per cent of your fees. In the UK, they will also charge VAT, which if you aren't VAT registered means they get 12 per cent of your fee. A few agents work on a monthly fee basis instead. Ideally they can improve your wages more than the percentage you're paying them. And by maintaining good relations with the producer yourself, you can get more repeat work. An agent isn't necessary, and many people work for years without feeling the need for one. A designer's relationship with their agent is more business-like than the media cliché of how actors and their agents work together.

It's important when negotiating not to sweat the small stuff – it can be tempting to spend time arguing over the smaller expenses, such as a taxi to the airport. I have seen fellow designers sour their relationship with a producer by arguing over the smallest of expense, sometimes just for the principle of it. Sometimes they'll successfully get their £25 receipt reclaimed, sometimes not, but often they'll just not get employed by the producer in the future. It's important to play the long game and absorb some smaller expenses (which will be tax deductible) to keep the long-term business.

Finally, the Contract

The negotiation process can be stressful, regardless of having an agent or not, and it can take weeks, sometimes months, of emails and phone calls until the contract is agreed upon and signed. During this time you may well be turning down other availability checks and offers for the same period of work. Most negotiations end satisfactorily with some compromise achieved on either side, or if not that, at least everyone goes into the contract better aware of its parameters.

Unless there are exceptional circumstances, don't withdraw from a booking you've accepted for the possibility of a better job. That opportunity may lead somewhere, or not, but you can be absolutely sure you won't get employed ever again by the person you let down. Work on a strict first come, first served basis. There will be painful moments where you have to turn down exciting-looking possibilities. But actually, it is difficult to predict which show will be most interesting, or most fun to work on: the good opportunity can turn out to be a poisoned chalice, and the less interesting show may lead to working with the director on a more interesting show in the future.

WHAT SHOULD A CONTRACT CONTAIN?

A contract should contain the following:

- Details of the parties the contract is between
- Details of what the producer wants from you, and when they want it
- Details of when they want you exclusively working on their project ('exclusive first call basis'), and of when you're not available
- Details of payments, expenses and per diems as appropriate, and a payment schedule
- How, where and when you will be credited. I often push against credits that just say 'Sound by' in favour of 'Sound design by'
- Who will own the copyright to the sound design
- Details of which venues and dates any licence to use the sound design are for
- What will happen if the producer wants to extend, tour or transfer the production
- What will happen if the producer wants to broadcast, live-stream, or otherwise record for future exploitation
- Details of promotional and archival use of your material. A promise to negotiate further for broadcast rights
- Who will clear copyrighted materials
- What will happen if the production is postponed or abandoned

GARETH FRY

AS YOU LIKE IT

By William Shakespeare

Edited for Regent's Park Theatre Summer 2018

PROLOGUE

It's raining. Everywhere. Constantly. The world is flooding.

Thunder into news montage of flood-related disasters

Full band

When that I was and a little tiny boy,
With a hey, ho, the wind and the rain,
A foolish thing was but a toy,
For the rain it raineth every day.

HH-Jucadl

But when I came to man's estate,
With a hey, ho, the wind and the rain,
To knaves and thieves men shut their gate,
For the rain it raineth every day.

Everyday
Everyday

+ 2 girls Amy + Joanne

But when I came, alas! to wive,
With a hey, ho, the wind and the rain,
By swaggering could I never thrive,
For the rain it raineth every day. gtr flourishes
The rain it raineth every day.

building into full company

Thunder crack here

F *When I came to my death bed,*
all *With a hey, ho, the wind and the rain,*
M *Toss-pots still had drunken heads,*
all *For the rain it raineth every day.*

3

SCRIPT ANALYSIS AND MEETING THE DIRECTOR

Having accepted the job, you will normally be sent the script. This may differ from what is eventually used to rehearse with, if it is still being worked on by the author, or being adapted from an older text. Scripts often evolve in the run-up to the start of rehearsals, and during rehearsals. A new play or musical can go through many drafts before it's ready for rehearsal. Scenes may be added, cut, or completely changed. The number of cast members may increase or decrease. Obviously, this can make planning tricky!

A revival of an existing work may come with licensing restrictions that prevent much editing, or even deviation from the original production. Existing works, particularly older ones, are often cut down, with lines or scenes removed. Most Shakespearean plays are full of references that were funny and topical to the audience at that time, but are meaningless, and not remotely funny now. *Hamlet* is a good example of a play that is sometimes played in its full length, around four hours, but is often cut down so as to be more acceptable to a modern audience, at under three hours! These cuts are often chosen by the director, either on their own, or in consultation with the artistic director or a dramaturg (though the latter is rare in UK theatre).

For some people, the world of theatre sound falls neatly into plays and musicals, with some people specializing in each. Whereas this can be true of some markets, the world we can work in is far more diverse than that. I work primarily on

WHEN WAS IT WRITTEN?

Research the era the story was written in. What was the style of performance and design for the time and place the play was written? If you read a Noel Coward play, or something else from the late nineteenth or early twentieth century, you'll notice that there are often quite long scenes often set in a single location. In Ferdinand Bruckner's *Pains of Youth*, written in 1926, the entire show takes place in one location – Desirée's apartment. Throughout the thirty-five minutes of Act One, we have seventeen different combinations of different characters arriving and leaving, in order all to have a scene in Desirée's apartment. Why? At the time there was a trend for having detailed, naturalistic sets. These were expensive, heavy, and difficult to change from representing one location to another. Instead the writer manipulates the story and characters so they all happen in the same room in various unlikely combinations.

Later in the twentieth century playwrights were increasingly influenced by film and television, which tend to have shorter scenes, and may be set across multiple locations. A modern play may have a larger number of scenes within it, set in different locations. There is less need for the writers to contrive reasons to get these characters in one room – instead we can find them in the location they might naturally inhabit. Because scenery is quite expensive, and it can be tricky to move between multiple naturalistic sets, other options can be used to create a sense of location. Sound design, as well as lighting and video design, allows us to set location almost instantaneously, and often at much lower cost.

plays, devised work, dance, occasional operas, and other spin-off areas such as radio and/or podcast drama. Whilst I don't often design musicals, I do a lot of work that features songs, live musicians, live singers, and many of the things that make up a musical, without them being labelled as such.

Many of the most successful shows are the ones that blur the lines of what genre you consider them to be part of. Whilst some musicals may eventually not require a single sound effect, and some plays may not eventually require any music, don't let the genre define your approach to it. It is always useful to examine the script to discover all the possibilities of what you might do with it.

SCRIPT ANALYSIS

Often a huge part of our job is to help tell the story, so the first time you read the script, ignore all thoughts of sound design and concentrate on what the story is telling you. If we don't take a moment to examine how the story is told, we can't really discuss how and why we can use sound to tell it. So, start by listening to the story. How does it start? When do we meet the various characters, how are they introduced, and how does their character, or our understanding of their character, develop over the course of the story? What techniques does the writer use to help us form an emotional attachment to these characters? What history of this world, these characters, their back story do we learn, and where in the script do we learn these details?

When are the threads of the plot revealed? How do they develop and intertwine? What are the moments of crisis and conflict? What are the moments that make our pulse race? When do we get those surprise revelations that make us re-evaluate something we thought we knew, or reveal something key to our understanding? Where do things that are ambiguous become clear? Where do the moods change? When and how do all the elements resolve? What is left unresolved?

Highlight all these moments in the script. Use the script to understand the story, and how the telling of it unfolds. Many scripts deviate to great effect from the conventions of script writing, so these questions may not always be the most pertinent ones.

It's worth noting that scripts aren't meant to be read, they're meant to be performed. I've read some scripts that are utterly indecipherable on the page but are utter genius when performed. It's fine to admit you don't understand something in the script. Directors are often interested in knowing which bits of a script are unclear, especially in new writing, so they can work to make it clearer. If they want to.

When I've finished the first read, I reflect on the themes and arcs of the show. What did it evoke in me? What are the overall themes? Is the author trying to achieve anything specific? Where did I get excited by it, where did I get bored? What thoughts or ideas did it trigger in me? Only then will I begin to ask myself how we might use sound design.

I then read the script a second time to highlight any things that on first reading seemed unimportant, but developed into something later on. This can become an opportunity to reconsider the questions we asked on our first read, knowing the full arc of the story. I'll also highlight any written or implied references to sound (I'm including music when I say sound).

It's always important to approach any written stage directions that mention sound with caution. Writers, with the greatest respect, don't necessarily know the best sonic way to tell their story. Following stage directions can often box you into the way the writer has imagined their play being directed.

The best stage direction I've come across is in Chekhov's *The Cherry Orchard*:

> They're all sitting, deep in thought. Silence. Only Firs's mumbling is heard. Suddenly a distant sound is unleashed, from the sky, the sound of a bursting string, dying away, sadly.

I like this stage direction because the author is conveying the emotional intent they want to achieve without prescribing how to achieve it. The sound technology available in Chekhov's time was very poor, so if he'd said instead, 'Offstage thunder rumbles', then we'd be stuck forever with the best of what was technologically available at the time of writing. Instead, Chekhov's stage direction allows us to understand the author's emotional intention to a degree, whilst remaining ambiguous in its execution to allow us to experiment with a range of ways to execute it.

Offstage thunder is a classic writer's stage direction. I take any stage direction about thunder to mean that they want some sound that indicates rising tension or foreboding. Fifty years ago, thunder would be one of the few ways of indicating that which most theatres could easily achieve. But now, we have dozens more ways to create something more interesting and less clichéd. There are, of course, times when it's perfectly valid to use thunder.

It's important to question any sound-related stage directions, as much to open up the discussion about whether it's the best way to tell the story, or if there are other approaches. I say this with utter respect for playwrights: I spend a lot of time analysing their work, discerning their intentions, so I can help tell their story in the best way possible. I do a lot of shows where the playwright is present in the rehearsal room and I may discuss their play with them to better understand it. It's often interesting to discuss which of the choices they've made are critical, and which are more arbitrary. Is Scene Five set in a library because a library has critical meaning to the show, or was it chosen arbitrarily out of many public locations where these characters might meet?

It can be interesting to run the script through an app that allows you to count the occurrence of each word. Has the playwright mentioned the word 'children' forty-seven times in the script on purpose because it is a significant theme, or because it was something about their own personal life they were thinking about when they wrote the play?

As I complete my second read of the script I am often looking for the things about it that interest me, that I connect with, or the things that make it unique or unusual as a story. Any of these may inspire some form of an idea for a sound design. But it's not unusual for inspiration not to have struck yet.

There are some key questions we should ask at this point:

- Why are we telling this specific story?
- Why is this specific audience coming to hear it?
- What are we doing when we tell this story? What is its intended effect on our audience? To inform, educate or entertain, or something else?

The answers to those questions vary from story to story, and there may not even be neat answers to them. We may not know the answers to these at this early stage, but we should keep these questions in mind throughout the creation process of the play, as otherwise our sound design will be built on weak foundations.

WHO IS YOUR AUDIENCE?

Any production will attract a different audience to it, so don't treat them like a homogenous mass. If you compare the audience of a Broadway play and a West End play they have different expectations of what they are there to see. If you compare the audience of an RSC Shakespeare to a dance adaptation of a Shakespeare, you will find different people in those audiences. Some venues are known for a certain type of work, and may well have developed an audience who like that type of work and come back show after show. Other houses may receive shows so wildly different from week to week that completely different audiences will come week to week.

THE FIRST MEETING

The first meeting with a director is critical, especially if you are working with them for the first time. It's important to go in prepared. If you haven't read the script recently, have a quick look through it, as there's nothing worse than not being able to remember the plot when you're discussing how to tell it! Know who the characters are, and what it is all about (the underlying themes, not just the plot). Do your homework on the author, and the context of the writing of the play. Re-read your notes in the script.

Sometimes life doesn't present the time or opportunity for all this, and you'll find yourself meeting the director with no more preparation than the information you can find on Wikipedia!

If you've not worked with the director before, check to see if they have a show on that you can go and watch, to see their style in action. It can be an interesting talking point: 'I went to see your other show last week, and I really liked the …'. Try not to be late, and arrive in a composed manner, and dress suitably. I rarely manage to achieve more than one of these, but aim for all three! There are many pre-existing negative connotations about sound being a technical craft rather than an art, so the more you can do to dispel that, the better. It is a sad fact, but the more you look and act like a theatre technician, the less a director is going to treat you like an artist, and the less they will entrust you with the authority to make artistic decisions. Consider how you present yourself, because you will be judged upon it. This is crucially important if you haven't been chosen specifically by the director.

Some of the most disastrous jobs I have done have been ones where the director has almost randomly picked my name off a list of sound designers that was presented to them by a venue. This means they may not know anything about me, my specialisms, my interests, the shows I've done previously, or anything – I'm just a generic sound person. Whilst my ego can happily handle that, it is a difficult point from which to start a creative relationship. It means the director associates you with the venue, and in this scenario, I'm often asked if I work full-time at the said venue. That isn't necessarily a bad thing, but it does mean that the director may be thinking of you as a facilitator rather than a creator, as a member of the venue staff rather than as *You*, as a member of their creative team.

In this situation it's important to work hard to push your image as a creative team member, rather than as a member of the theatre production staff. In this scenario, I work hard to gain their trust as a creative team member, rather than as someone they can give a list of sound effects to. I'll push to have meetings happen away from the venue where practical. I'll concentrate on concepts and the study of the text, and veer away from discussing technical, practical implementation. It isn't always successful, however, particularly if it's a script that I don't particularly connect with, or a

WHAT DO YOU DO?

Public perception of sound design is limited – you will spend many years explaining to your parents what you do. You may well get those 'I'm worried about you' looks when you visit at Christmas, which many people who have careers in the arts get, regardless of how successful their careers are.

In 2014 the Tony Awards, one of the most high-profile theatre awards, focused around Broadway shows, decided to drop their sound design categories. The unofficial reason given was that 'Many Tony voters do not know what sound design is or how to assess it … and some administration committee members believe that sound design is more of a technical craft, rather than a theatrical art form that the Tonys are intended to honour.' Fortunately the Tony Awards reversed this decision for the 2017–2018 season after a lot of discussions and petitioning.

We do have to be aware that many people, even the people we work next to every day, rarely know much about what we actually do. It's therefore important to correct misunderstandings and to inform wherever possible.

director with whom I find I don't personally connect (or vice versa).

The Director's Concept for the Show

The first meeting is where you hear, perhaps for the first time, the director's concept for the show, what they're planning to do with it. If you're unfamiliar with the process a director goes through to develop a show, I highly recommend Katie Mitchell's book *The Director's Craft: A Handbook for Theatre*. Her description of using sound and music feels reductionist in its brevity, but I know from personal experience that these form a key role in her directing process.

The director may have ideas about sound or music already. Listen to them carefully, even if you feel they are not fully formed, and work out what they are trying to achieve with them. Do the ideas you had on reading the script look to achieve the same things? Listen to the language the director is using to talk about sound – are they using cinematic references ('close-ups', 'zoom out'), or musical language ('crescendos')? Analyse how they talk about sound, and use the same terminology. Establish the best language to talk about sound with them.

Don't be afraid to expand their vocabulary, but avoid jargon. I think in my whole life I have only met one director who used the word 'diegetic' in a conversation. It's a great word, but virtually no one knows what it means, and most can barely remember it when told it. It's a good example of a word I might use internally to think about sound, but not one that I'd use when talking to a director, as it often ends up confusing the conversation rather than clarifying it. (A diegetic sound is typically one that appears to come from the world of the story, so for example, music playing on a radio would be diegetic, whereas underscoring music would be non-diegetic.)

Don't worry at this stage about getting too specific – it's all right to be vague. Talk about sound more experientially: 'I want it to sound like that moment after you're told the news of a traumatic effect' is a far better way of describing what you might want to achieve than going into a description of how you might achieve it.

It's often useful to find out how musical your director is. Like sound designers, directors may be incredibly musical, or not at all. Some may know everything about music and how to use it, but have no idea about how to use any other type of sound. Some may be pitch perfect, some may have the most immense knowledge of certain genres of music, or of vast swathes of music, while some may have none. You yourself will sit somewhere on the same range of none, to all. Establishing where your director sits can be useful in working out how to discuss ideas with them. Don't be afraid to acknowledge if the director knows more about music or a certain genre than you do. Nobody can be an expert in all fields, and it's important not to pretend that you are.

Demonstrate you are a Creative Person

This first meeting is your opportunity to demonstrate that you are a creative person with whom the director can collaborate. That's a lot of pressure, so be careful not to overdo it! Let the director know if there are relevant things you can bring to the table, whether it's your hobby as a bell-ringer, or your holiday trip to the country where the show is set. Talk about ideas of theirs that you like, or connect to. Be positive, open-minded and enthusiastic. Don't be afraid to mention an idea or opinion you have. Don't be afraid to wade through the obvious, stupid ideas to find the way to the interesting, less obvious ones. Don't be afraid to say, 'We could try ... Actually, no, that's a stupid idea.'

Don't stamp on an idea just because someone else has done it before. There are few truly original ideas out there. If an idea or concept is brought up that has been done recently and noticeably by another director or sound designer I may mention that to protect them from appearing to copy someone else. If it's not so significant, or is less clearly a derivative, I'll keep my mouth shut: nobody likes being told 'that's been done before'! And most things have been done before, in one form or another. I might mention that I've tried something similar in the past and whether, and why, it was successful, or not.

Talk about your initial reactions to the script, gauge the director's reaction, and adapt accordingly. They will be trying to work out what you'll be like to work with – whether you're going to respond positively to their ideas, whether you speak the same language, hold the same opinions about theatre, whether you can fulfil your commitments successfully.

At this stage you can be discussing vague concepts – so don't squash ideas just because they are not practical or financially achievable. Explore where they can lead, bounce the ideas around some more, until they land on something that *is* achievable. Don't lie about being able to achieve things you don't think you can achieve, but be confident about things you think you can learn that you haven't already done before. Many of us have taken jobs not knowing how to do them and worked it out as we went along. Preparation is key to this though.

It's all right if you don't connect with the text or with the director's vision. I have designed plenty of shows where I haven't particularly connected with, or even particularly liked the script. If you're stuck for inspiration you may have little to offer to the conversation, but it's fine to say that you'd like to reflect on everything they've told you – it can be a lot to take in – and come back to them with some thoughts later.

Show that you have a sense of humour, if it feels appropriate. As well as selling yourself as a creative person, you are trying to build up a personal relationship with the director. If you're confident about it, talk about the politics of the play. Talk about how they came to be doing this show (though be careful how you phrase this one… 'How on earth did you end up directing this show?' can be easily misinterpreted!). What drew them to this script? This is also useful for finding out if this is a pet project of theirs, a script they've been wanting to do for the last ten years, or whether they were offered the job to direct this script by the venue, and actually don't care for it much.

Rehearsal Processes

It's important to establish how the director likes, or plans, to work, when they'd like you to be around, when you can actually be around, and what level of support you will provide for rehearsals. Some shows may be complex and may require you in rehearsals with a large sound system from day one of rehearsals. Others might not need anything. Some directors like plenty of sound support, some may prefer to focus entirely on the acting. The latter doesn't mean they're not interested in sound, but just that they want to compartmentalize how they work on the elements.

There may also be other rehearsal room processes to find out about. If your play has a celebrity actor in it who doesn't usually act in theatre, then they may want as few people in rehearsals as possible. If there are scenes of a sexual nature, or a great deal of nudity, access to rehearsals may also be limited. Some directors are open with their rehearsals and are happy to have people coming in and out; others like their rehearsals closed, a sealed off, safe space.

If you are working with a composer, that may be a new relationship to establish, too. Schedule a meeting with the composer after the first meeting with the director, so you can work out who will do what, and how and when. How much will they self-produce music, or will you get involved in that? Who will you collaborate with, and how, on the blurry middle ground that exists between music and sound?

Between the First Meeting and the Start of Rehearsals

You can follow up after the first meeting with any ideas you might have had, or send them film clips that demonstrate concepts, or anything you discussed. It's important to carry that first meeting into a continued dialogue, so the director is including you as they develop their ideas for the show, both relating to sound and otherwise.

Between the first meeting and the start of rehearsals is a crucial time, when the creative team have to take creative concepts and approach how to make them into a practical reality that can be built, costed and rehearsed. It is the time to establish what sort of show you're doing, and how to approach it, also to talk to the other creative team members to find out what they are doing. What is the lighting designer planning to do? What is the set design, how does it evolve over the show? What sounds do you need to emanate from the stage, where will you need speakers in the set? The earlier you talk to the set designer about speaker positions, the more likely they can find a way to integrate it into their design – the later you leave it, the more of an imposition to their set design it will be.

Unless you're doing a devised show, where the show is being made up as you rehearse, you should be starting rehearsals with a fair degree of the concept established between yourself, the director and the creative team. That doesn't mean you know everything about the show by that time, but you'll have a starting point in place.

When I look back on most shows that haven't been fun to work on, I can usually trace the root cause back to this part of the process. Sometimes it's because somebody forgot to tell me some crucial detail that would prove pivotal to the show not sounding good. Sometimes the director and I didn't speak enough during this stage, so we weren't properly prepared for the start of rehearsals. Sometimes I underestimate the scale or ambition of the show, or the time required to support it, so book in other work, leaving me fighting to support it. Sometimes I haven't spoken early enough to the set designer to get good speaker positions in their set.

If I'm working with a new director, I might not find the personal connection with them to properly talk about sound, and it then becomes a struggle to communicate through the rest of the process. Usually when a show isn't fun to work on, it isn't anything to do with sound equipment or acoustics, it's down to the people.

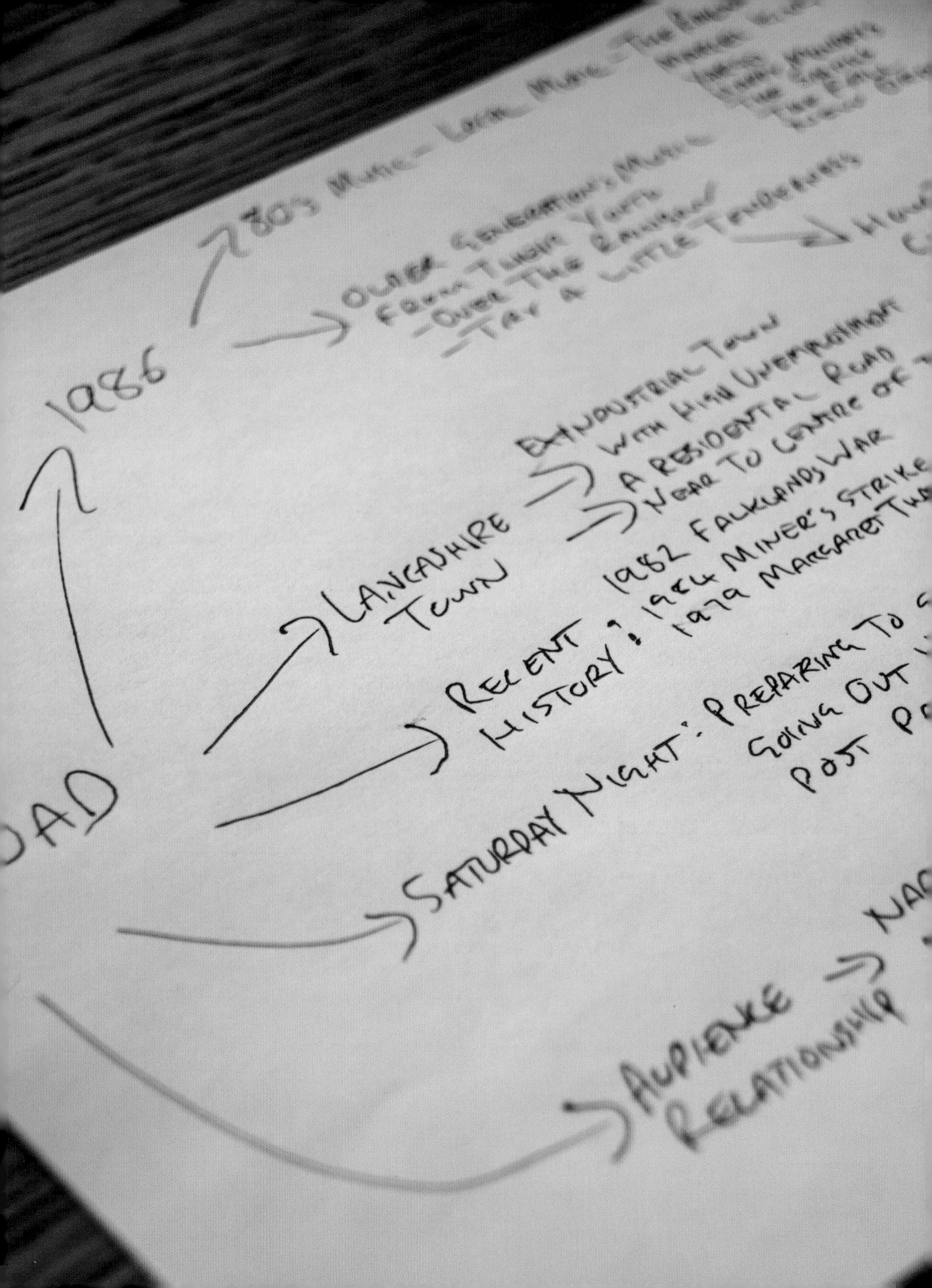

80's Music - Local Music - The Band...

↗ 80's Music

- OLDER GENERATION'S MUSIC
- FORM THEIR YOUTH
- OVER THE RAINBOW
- TRY A LITTLE TENDERNESS → HUM...

1986

INDUSTRIAL TOWN
WITH HIGH UNEMPLOYMENT
A RESIDENTIAL ROAD
NEAR TO CENTRE OF...

→ LANCASHIRE
TOWN

DAD

→ RECENT : 1982 FALKLANDS WAR
HISTORY : 1984 MINER'S STRIKE
1979 MARGARET THA...

SATURDAY NIGHT : PREPARING TO G...
GOING OUT W...
POST P...

AUDIENCE → NAR...
RELATIONSHIP

4
CONCEIVE AND EXECUTE

Having a 'concept' is a term I use to include many things, but in essence I'm talking about how I want the show to sound.

On some shows you may start with a concept, one that applies purely to the sound design, or perhaps one the director has come up with, or perhaps one from the set designer that comes from the style, period or place where the play is to be set. From that starting point, the rest of the process (the rehearsals and the time spent in the theatre) can be seen as working out how to develop and execute that concept. I tend to refer to this workflow as 'conceive and execute'.

On other shows, in particular devised shows or shows that follow that sort of development process, you may not be starting with a script or any sense of what the eventual show will be. In this workflow you may be heading into rehearsals with a few notions or reference materials or some starting point for the show, but little idea of what the eventual show will be like. This workflow I call 'react and refine'. We'll talk more about this workflow in a later section as it tends to be more focused around the rehearsal process.

Whilst some shows may clearly fall into one category or another, many sit somewhere between the two and require you to adapt your process to the demands of each show.

There are many inspirations that you can choose from, to develop a concept. Some may be rooted in the text, some in the direction, some in the set design, some in the performance, some in the venue, and some in the audience relationship. And they can vary from high art to incredibly pragmatic things. Whilst you have to balance your imagination with what is possible, don't let reality get in the way of your imagination when you are starting off. Let your imagination go on its flights of fancy and see where they land. If you start imposing harsh realities on your imagination from the start, you'll never take off.

Sometimes you'll come up with a concept straightaway, and sometimes it may feel as if the show doesn't need one. What follows isn't the thought process that I necessarily undertake for every show, but it is here as a launch pad for your thinking. There are other ways to approach looking at a text beyond these, but they are useful ways to examine the show from different angles, to see where ideas might begin, and how they might converge.

CONCEPT FROM THE TEXT

Having done some basic script analysis already, further researching the author, and also the political and sociological context in which they wrote the piece, can be illuminating as regards finding themes and ideas. Reading or researching the playwright's other works can also be interesting as regards finding common themes that crop up repeatedly. You might try to find answers to the following questions:

- When is the play set?
- What was the world like then?
- What was happening politically then?
- What technologies were in common use then? Were there telephones, gramophones, radio, television, electricity, gas lighting, automobiles?

OPPOSITE: Brain-storming for Jim Cartwright's *Road*.

- What was popular music then?
- Were there any niche music genres associated with the world of this piece?
- In what season, and at what times of day, does each scene take place? What happens between each scene?
- What has happened immediately before the story begins?

- Where is the play set?
- What was the geography of the world like, where did the borders of the relevant countries lie then?
- Is there anything significant in the local history of the locations?
- What are the dominant, or interesting, sounds of those places?

- Who features in the story?
- Are there interesting sonic traits to the people in the show, their actions, their obsessions, their dreams, their occupations?
- Are there recurring or significant words, or objects mentioned in the script? If the word 'water' is mentioned multiple times in the script, then that might be something worth exploring
- How does any of the above evolve over the timeline of the play?

You can also ask more abstract questions:

- How orienting, or disorienting, do we want our sound design to be? As an example, if we want to evoke the perspective of someone going mad, we can create a disoriented perspective of the world, jump cutting all over the place and ignoring our societal conventions of what something sounds like, or how loud it is
- How would a dream-like version of this world appear?
- What is the Light, and what is the Dark version of this world?
- What would you remember of this world if you were trying to remember it twenty years from now?

- Do we follow one protagonist, or a number of people?
- The way we hear the world – and the way a character might – is dependent on, and changed by, our experiences in it. How would character X hear this world? How would character Y hear it? What would they focus on, what would they ignore, what would grab their attention? If character X has been in a genocide, would they hear dogs barking or sudden impact sounds differently? If character Y almost drowned once, would they hear running water differently?
- Which is the interesting dramatic moment: the moment when someone does something, or the moment when they *choose* to do something?

CONCEPT FROM THE SET

Sometimes there will be sound effects mentioned in a script, and these should always be analysed and questioned.

> SFX: A car pulls into the drive, the car door opens, and feet are heard walking up to the front door. Keys jingle and Bob enters.

> Bob (shouts): Hi, I'm home!

This sort of stage direction can often feel like a hangover from the contrived writing of drawing-room box sets – we need to hear something for the plot to advance, so it is written as a stage direction in order that we hear it. The presence of this in the script, to the exclusion of what else we might be able to hear, leads us to ask questions. Do we really need to hear the car pull up, or the feet outside? What is this contributing to the story? How much can we hear of the world outside the house? Should we hear every car that goes past? If we were to hear only this one car, and not all the others that we might realistically hear, then we are setting ourselves up for a very specific language, where we have these orphan sound effects – sounds that just come out of no-where, with no 'language' to set them up.

This is fine if your style of storytelling isn't natu-ralistic, but often this type of stage direction ap-pears in the most seemingly naturalistic of plays. But if you only put the sound effects mentioned in the script in your show, then you are going to end up with a very fake, artificial sound design which isn't naturalistic! Sound effects often sound like sound effects when they're orphaned, rather than being part of the world of the show.

Early on, discuss how to deal with these or-phan sound effect stage directions. It might be useful to build up a language where we *do* hear cars passing by outside, so when one pulls up to the house it isn't odd. Or maybe we don't need to hear any of this. Does the car arriving element of the stage direction actually contribute to the story? I might suggest we have some paving slabs outside the 'front door' so we can acousti-cally hear the actor approach the front door, jan-gle their keys, and unlock the lock, and not have any sound effect at all.

This imaginary stage direction brings up a key question, especially when dealing with naturalism, namely how much of the world beyond the con-fines of the set do we want to hear? How much of the world of the play is the set going to contain?

Let's take a basic example of a small stage, which contains a set that is a room of a building:

- How much do we want to hear of the building around the visible room, the hallway beyond, the rooms on either side and above it?
- How much sound does the building itself make? Is it a new building or an old one? Does the plumbing make any noise? Is there air condi-tioning? Does it move and shift and creak at night?
- How insulated is the building from the ele-ments? Does wind whistle through the gaps, or is it hermetically sealed?
- Who are the other occupants of that building? What are they doing across the arc of our story, and how much can we hear them?

- How much do we want to hear of the outside world beyond the building? Is there a window or door out to the outside world? What wildlife exists outside?
- What is the world beyond that building? Is it urban or rural? What sort of neighbourhood or activity is audible? How much do we hear traffic and aircraft?
- How much pressure should the outside world place on the inside world? Are there any events happening in the outside world that we should hear in the room? Is there a war raging outside, or a school playground next door?

You can choose many of the answers to these questions according to your own desires. Your choices can be significant. To take our last ques-tion, having a war waging outside might sound like a high-pressure event and a children's playground less so, but if the story you are telling is about a couple trying to conceive a child, and you decide they live next door to a school playground, then the resulting soundscape could be highly stressful for the characters of your story.

There are many plays where the story onstage doesn't make sense without a sense of the world offstage, which is something that can rarely be easily conveyed via the other design disciplines as easily as it can be done with sound. But just because it's the easiest method doesn't always make it the best one.

What is audible to the characters and what is audible to the audience do not have to be the same thing. In our example of Bob's car pulling into the drive, our actors can pretend that their characters hear the car arriving without the sound of the car actually having to be audible to anyone.

Sometimes it may offer nothing to the story to extend the world beyond the set. Indeed, some stories seem to happen in an isolated bubble of their own reality, so it's equally valid to say that we can't hear anything beyond the walls of the set.

Are there physical things we can do to help meld the reality of the set and the sense of the off-stage world? It's easy to destroy the sense of the offstage world if an actor walks offstage and we hear their feet walking away on a creaky wooden stage floor. If they're supposed to be walking off into a garden, then you can make a gravel pit offstage, so they can walk off in that. It carries the reality of the set further than the bounds of visibility.

CONCEPT FROM THE DIRECTION

How is the show being directed? Directors often bring extra layers to a text in how they direct the show. This can be by subtly shifting the perspective from which we see the story told, or by choosing how to set it in the world. There are hundreds of directing choices that can be made with any text, which can change the telling or interpretation of the story either subtly, or radically.

Nick Hytner chose to bring his production of *Othello* into the modern day, starting off in a modern London pub, through to a military camp in Cyprus. This decision opened up a world of twenty-first century music, and modern military sounds, vehicles and telecommunications. The offstage world is of a modern military base with helicopters buzzing around.

Scott Graham and Steven Hoggett chose to set their production of *Othello* in a pub on a council estate. Here the war is between postcode gangs, and the power struggle is within the gang's leadership. The onstage world is jukeboxes, fruit machines and televisions, and the offstage world was joyriders buzzing around in their cars.

The aural world doesn't have to follow the same design decisions as the visual world. Whilst adding a soundtrack of twenty-first century music and warfare to a period production of *Othello* might seem incongruous, it doesn't mean it wouldn't work. It's all about finding the energy that works with the performance.

Where a production doesn't visually place itself into a particular period or geography, you have more freedom to experiment with placing it in one aurally. Whilst the set, costume, lighting and video designers are often working towards creating a shared visual aesthetic, we can choose to contrast, or juxtapose that aesthetic aurally. For example, the visual design may be going for realism, but our sound design might just follow the emotions of the characters, ignoring any naturalistic elements. We share our aural world with the performers, and it is with them that we must create something that works together first and foremost.

Is our production being directed to an established theatrical style, or a combination of styles? There are many practitioners, such as Brecht, Stanislavski, Meyerhold, to name a few, who can be said to have developed unique theatrical styles. Much current UK theatre, TV and film is done in a sort of faux realism, existing in the real world, whether in a contemporary or historical version

Othello at the National Theatre. Directed by Nick Hytner. Designed by Vicki Mortimer. Lighting design by Jon Clark. JOHAN PERSSON

OPPOSITE TOP: Frantic Assembly's *Othello*. Directed by Scott Graham and Steven Hoggett. Designed by Laura Hopkins. Lighting design by Andy Purves. MANUEL HARLAN

of it. Whilst we may create realistic environments, and realistic portrayals of characters within them, the actual plot of many of our productions is anything but realistic – it is often a wild exaggeration of what could possibly happen if a certain set of characters met in very certain circumstances.

This is not a criticism, and many people create work in many different styles. But it is the style currently people default to when telling a story, because audiences can relate more 'easily' to a story happening in a reality closer to their own, than, for example, the same story being told by the masked forms of commedia dell'arte. Of course, 'easy' is not the same as 'best', and there are stories that are best told through commedia dell'arte than through realism. Discuss with the director if they are directing it with any particular style in mind, or if they generally work to a specific style, and what that means for the world of music and sound.

CONCEPT FROM THE SHOW ITSELF

Finally the concept and execution of the show may emanate from the performance itself, the venue and the audience relationship, when the following questions may be asked:

- How will the show be performed?

- Is it a one-person show? Is it acted out?
- How are the performers bringing the story to life?
- Will there be a sense of a 'fourth wall'?
- Will there be soliloquies or monologues? Do we break out of the world of the story for these moments?
- Do the performers break out of the performance space into the auditorium? Will there be audience interaction?
- Will there be elements of improvisation? Do we need to allow flexibility in our design, and in its operation, to allow for this?
- Is there a narrator? What is the world the narrator is in? Is it first-person or third-person narration? What time, geography or world do they exist in? What does their existence do to the world they are narrating – does that place everything else as a memory piece? Is the narrator conjuring up the world they are creating? What power do they have over the world they are describing? How do we distinguish between the narrator and the world of their narration? Is the narrator reliable?
- How are we placing our show in the venue? End on, thrust, traverse, in the round, promenade? Each format brings different possibilities and challenges
- What are the characteristics of the venue? Does the venue impose anything on us? Is it a neutral space, or does it bring a story of its own to bear on the world? For example, what is the effect of telling a story about working-class characters in an opulent auditorium, or vice versa? An open-air theatre is often a noisy place, varying by time of day, and from day to day – how might you create an urban soundscape if the venue is contradicting that visually and aurally?
- How formal is the venue? A conventional theatre can be quite a controlling environment. An open-air theatre where people bring picnics to eat whilst they watch the show is more informal. This forms different audience relationships between the audience and the story.

5
MUSIC AND THE BLURRY WORLD OF SOUND

There are many ways we can use music to help tell a story.

Whilst we can often think of 'sound' as sounds that might have some naturalistic origin in the world, 'music' defies being explained so simply. We struggle even to define what music is. As human beings we have a complex relationship to music, as we know it can have quite a direct emotional connection with us that can bypass our rational brain. We often turn to it to express our emotions when words struggle to convey them, in times of joy and sadness. We know its effect is different on us depending on our own experiences, memories and emotional state – for instance, the same love song can make us happy or sad depending on our past experience or connections with that song.

We know music has many connections we have learnt, that don't necessarily cross different cultures: the theme tune to *Jaws* is something most people in Western Europe and the USA will know well to mean 'shark', but one can't assume that everyone has that association.

We use music to manipulate our own emotional state – to hurry us along as we go for a run, or do a work-out, to send us to sleep, to meditate. We may well have gone up to our room and turned our music up really loud when we were younger and in a strop!

Our experience of music is changed, and often defined, by repetition. Have a think about your favourite piece of music – the first time you heard it, was it instantly your favourite piece of music, or did it grow on you as you listened to it repeatedly? Sometimes we may hear a piece of music and it just sounds like noise, but after repeated listens we begin to pick out the patterns within it – what we are hearing is unchanged, but our brain's response to it has, and so has our relationship to it.

Indeed, one of the functions of an overture at the beginning of a show is to introduce the musical themes to the audience so when they hear them during the show it's not for the first time, it's something they're already familiar with. It's an interesting aspect that if we repeat a sound over and over, it can sound as if we've lazily copy-and-pasted the same sound effect several times. But arrange it into a rhythm and it can become musical, and we can enjoy the repetition.

There are many ways we might use music in a show. Music can create a shared energy, a shared emotion in our audience. We can use a piece of music to bring our audience together, to be more attuned to the story and to each other. Music is a great way to create an ensemble, both onstage and in the audience. Many of us are happy to let ourselves go into the embrace of music, to tap our feet, to sing along, to dance. Music can often bring people out of their shell in a way no other medium can.

Music can continue the energy from one scene to another, covering a prosaic activity such as a scene change or costume change. It can make the transition between the mood and energy of one scene to that of another – we may end one scene

OPPOSITE: Gareth Fry bowing a thunder sheet to create a dense, abstract sound.

SUCKER PUNCH AT THE ROYAL COURT THEATRE

Roy William's play *Sucker Punch* is set in the world of amateur boxing in the 1980s. The director, Sacha Wares, asked me if I could make a soundtrack for the trailer, which was visually simple, with Daniel Kaluuya skipping on the spot. We wanted it to build to a crescendo for the end of the trailer. The whole creative team had previously visited a boxing match to learn more about the sport and experience it from the audience's perspective. I'd been struck by the sounds of the sport, the rhythm of punches and the sound of breath and boxing gloves.

For the trailer I started off with the looped sound of Danny skipping on the spot. I recorded some sounds from the rehearsal room (which had a boxing ring in it) of thumping the floor, a punchbag, lots of boxing gloves, and made them all into rhythmic loops. I created a soundtrack using these loops, further layering on boxing bells, crowds, and a variety of voices speaking text from the show. The result sounds, to all intents and purposes, musical, but it doesn't use a single musical instrument.

Sucker Punch at the Royal Court Theatre. Directed by Sacha Wares. Designed by Miriam Buether. Lighting design by Peter Mumford. PETER MUMFORD

in mayhem and chaos, and start the next in serenity and calmness. Music can take us on a journey.

We can use music to set time and place, whether that's bluegrass or grime, eighties new-wave pop or forties Big Band swing. That music might exist within the world of the play, on a jukebox or radio, or it might exist outside the play, in the preshow music, as underscoring, for a transition or otherwise.

Music has functions in society we can draw on, from the *Here Comes the Bride* wedding organ,

muzak in a lift, Big Ben ringing, to a cheesy radio jingle.

We can associate themes and motifs with certain characters or situations. We are familiar with this in films, from the Harry Potter whistle to the many layers of character themes John Williams layers into a Star Wars film. Interestingly, you may notice a shift away from this in film music, with many of the Marvel universe movies doing continual underscoring in a way that doesn't grab your

THE BARBERSHOP CHRONICLES AT THE NATIONAL THEATRE

This play moves between a number of barbershops, with every other scene set in a barbershop in London, and the others set in barbershops in a variety of African countries. Director Bijan Sheibani was keen to use music in the scene changes to help guide our sense of location. For almost every scene change into London we would have a British Grime track playing, which would often fade into the HiFi speaker that was onstage in the barbershop set design. For each scene change into Africa, musical director Michael Henry arranged and taught the cast a series of acapella songs that incorporated the name of the town or city the next scene was set in. The music set the location, and created a tonal shift between the London and African scenes.

The Barbershop Chronicles at the National Theatre. Directed by Bijan Sheibani. Designed by Rae Smith. Lighting design by Jack Knowles. MARC BRENNER

attention the way a motif might. Neither of these approaches is right or wrong.

Whilst I'm referencing film music a lot here, it's often difficult to use film music in a theatre show because it might be too epic, or it has musical dynamics that correspond heavily to the way the film is edited, or an actor's performance within the film. Writing music for theatre is an art in itself, and something I'll leave a composer to write a book about.

BLURRING THE LINES

I've alluded to the grey area that exists between what we might strictly call music, and what we might call sound. There are many sounds that have a musical nature, in that they evoke music or stimulate an emotional response in us. We probably know this from personal experience. Studies have shown that the sound of a baby crying makes us agitated – it puts us into a heightened alert state. Also, our hearing is most sensitive to the frequencies that a baby cries at, amplifying our emotional response. The wail of a police siren, the rhythm and pitch of a cellphone ringing, are all in that same frequency range and have similar rising and falling patterns – these are sounds that are designed to get our attention by tapping into our sensitivity to a baby crying.

We can abstract sounds to create something that doesn't have a discernible naturalistic origin, but still feels organic and of the natural world. I make a lot of these sounds by slowing down real-world sounds by extreme amounts (there is more about this in Chapter 7, 'Content Creation'). I often use the resulting gently undulating, drone-like sounds to underscore a scene in a way that might add an edge to it without being quite as specific or apparent as a piece of music might be. Using less melodic or structured sound doesn't push the performer to react to the underscoring at all – there are no dynamics to influence them, so they can go with the dynamics of the story.

We can also abstract the sounds musical instruments make, whether that's something such as John Cage's 'prepared piano', or more abstract sounds again, such as bowing a cymbal. A lot of fun can be had experimenting with instruments to get them to produce sounds you wouldn't ordinarily hear from them.

If I'm working with a composer for the first time, one of the things we might establish early on is where, or if, we will draw a line between music and sound. The soundscape side of things is very interesting to me, so I will often offer to take that on. We might describe which moments in the show might be achieved primarily with music, or with sound, or with both. It can be quite a tentative negotiation process, dividing up the work between you.

I've worked with some lovely composers, repeatedly on many shows, by which point neither of us are fussed about boundaries and who does what, and we may well end up passing both our creative work back and forth between us as we process and develop what the other has done.

Often we are able to feedback to each other, generously but honestly, about each other's work, being able to hear and analyse the other's work with more objectivity than we can analyse our own.

We can also offer each other solutions to the problems we are facing. If there is a tricky time signature change the composer is struggling with, I can cover it with a sound effect. If there is a sound effect I'm struggling to make convincing they might be able to incorporate it into the musical world. In an ideal world, music and sound shouldn't ever sound as if they were done by different people.

THE EMOTIONAL JOURNEY

One of the most powerful ways we can use sound and music is when they are telling the emotional journey of the story. Many of the best stories engage our emotions as much as our intellect. Audiences often don't have time to develop a real emotional attachment to a character, but nonetheless we want our audience to care about the characters. Writers often use storytelling shortcuts to give the characters opportunities to show their worth, or their failings.

This can be seen in countless movies, in the opening shots: the camera pans across a room, past a photo of a policeman being decorated with a bravery medal, a wedding photo, then to a crumpled news article with the headline 'six-year-old son killed in tragic accident', then over some torn-up divorce papers and empty whisky bottles, and finally ending up on the dishevelled, semi-clothed form of someone asleep on the floor in a drunken stupor.

As well as giving us a fast (and somewhat cliché) back story of this character, it is also using highly emotive events – the death of a child, divorce, languishing in depression – to lead our audience's emotions, to have sympathy, to care about this poor character. This is a crude example but used surprisingly often. Even with more sophisticated stories we often lead the sympathies of the audience using similar techniques.

Alongside these emotive writing situations, music is often at the heart of how we engage, guide, and occasionally outright manipulate our audience's emotions. The musical equivalent of our camera pan example is the great swell of strings at the climax of a Hollywood rom-com that can have tears welling in our eyes even if we haven't cared much about these characters so far in the film.

Music makes me forget myself, my true condition, it carries me off into another state of being, one that isn't my own: under the influence of music I have the illusion of feeling things I don't really feel, of understanding things I don't understand, being able to do things I'm not able to do ... Can it really be allowable for anyone who feels like it to hypnotize another person, or many other persons, and then do what he likes with them? Particularly if the hypnotist is the first unscrupulous individual who happens to come along?

Leo Tolstoy, *The Kreutzer Sonata*

As we broach this topic we confront the ethical dilemma of the storyteller: how much do we want to guide our audience's emotions as we tell our story? Most people's first reaction to a question phrased this way is to say we shouldn't, we should let them make up their own minds. But is that really what we tend to do?

The Subjective Brain

It is easy to forget how different our hearing system is from our visual system, and how differently we use the two. For example, our hearing system is still active in some stages of sleep, standing by to wake us up as we slumber unconscious with our eyes shut. It's often an audible sound that wakes us up each morning, whether an alarm clock or someone whispering our name.

As human beings, we often use our eyes to focus on what is in front of us, whereas we tend to use our ears to remain aware of everywhere else, off to our sides, behind us. Our hearing system is always 'switched on', and because we can't focus our ears in the same way that we can focus our eyes on something, we physically hear more things than our brains can process. We have therefore developed a sophisticated filtering system that our brain applies subconsciously to choose which sounds we pay attention to. Stop reading this for a moment and count how many sounds you can hear. Were you consciously aware of all of them a moment ago, or had your brain filtered them out of your attention?

Our brain is adept at choosing to ignore sounds we don't consider relevant to us, whether that's the rumble of traffic or our own breathing. This filtering out happens at a subconscious level without us being aware of it.

Have you ever thought that someone had said your name, but when you turned around, nobody had? That's your brain subconsciously listening to fragments of noise, searching for meaning in them, and screwing it up. You've probably also heard your phone vibrating, but it didn't. Or your front door bell ring, but there was no one there. Exceptions aside, our brain is really good at interpreting meaning from partially heard fragments of sound, and filtering sounds out that would otherwise cause us sensory overload.

In other words, what we think we hear bears little resemblance to the real world. Listening is a subjective act. How and what we hear, or rather pay attention to, depends a lot on our emotional state of mind. This knowledge is something we can really lean on in thinking about how we can use sound to tell stories, particularly the emotional aspects of the story.

For example, we can reflect the emotional state of a character by choosing what sounds they might hear. If you've ever been alone in a house late at night you might suddenly start noticing the sound of the plumbing, or the structure of the house shifting around. These can be quite unsettling sounds. You might have been alone in a house late at night but in a jolly mood and maybe you didn't notice the sound of the plumbing and the house shifting – the sounds were still happening, your ears were still hearing them, but you weren't paying attention to them.

How good would a story be if our audience didn't feel anything for it, or the characters within it, and what happens to them? Is there any such thing as telling a story without leading the emotions of our audience? Even when we tell the story of a factual event, we can never tell it objectively, we are always telling it from one or many subjective points of view.

As you consider telling the emotional journey of the story, it is good to reappraise our relationship with the audience, to re-examine why we are telling this specific story, and why this specific audience is coming to see this specific show. Different audience members have different reasons to come to see any show. What they have in common is that they have bought a ticket to hear our story, to hear our take on it, and for that story to make them feel something, whether to escape their reality, to go on a ride, or to have their reality illuminated, or thrown into relief.

> There is an unspoken contract between magician and audience, according to which deception is both allowed and expected.
>
> Derren Brown, Foreword to *On Deception*, Harry Houdini

When the audience enter our theatre, I believe they come to be taken on a journey, both intellectually and emotionally. In placing their trust in us, we must use that carefully. If we go too far, or if we do it so crudely the audience are overly aware of what we're doing, it can cheapen their experience, it can make them feel they're being manipulated.

If we consider ourselves to be in a position to tell the emotional story of the show, we should weigh up how much we need to do it – how much is already evident in the story or the action? Sometimes the story will need an emotional lift here and there, sometimes not. Do we want to punctuate certain moments in the story, or do we want to illustrate the journeys between those moments? Do we want to punctuate our biggest emotional moment with loud music or a deafening silence?

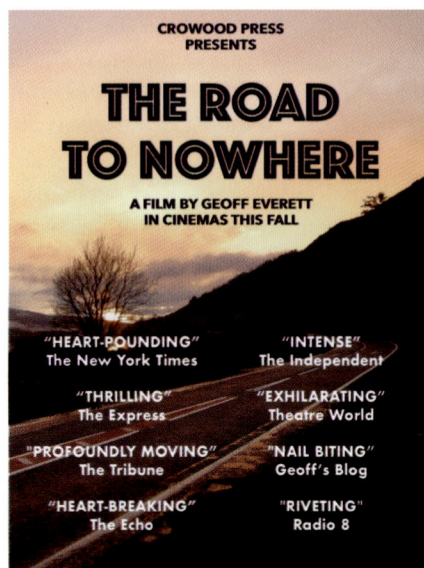

Movie posters often feature quotes pulled from reviews to sell the film to its potential audience. The pull-quotes are often the emotions the critic felt watching the movie, that the audience may want to go and feel too.

Not everyone responds the same way to the same stimuli. If we use one technique heavily over another to draw in certain audience members, to create certain emotions, we risk alienating those who don't respond to this technique.

I don't particularly like the sort of emotional manipulation as seen in the Hollywood string crescendo. But it is absolutely a technique I've used when I felt it was justified. Sometimes people don't mind their strings being pulled so long as they're not too aware you're pulling their strings.

Our initial script analysis and concept development will reveal many of the possible emotional stories that we might tell. We can also ask more specific questions:

- Do we want to illustrate the emotional journey of the character, or the audience?
- Do we know only what the protagonist knows, as they know it, or do we know more than them?
- Do we want to illustrate their thought process, their choices, their actions, or the impact of their actions?

- How does a character's internal and external world differ – which one might we illustrate? For example, a character's internal world might be 'death metal', but they may have a serene 'classical muzak' exterior

The style of emotional storytelling I gravitate towards is to punctuate certain moments in a way that gives things weight without explicitly leading the audience to feel a certain way. I don't tend to use traditional musical instrument sounds for underscoring, though we know that can be effective. I prefer abstracted sounds, sounds that exist halfway between sound and music, sounds where you can't identify the source. Often the emotional storytelling I do is on the edge of the audience's perception. It may be very low frequency or very high frequency, and it will often be introduced slowly and shift slowly. This way it never grabs our attention but nonetheless has an emotional impact on us.

As we look at using music, whether composed or found music, to tell the emotional story, we should consider our choice of instrumentation. Culturally we have grown accustomed to certain styles of music being used for certain types of movie, to signify certain things, whether that's the epic symphonic orchestra sound that is prevalent in big action movies, or the jagged strings of a horror movie. We can draw on these conventions if we want to – again they can be quick storytelling shortcuts, such as the string stabs from *Psycho* or the approaching shark in *Jaws*. Will some frenetic jazz or atonal music give us 'madness' because we've heard that in countless films? In the same way that we can use stereotyped sound effects to our own ends, we can also use stereotyped music, to reference their original context or to play against them.

There are many ways to underscore, with many different types of sound, with many different types of music, with abstracted sound, with abstracted music, and we should consider all these possibilities.

Some directors can be cautious of using underscoring. We've probably all heard it done really badly. If our director seems cautious, then take an equally cautious approach to it. You may consider waiting until you get into the theatre and introducing it there, in its more controlled environment.

6
PULLING THE IDEAS TOGETHER

As you establish the ingredients of your design, you should consider the following:

- How can you move between them?
- What are the polar opposites of each of your elements?
- Which are the most clichéd or obvious elements, and can they be excluded? I did a play recently that had a lot of magic in it, so the first two rules I set myself were to avoid any wind chime sounds, and to avoid using 'whoosh' sounds. These rules made my job immensely harder, but pushed me to find more interesting sounds and to explore different routes, rather than to head straight down the easy path. I did end up using some whoosh sounds, but no wind chimes!
- We can also use the language of cliché, of stereotypes, so we can subvert them and work against them later
- If you want something that is good, you're probably going to have to avoid the safe and easy route. Embrace risky ideas first, knowing that if they don't work out you can revert to 'safe and easy' later

These are all just ways to think of ideas, ways to locate something interesting in the script. If the sheer volume of questions here is causing you anxiety, worry not. None of these questions necessarily needs an answer. Maybe none of them will deliver anything useful for the particular script you are reading. A sound design doesn't necessarily have to be formed around ideas or your response to it. It doesn't have to provide all the meaning, all the context, all the answers. A simple response to the text can be as beautiful and artful as a complex response. Some shows really don't need anything

more than some scene-change music and a doorbell. Take your time to go through the thought process of analysing and thinking about the script, but there's nothing wrong with coming to the conclusion that it doesn't need anything.

I like to think of sound design as a voice that exists alongside and amongst the performers' voices. Sometimes we may choose to speak up, to come to the foreground, and sometimes we may be whispering away in the background. If you gain the trust of the director and cast, they will make space for your voice. I spend a lot of time working out how loud the voice of the sound design should be. For some shows it will be a loud voice, and for others not. This choice is as much a part of the art of your design as any other, if not one of the key parts.

I may talk sometimes about not wanting the audience to notice the sound design. Sometimes I don't want them to notice because I'm wanting to do something manipulative. Sometimes it's because I want to do something that subverts their expectations. Sometimes it's about disconcerting them. But what it's not about, is avoiding risk. It's not about being afraid to be in the foreground. It's not about being ashamed of our soundtrack. I often hear people say the words 'if the sound is good, no one will notice it'. This is nonsense. Yes, if all the elements of a story are working well, then no single element may stand out. But that's not the same thing. There are times when one should be bold with sound, and bold with music. Don't be afraid to suggest that the sound should be in the foreground to best tell part of the story.

Developing a concept should be a collaborative approach, not something you do all by yourself. You may develop a few different concepts – share these with the director, decide what to pursue together. Sharing and discussing ideas is a key part of developing a relationship between yourself and the director. Play them different ideas, different versions of things. Find out which versions they respond to and which they don't. This is a large part of how you discover their tastes, through their responses to your ideas. They may well suggest ideas you might never have thought of alone. Putting your ideas out in a rough form can feel quite a vulnerable thing to do, but it's only through making yourself vulnerable that you will discover the strength that is collaborating together as a team.

As you develop a concept it's easy to become obsessed by the internal logic of it: 'We can't do this because we've already established that…', or 'We've set our production in 1870, telephones weren't in common use at that time, so we can't…'.

> Logic is dull.
>
> Alfred Hitchcock

Don't let your concept limit you, don't let it force you into only being able to make certain choices because it is logical within itself. Our concept is a method to better tell the story. You make the rules of the world you create, so you can break them. If it better helps to tell the story, use your artistic licence, be irrational, be inconsistent, be unrealistic, be inaccurate. If the story is compelling then the audience won't mind. If your story is representing real people and real events, then be respectful.

> There are painters who transform the sun into a yellow spot but there are others who with the help of their art and their intelligence transform a yellow spot into a sun.
>
> Pablo Picasso, Sergei Eisenstein (1957)
> (Film form [and]: 'The film sense', p. 127)

Whilst it is useful to conceptualize our ideas, it is also important to play. Give yourself time to experiment with different sounds, with different FX units to see what happens. Process them, then process them again, and again. Can you remove the identity of the sound whilst retaining its essence? How can you layer the sounds with other sounds? When searching through sound effect libraries, play through the tracks that fall just outside your search criteria to see if there are interesting sounds there that are similar in sound to what you're searching for. Finding sounds that have the right energy is often more important than finding the most accurate version of a sound. Give yourself time to explore interesting mistakes.

CINEMATIC INFLUENCES

Looking at the use of sound design in cinema can be useful for talking about, and inspiring directors with, the possibilities of sound design. Part of this is because there isn't an equivalent repository of theatre shows you can show a director, to demonstrate sound design alongside a performance. There are many great examples of sound design in conjunction with performance, and a few minutes with a search engine can help you find many of them.

It is worth remembering that cinema is a different media, with a different relationship with the audience, and so the sound design is different too. Be influenced by it, but don't copy it. You'll often see sound effects and production elements being marketed as 'cinematic'. Some of these work well, but many of them, particularly those designed to accompany a trailer about giant alien robots or the total destruction of every known landmark on the planet, will just sound too big for theatre.

Here are a few films I find myself referencing often, in no particular order.

Contact: The opening five minutes is a great example of rewinding in time via archival footage, followed by lovely abstract sound design and a protracted silence. Sound design by Randy Thom.

The Godfather: Al Pacino finding the gun in the restroom: a great use of a naturalistic sound to indicate the internal emotional turmoil of a character. Sound design by Walter Murch.

Shaun of the Dead: There are many great sound sequences in this, but the scene transitions early in the film are a great example of how you can use diegetic sounds for transitions – for example, spreading butter on toast. It is also a good example of using one sound to mask another. The images of toilets being flushed, toast being spread, and so on, are used, along with their sounds, which seem to be driving the scene changes, but if you close your eyes you'll notice there are several 'whooshes' played at the same time, providing a lot of the energy and momentum, which we don't notice because our attention is caught by the visual elements. Director Edgar Wright's films often use sound well, with *Scott Pilgrim* (referencing of eight-bit sound and gaming, and blurring of transitions between scenes) and *Baby Driver* (with its integration of music, sound, editing and choreography) are both worth watching. Sound edited by Julian Slater.

The Sixth Sense: When the boy is heading to school but can't bear to go inside and stands outside. There is a great abstraction of the school bell here, which reverberates out with a long decay that slowly pitches down over time. There is a lot of use of room tones and human breaths as underscoring and transition elements. Sound design by Michael Kirchberger.

Eraserhead: Many of David Lynch's films provide interesting views of often disorienting worlds, but *Eraserhead* has many nightmarish tones worth exploring. Sound design by Alan Splett.

Tarkovsky's *Stalker*: Just watch it.

Klimov's *Come and See*: There are two notable sections, the first when the boy temporarily loses his hearing, due to a nearby explosion – an effect that is now often used, albeit much more briefly than here (see *Saving Private Ryan*'s opening beach scene as a more modern take on a bleak battle scene); and the section with the pile of bodies.

Atonement: The opening credits demonstrate a lovely interweaving of musical and sound effect elements, reflecting the role that storytelling takes in this story. Notice how the carriage return becomes a door opening sound. Composed by Dario Marianelli.

Wall-E: This Pixar film has little dialogue for the first thirty minutes, and is a masterclass in character voice design, and how sound can be used to communicate emotions without dialogue. Sound design by Ben Burtt.

Arrival: This is another great example of the use of sound design and music to create a sense of character. The lines between the sound design and music are often difficult to discern. Sound editing by Sylvain Bellemare, composition by Jóhann Jóhannsson, creature voices by Dave and Michelle Whitehead.

Cinema has developed its own language of using sound that is often inconsistent with reality. Sometimes we've heard the trope so often that it changes our sense of reality – for example in cinema, thunder is always heard at the same time as we see lightning, swords and knives make a metallic 'schwing' sound when unsheathed and when moved around, microphones always feed back when you start to speak into them, every computer beeps as it displays text on the monitor, and so on.

Movie sound is often incredibly unrealistic because it is often telling more about the emotional story than the naturalistic world. Movies are notoriously fluid with historical accuracy. Generally speaking, our audience members don't really care about this. There are exceptions – for example, American war films – where history is rewritten for dramatic purposes in ways that can offend those with an invested stake.

7
CONTENT CREATION

First of all, let us make clear that no one likes using the word 'content' when talking about our work, because it is generally something that we create with much love and artistry. The word is used in other creative industries often to differentiate between the content, and the system or infrastructure it will be played back on. It feels like a word that cheapens our work. However, it is better than saying 'the sound files', and less pretentious than saying our 'works of art', especially if SQ 1 is a doorbell sound effect. But let's not get too obsessed with the name, because there are far more productive things to be occupying ourselves with, such as making content!

It is to be hoped that we have had plenty of ideas about what sounds we might like to include, but how do we go about making them?

Generally, we need some source for a sound: it may be something we record, either an actual thing, or something we fake using Foley sound techniques; it may be a sound we source from a sound effects library or other pre-recorded source, or it may be a sound we've made using synthesis and modelling techniques. Then we'll take that sound and tweak it until it sounds good or appropriate. What sounds good is entirely subjective to your personal taste – and beware of being seduced, especially when working away from the rehearsal

OPPOSITE: Location recording. SARAH AINSLIE

room, into making something that sounds cool or epic, rather than something that's appropriate.

I often have in my head some sense of how I want something to sound, based on the ideas I've had about the show. Turning those ideas into a reality is often about finding the right ingredients. We live in a vast, complex world where there are often many variations to be found of any one description of a sound, and it can take a while to find those variations and search through them to find what you want.

SOURCING SOUNDS

When sourcing sounds, an important consideration is, how accurate do we want our sounds to be? If we are doing a naturalistic play that is entirely set in a forest, then we might want to have birdsong that is accurate for the country, season and time of day. Most audience members won't notice either way, but at some point there will be someone who notices the inaccurate sound effects, and you will spoil their night. I once spoke to a soldier who'd returned from Iraq the previous week who told me that my 'incoming shell' sound effect wasn't accurate…

But you must weigh up how much time you have to spend. Typically a *movie* sound design team may have a couple of months to assemble ninety minutes of sound, whereas we'll be lucky to have a couple of weeks and 1 per cent of their budget for our two and a half hours of drama.

Is total accuracy a good use of your time? It is easy to spend so long trying to 'do' accurate realism that you don't give yourself enough time to create the often more important emotional storytelling.

If we are doing a less naturalistic production, then we can free ourselves further from the burden of accuracy. Personally – and I know this will make some people furious – I have little patience for accurate birdsong. I have a stock of four birdsong sound effects for dawn, day, evening and night, and I use these for just about everything. To be fair, most of my shows will have many layers, and the birds are unlikely to be a prominent one. If they are prominent, or if I'm creating a world outside a typical European setting, then I'll put more time and energy into finding something appropriate.

It is totally acceptable to create a realistic sound design, but don't fall into it by default without considering how, to what extent, and when you want to be realistic, and what other choices you could make instead of being realistic. Don't get bogged down in the details of recreating some version of reality if you haven't yet worked out how to do the emotional heart of the show.

All bad art comes from returning to Life and Nature, and elevating them into ideals. Life and

THE WAPITI

I was doing a show set in Africa. I searched through a sound effects library and found a collection of recordings of various wildlife from Africa. I copied these off my hard drive and into my show folder. The director particularly liked the plaintive call of the wapiti, which I assumed was some form of bird. I did another show set in Africa with the same director, and he again asked to use the wapiti bird we'd found for the last show. In a quiet moment I used 'Google' to find out what a wapiti was, and was surprised to find out it was a North American elk. Obviously when I'd originally copied across the files, I'd accidentally selected an extra file that wasn't from Africa. Therefore geographically it was wrong, and the species was wrong – but emotionally it worked for the scene, so we kept it in.

There were many genuine African bird sounds that we discarded using because, whilst they were accurate, they were attention grabbing because of their unfamiliarity.

If it sounds good, it is good.

Duke Ellington

Nature may sometimes be used as part of Art's rough material, but before they are of any real service to Art they must be translated into artistic conventions. The moment Art surrenders its imaginative medium it surrenders everything.

Oscar Wilde, *The Decay of Lying*

SOUND EFFECT LIBRARIES

When I'm looking for sounds I often start with my sound effects library. Even though it is 5TB in size, my searches often don't turn up what I need. There are a range of sound effect libraries to choose from, both larger 'general' libraries, which offer a broad range of sound effects, or more specific libraries, which often feature one specific type of sound with a lot of variations of recordings of that. These can all be found online. Some of the libraries available are quite old now, recorded back in the 1980s or earlier. Some of these are great for shows set in the earlier twentieth century as they contain recordings of sounds that were around then. However, they can be bad sources for anything that has developed sonically over the years, such as phone rings. Some of the recordings can be relatively noisy, or lacking in dynamic range, due to the limitations of the equipment they were recorded with.

Sound effects are not cheap – they are often costly to record, so it is common for sound designers to build up their sound effects libraries gradually over the years. Increasingly you can purchase individual effects online, and we are also seeing subscription-access services emerge. Many people buy a general library, and add additional specialist libraries as and when they need them. Sound Ideas and Pro Sound Effects are two of the main suppliers of general libraries. ASoundEffect.com and Sonnis.com sell a lot of the specialist libraries.

When you 'buy' a song or a sound effect you are only ever buying a licence that lets you play it in certain settings – you never actually own the song or sound effect. If you buy something off iTunes it won't come with the licence to use it in a theatre show, or in anything else (they are also often lacking the metadata that allows them to be searchable by applications such as Soundminer or Basehead). Many consumer sound-effect collections don't allow you to use them commercially, so ensure that you 'buy' sound effects that come with a licence for theatre or commercial use.

The larger shows may require you to provide a list of the effects you've used and proof of ownership, to protect your employer from prosecution for using pirated sound effects.

LOCATION RECORDING

What makes a useful sound effect recording? How will we use it? What is the relationship between the sound and the stage?

If, for example, there is a big stage where we're playing the sound of a station, then having voices in the foreground of that recording will create a disparity – you can hear a voice in the foreground but there isn't a person on stage, or any sense of where that foreground person is. A more ambient recording of a station, with no distinguishable voices, recorded from somewhere high above the concourse, might be better than one recorded on the concourse. If you're playing a sound in the foreground for a transition, then that ambient recording might sound bland. Here you might want foreground detail.

When we record on location it is good to record as much material as possible because it is difficult to judge *in situ* what is going to work later. Listen to what is in the foreground of your recording, what's in the middle distance, and what's in the background. Record the perspectives you need, then record a few with different relationships between those layers. There have been countless times on location when the recording I thought was going to be less useful has been the one I've ended up using in the show.

The cost of recording equipment has dropped dramatically in recent years – everything has got smaller, and the quality has increased. But most handheld recorders do not have great microphones on them, so it is always a good idea to buy one with XLR inputs, and then buy a half-decent professional microphone that you can plug into it.

Ric Vier's book *The Sound Effects Bible* is a detailed exploration of how to create and record different types of sound effect, both in the studio and on location.

The key problem for location recording is the sheer level of background noise that exists in the modern world. Finding a way to control our environment, to silence any nearby noises, can be tricky. Moving whatever we want to record to a quiet location can also be tricky. We can sometimes use directional mics (and sometimes even contact mics) to get a recording with less noise.

WHAT TO USE?

I use a Sound Devices MixPre10-T, with a Sennheiser MKH50 and an MKH30 in an M-S pair in a big windshield. It can cope with really strong wind, but it's not great for discreet recording. For many years I used a small Zoom recorder with a Rode NT-4 stereo mic.

Gareth Fry recording at high speed on an Austrian log flume ride.

We must be careful about what we record. People have the right to privacy, so we can't record someone's conversation in the street and then play it to the world. We could ask those people before or after we record them if we can use the recording of them, but that may be tricky to do.

The world is full of objects making their own sounds, whether it's smartphones or self-service checkouts, often created by a fellow sound designer somewhere in the world, and these are predominantly copyrighted sounds.

Increasingly we are finding that what we imagine are public spaces is actually privately owned land where the owner won't allow us to record without permission. In large parts of London, such as the Southbank, City of London, and anywhere on the London Underground, we will get shut down for trying to record. You may also run into trouble recording near areas that are security sensitive, such as military bases, airports or schools. We can seek to get permission from the owner, but this can be costly and can take time, so we may often resort to covert recording techniques.

When we decide to record something we also need to allocate time to edit those recordings, and to add all the metadata (a detailed description of what's on the recording) to the file.

FOLEY AND STUDIO RECORDING

Location recording can be thwarted by many factors. Sometimes we can't record something because it's native to a faraway country we can't afford to get to. Perhaps it's something from hundreds of years ago. Perhaps what something actually sounds like isn't what we want it to sound like. Perhaps we need the sound of something that has never existed. Then we need to fake the sound.

'Foley' is the term that has become associated with making sound effects in a studio, and sometimes live onstage. The term comes from cinema, but many of the techniques date back through centuries of generating live sound effects for theatre. Frank Napier's 1936 book, *Noises Off*, details how a lot of these were created live for theatre, from simple thunder sheets and rain machines, to the seven stage-crew who would create the sound of a ghost train for the production *Ghost Train* at the Garrick Theatre, London, using a variety of garden rollers, air canisters, slats of wood, chains, mallets and some sandpaper.

The stereotype of Foley is the coconut shells for horse's hooves, and the snapping of celery for a bone breaking. These can actually be quite convincing done well. There are many techniques for creating naturalistic sounds.

We can create more abstract effects, too, and in my time I've waved a duvet around to create the flapping wings of a dragon, and roughly caressed lettuce to create the sound of a plant growing rapidly! Using Foley sound techniques, we can create sounds that just don't exist, or aren't possible to record. Ben Burtt has produced a great featurette film to accompany the film *Wall-E*, which looks at the use of these techniques for animated films.

There are a couple of books available that go through some of the best techniques to produce different types of sound, such as *The Foley Grail.*

Finding a studio that is well sound-proofed (to make it as quiet as possible) and well sound-treated (to make the acoustics as dry as possible) is essential for this.

PRODUCTION ELEMENTS

We talked before about sounds that have a musical nature, the sounds that might evoke a musical, emotional response in our audience but for which we don't have an identifiable source. These sounds are sometimes referred to as production elements, abstract sounds, tonal sounds. We can be less vague when we start categorizing these sounds more: drones, risers, stings, booms, whooshes, and so on.

These production elements are available for purchase on the internet or can be made yourself.

A drone can be made out of many things simply by slowing it down a number of octaves. This can be human speech, drawing a bow across a violin, a cymbal or waterphone. We can make many

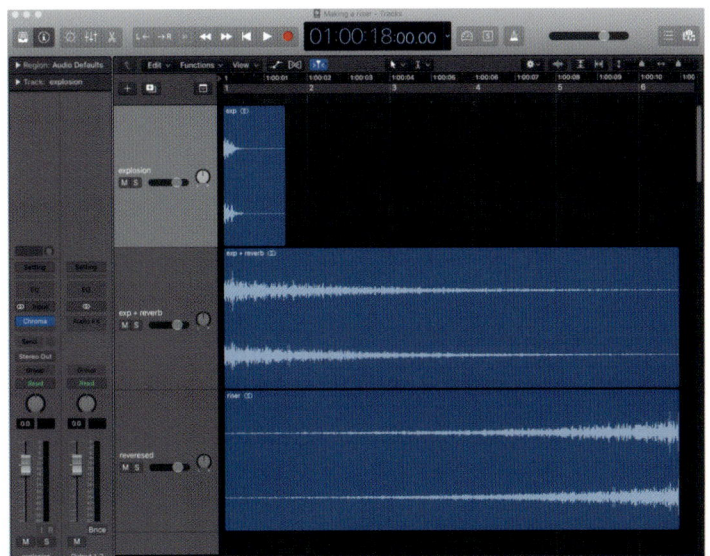

A riser effect can be created by using some sound with a strong impulse (Track 1), adding a long reverb to that impulse (Track 2), and then reversing that sound (Track 3).

LIVE FOLEY

One of the joys of live Foley is how performative it is, and how responsive it can be to what's going on on-stage. It can be difficult to be truly responsive playing back recorded sound effects.

Performing Foley is a real skill, requiring the artist to take on the character of who they are Foley'ing for, and to have a real sensitivity to the sound they're making. I have used live Foley in a number of shows, most successfully when employing a real Foley artist to do it, but I have also trained actors in how to do it. Some people really take to it, and others don't.

Foley sound is often about making sounds that have the right energy for the action. It's important to locate the amplified Foley sound as close to any visible action it's accompanying so they can support each other. Even the greatest of Foley effects will sound fake if played through the wrong speakers.

The Foley set-up for *Die Ringe des Saturn* at the Schauspiel, Cologne. Directed by Katie Mitchell. Designed by Lizzie Clachan. Due to the open nature of the stage, it was difficult to get the Foley mics loud enough, so wherever possible we tried to have as few mics on at any time.

interesting sounds with a cello bow, some rosin and occasionally a contact microphone.

We can create a riser effect by using some sort of sound, often one that starts with a sharp attack. Put that through a thirty-second reverb effect, then bounce that file out and reverse it.

You'll get a sound that builds up from nothing over thirty seconds to a big crescendo. You can alter the reverb time to create longer or shorter risers.

You can make a boomer from dropping a mic on to a table and EQ-ing the result. Whooshes

In the studio we might mic up Foley objects using a microphone 50–100cm away from what we're record-ing, so we don't get too many close-mic'd artefacts – in the same way we might mic up a musical instru-ment such as a flute or piano from a small distance to get a more natural sound, so the fingering or pedal sounds are less obvious. In the studio we don't have feedback to worry about. Typically in live sound we must either put Foley effects in a drum booth or soundproof box, or mic them really close to get enough gain before feedback. We will often process the Foley, trying to make it sound more ambient using the tools we'd use to do the same with a sound effect (*see* next section). We may add different reverbs and EQs to different effects, too.

An almost-soundproof Foley booth, for the opera *The Magic Flute*.

can be made in a variety of ways, though a huge number of sound libraries and whoosh-generating synthesizers is available.

One of the current vogue production elements is hybrid effects, many of which are naturalistic ef-fects or musical instruments run through extreme distortion pedals.

USING YOUR VOICE

Most of us are quite good at using our voice for vocal mimicry. These effects can be great for more cartoon-style effects. I often have quite specific ideas about how I want something to sound, and often just can't make it happen using our other techniques. If I can, I may record myself making the sound I want, and then use effects plug-ins to disguise the vocal nature of it. Often when I lay this in with actual recordings it can make everything sound just right.

RECORDING A VOICE-OVER

There are many reasons for us to record a voice-over. It may be for narration; it may be some form of scene that is playing in our offstage world; it may be a fake TV or radio station – actual TV and radio content is copyrighted, and complex and expensive to license, so it's often easier to make our own. We may end up recording multiple versions of the same thing with different actors to deal with all the possible combinations of understudies and covers who might go on.

I often find myself working one-to-one with a performer in the recording studio, as they are often scheduled when the director is busy in rehearsals. Consequently, I often find myself directing them to a degree, not just for vocal delivery and mic positioning, but also for character, accent, storytelling and everything else! It's important then to have the studio ready and working before anyone arrives. I give myself thirty minutes to get myself set up and tested, and more if it's an unfamiliar studio or if there will be complex foldback requirements.

Make sure there are printed copies of the script to record, in a large typeface and typed out for announcing. Check how to pronounce any unusual or foreign language words or names. Decide whether the number '1,500' is to be spoken as 'one thousand, five hundred' or 'fifteen hundred'. It is your responsibility, not that of the performers, to make sure you record everything you need.

Welcome the performers into the recording studio, get them relaxed and comfortable. Some performers deal well with being in a studio, others can clam up in such an unfamiliar environment. It's not uncommon for unresolved questions about character, accent, intentions or plot to come to the fore in the recording studio, as often we are committing

their current interpretation of the character to tape in perpetuity. Dealing with this, giving feedback on what they are doing and what you need from them, requires a lot of sensitivity and tact. It can also involve doing many takes to get them to produce something usable – 'Let's try one with a little bit more pace', 'Now let's try one that's a bit more threatening'. If there is an unanswerable question, just say 'Why don't we record it both ways?'

When the performer is on one side of soundproof glass and you're chatting away to someone else on the other side, they can often misinterpret that as you negatively discussing their performance, regardless of whether you are, or not. Keep talking to them, keep them in the loop of what you're discussing in the control room, don't let them feel isolated and cut off. Give lots of positive feedback.

READY, AIM, CHOOSE

A theatrical gunshot is often a tricky sound to choose how to do best.

A gunshot is a very high volume and very short sound. What we normally hear is the explosion of the gunpowder in the chamber, followed by the reverberation of that sound in the space we're in (possibly an echo off a distant surface, too).

The sound effect of a gunshot often sounds bad because most speakers can't reproduce the high volume that is required for the initial gunpowder explosion. If we use a blank cartridge in a real gun, this can often sound so loud in the confined space of a theatre that it simply shocks our audience so much that they don't really pay attention to what happens in the five minutes after it is fired. Whilst the sound effect might not sound as good, it can often better represent the sound of a gunshot than an actual gunshot can. Which we choose will depend on the size of our venue. We may perhaps even choose to mix live and recorded sounds – perhaps using the impulse of the live gun, with a recorded naturalistic or abstracted tail. Real guns can be quite unreliable, so we often have to provide backup for the real gun.

It's useful to record a voice-over, or anything else, with multiple microphones to give options later on in the production process. This photo shows the author recording with a Neumann U87 large-diaphragm mic, a Sennheiser Ambeo ambisonic microphone, and a Neumann KU100 binaural head. In this instance, the voice-over would probably also be used online in some form.

When you're ready to record, say something like 'We're rolling, whenever you're ready…'. Don't tell them to 'Go now!'

Often a performer may struggle to do a speech in one take, so you may have to break it into fragments to record it. However, it's important not to make the fragments too small as it won't flow together when edited. Once you've recorded all the fragments it can be useful to have a go at the complete speech again. Sometimes they'll be able to do it then, or at worst it gives you something to work the fragments into. If you're unsure whether you've got a usable take, do a quick edit to check before releasing them. Better to have them wait for ten minutes than have to call them into the studio again.

Depending on the material you're recording, it can be easy to end up with something that sounds very obviously recorded in a studio. I might ask the performer to project a little more, to imagine they are in a theatre and projecting to the back of the stalls, rather than delivering it to the mic a few centimetres in front of them. This will match their vocal delivery more closely to what we might hear from someone in the theatre.

You can also take a radio mic into the studio and record through that to match the signal chain of the theatre, rather than record with a studio mic. This works very well for recording click tracks so the recorded track sits better in the mix with the live vocals.

Once you've got what you need, always get another clean take. We call this the 'safety take' – an additional good take in case we find a flaw with the original.

When you come to editing your voice-over session, start at the end and work backwards. This way you start off by editing the final, and often best take, rather than working through all the moderate takes first.

We could double the length of this book if we started talking about recording musicians in a studio, and there are plenty of existing resources for that. Many of the same psychological strategies should be observed, as would be when working with actors.

SOUND SYNTHESIS

There are many different types of sound synthesis engines available to create sounds from scratch. You can use these to create tonal or abstract sounds, or more obviously musical sounds. Synthesizers can be powerful tools because you can make subtle modifications to the sounds to allow them to subtly alter in timbre to match changes in performance. Synthesis tools can also be used to process existing sounds, with interesting tools such as Krotos' Reformer plug-in allowing you to use your voice to modulate existing sound effects.

Sound effects can be synthesized, a technology that is becoming more sophisticated due to its use in game audio. The software pictured here is LeSound's AudioWind, who also produce similar plug-ins for creating fire, footsteps, electricity and engines.

As computer game technology develops we are seeing more advanced forms of procedural audio to synthesize sound effects in real time – for example, synthesizers that can model a jet turbine, or wind, rain or fire, where we can specify the engine speed, or we can choose how heavy the rainfall is, and what surface it is raining on. Whilst not perfect, these technologies are developing and allow for a lot of interaction with a performer or with the sound operator.

PROCESSING SOUNDS

We've sourced our sounds, now it is time to start tweaking them, to make them more appropriate to our sound design. This means talking about computers, sound-editing software and plug-ins (software you can add to other software to extend what it can do).

One of the key problems with using sound effects, and often location recordings, is that they are often recorded as close to the source sound as possible, so as to eliminate other noises, or the acoustic of the recording environment. Sometimes that's fine, but sometimes these sounds may need to sound part of the offstage world. For this, a more ambient recording might be desirable

but is perhaps unobtainable. Assuming the latter, we can simulate that extra distance, to make it sound as if it were recorded from further away than it was. This can be done by using sound-processing software such as TDR Lab's Proximity plug-in, which simulates the effect of air absorption over distance. This means that as we get further away from a sound it doesn't just get quieter: as the distance increases, the bass and treble frequencies drop off more than the middle frequencies.

A close-up recording of something will also accentuate more of the transients of a sound. For example, a recording of a person up close will feature more of the sounds of their mouth, of their clothes moving. A recording from a metre away will have less of these elements and more of the voice, which projects away from the body more

TDR Lab's Proximity plug-in is excellent for making things sound further away, by simulating air absorption loss over distance. Turn the Original Distance knob up to 10m, then experiment with bringing down the Distance Fader.

than the other sounds. (This is also a reason why radio mic'd cast members can sound artificial when they are close mic'd and amplified to a delay speaker near us.)

Occasionally you can use a transient processor, such as SPL's Transient Designer, to reduce the attack of sounds to make them feel less close. Another tool I find really useful is Audio Ease's Speakerphone. It has a reasonably unique module called Cover, which simulates the effect of your sound being muffled by something. My most used preset is the 'eight blankets and eight bricks' setting, which simulates your sound being played through a speaker that has eight blankets placed over it, with eight bricks on top of them!

These tools, along with using some EQ and some room reverb, can make many close-mic'd sounds more usable, more able to sit in our world.

There are many other ways we can process sounds: first, and obviously, we can make lots of edits and crossfades. Then Compressors are an incredibly valuable tool, both functionally and creatively; look up an online tutorial, or spend some time fiddling round with one.

We may want to thicken up a sound, often to add more bass. There are specific plug-ins to do this, such as Wave's LoAir. We can also copy our audio regions to a new track, transpose it down a few octaves whilst preserving the speed of playback, and layer it with the original.

ABSTRACTING SOUND

Abstracting sound is one of the most fun parts of sound design. There are lots of techniques to play with, and the key word here is 'play'. It is often

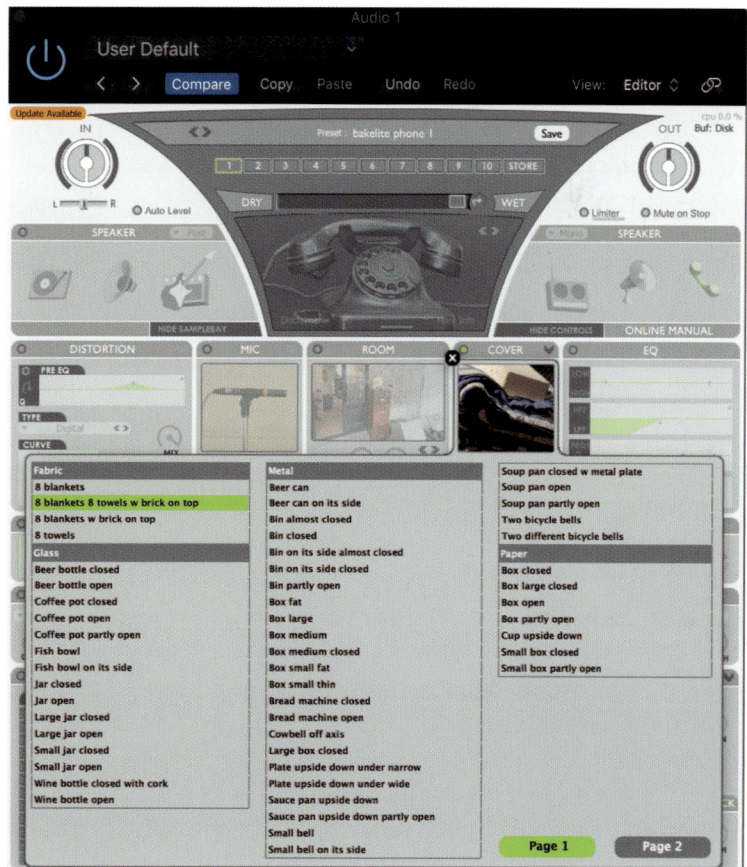

Audio Ease's Speakerphone plug-in showing the Cover module, useful for muffling a sound.

difficult to predict what you may end up with, and it's amazing what you can create by accident. I use the techniques described below.

Abstraction of Volume

We can create weirdly abstract soundscapes by using entirely naturalistic sounds, but playing the constituents' ingredients at levels that defy our expectations. We expect certain sounds to be at a certain volume and we can be surprised when they aren't. Horror films play a lot with our expectations of volume: imagine the protagonist, slowly walking down the dimly lit corridor – they are afraid, we can hear their breathing, their footsteps louder than normal. They creep further down the corridor, knowing the serial killer is probably lurking round the next corner. And. Suddenly. A cat jumps out, meowing loudly, at full volume, making us jump in our seat.

> We sat around in the living room describing the loudest things we'd ever heard. One said it was his wife's voice when she told him she didn't love him any more and wanted a divorce. Another remembered the pounding of his heart when he suffered a coronary. Tia Jones had become a grandmother at the age of thirty-seven and hoped never again to hear anything as loud as her granddaughter crying in her sixteen-year-old daughter's arms. Her husband Ralph said it hurt his ears whenever his brother opened his mouth in public, because his brother had Tourette Syndrome...
>
> *The Largesse of the Sea Maiden*
> Dennis Johnson

Time Passing

You are in control of the speed a clock ticks at. You can make it fast or slow. You can vary it in speed. In doing so, you are in control of the sense of time in a play. If you want a moment to drag out, you can extend the gaps between the ticks. If you want a moment to seem like it is racing by,

you can do the opposite. If you want the world to slowly go weird, you could slowly stylize and abstract the tick of the clock, in an unnoticeable or a noticeable way.

In life, things often take longer than we need them to take. Someone getting into a car and driving off can take about forty seconds normally, but we might need it to take five seconds. We can do this by simply editing out the silences, or by cutting out moments without significant change. At other times we may be able to use time-stretching techniques to speed things up or down.

Live Abstraction

We can work with the performers to abstract the sounds that they are making live onstage. If they are doing something repetitive, we can slide in and out of a rhythm, or make what they're doing somehow more dissonant. Consider any sound they're making, whether it's the cutlery they use to eat a meal, or the way they may be writing on a piece of paper, as like playing a musical instrument, that can be varied in all the same ways.

Morphing Sounds Together
Convolution Reverb

Convolution reverb plug-ins, such as AltiVerb and Space Designer, work by someone going to a real place, firing a starting pistol, or playing swept pink noise and recording the result. The recording, known as an impulse response, can be loaded into the software, and any sound you play through it will sound as if it is being played in the acoustic space the impulse response was recorded in. This is extremely useful for recreating a natural space. But you can load in any sound as the impulse response, which will then affect any other sound played through the plug-in. Sharp sounds often work well. You could also load in the sound of a snake hiss, and then any speech you sent through the plug-in would sound somewhat hissy. You can play with the wet/dry balance of the plug-in to create a sound that is heavily modulated by the input signal.

SIDE-CHAINED NOISE-GATES

Noise gates can mute, or dip, the level of a sound according to the volume of the incoming sound. Normally they respond to their own input, but we can set up the 'side chain' such that it responds to another sound. For example, my idea is to have a heartbeat, but instead of the regular bump-bump sound, I want it to be composed of a crowd cheering. I start with a continuous crowd cheering sound, and a heartbeat. I insert the noise gate on the track with the continuous crowd, but I would set its side-chain (or key) input to the track that has my heartbeat on it. I would set the threshold of the gate so it is triggered by the heartbeat, and set the attack and release

time so that the crowd cheering sound fades in and out relatively rapidly.

CROSSFADING SOUND

Our brains often seek to identify a sound when we first hear it, and having identified it, we move on to listening to the next new thing we hear. This means we can do a bait-and-switch on the human brain. As an example of this, you could start the sound effect of a car passing on wet tarmac, but have it crossfade to the sound of a wave crashing on a shore.

MAKE IT WEIRD

Most sound plug-ins are designed to make quite subtle, sculptural changes to a sound. But often we need more radical changes.

The track labelled Audio 1 is a recording of continuous crowd noise. Track Audio 2 is a heartbeat recording. A noise gate plug-in is inserted across the crowd sound on Audio 1, but the side chain is set to receive audio from Audio 2 (the heartbeat). The noise gate then turns the volume of the crowd on Audio 1 up and down in time to the heartbeat, creating the effect you can see on track Audio 3.

The fifty-five second reverb: A wash of reverb across sounds can be effective at making everything sound a little weird. By using a fifty-five second reverb time we are definitely out of naturalistic reverb simulation. You can apply it to single effects to make them stand out amongst an otherwise naturalistic background. Adding it to a school bell, or a ringing phone, or some other sound that has a harsh attack, can create really interesting tails.

Delay and filter effects: Both delay and filter effects can be exaggerated to create stylized effects. There are a few specific effects suites (such as GRM Tools, OhmBoyz, Soundtoys) designed to work at the more extreme end of the spectrum. Guitar-pedal filters are often designed to be less than subtle.

Audio Ease's Speakerphone: This is one of the plug-ins I use most often. It has a huge toolset to allow the manipulation of sound, from simulating your sound being played through a variety of loudspeakers, in a variety of acoustics, with specialist modules to emulate gramophone wow and flutter, radio interference, and cellphone interference. Whilst many of these can be used to make something naturalistic, they can also be used more abstractly (such as the birdsong in the opening of *Dancing at Lughnasa* discussed elsewhere). You can obtain similar results with some other plug-ins, but few offer the ease and flexibility that this module does.

Spectrasonics' Omnisphere: This synth has developed over the years, starting out as a CD set called Distorted Reality, into Atmosphere, and most recently into Omnisphere. It contains a large

Spectrasonics' Omnisphere synth contains a huge library of abstract and stylized sounds, plus powerful manipulation tools.

PLUG-INS IN THE LIVE ENVIRONMENT

Ableton Live and Apple's Mainstage are both good tools to use as plug-ins in a live environment.

You need to be careful about system latency. The more complex an effect is, the more latency, or the more delay it may introduce between the raw and the effected signal. Some soundcards have higher latencies than others. For example, the Dante Virtual Soundcard has a higher latency compared to its physical PCIe soundcard.

We avoid using Pro Tools and Logic in a show environment as they are not designed for it. They crash more frequently and are not optimized for live use, so, for example, don't start playing sound as soon as you press 'play'.

Apple's Mainstage software is a popular computer-based effects processor, allowing the full suite of Logic Pro's effects and software instruments to be used in a live environment, alongside other AU-based effects units and instruments. It is also popular with band keyboard players to expand the sounds they can play.

range of already abstracted effects, and stylized playable instruments. It is an excellent source for weird drones and tones.

Layers and layers: A lot of the time I will combine many of the possibilities above and layer them up to produce a denser sound. Whenever I produce a layered sound I will bounce it out as its different layers, so I can experiment with different volumes for each layer within QLab.

THE EQUIPMENT YOU NEED

You need a certain amount of equipment to get started as a sound designer. Fortunately, the initial investment becomes more affordable each year. These are my recommendations for someone starting out to have access to.

An Apple laptop: Whether you're a fan of Apple or Microsoft is largely irrelevant, as the industry standard software (QLab) for theatre sound playback is Mac only, and you're inevitably going to spend a lot of time using that software. Macs can run Windows either simultaneously via an emulator or can be rebooted to run it natively via Bootcamp, so you can run both operating systems on one machine. Get the most amount of memory and storage you can afford. This will be the heart of your ability to earn money and where you'll spend many hours a day, so don't skimp on it. Purchase a portable 5TB hard drive to back it up, and an Ethernet adaptor to plug into a wired network.

Apple Logic Pro software: Reasonably priced, regularly updated and one of the top three Digital Audio Workstations (DAWs) that people use to record, edit and create sound with. Pro Tools is the more expensive industry standard, but I prefer Logic. It comes with a massive array of built-in plug-in effects and many software synthesizers.

Zoom recorder with XLR inputs, such as H4NPro: These are excellent small handheld recorders, though you may find them a little hissy for quiet sounds. If you can afford to, buy a Rode NT4 stereo mic with a Rycote mini windjammer, to get better quality recordings. If you can afford it, Sound Devices recorders are a popular choice for higher quality recordings with exceptionally low noise. Both the Zoom and the Sound Devices can be used as a soundcard for your computer, too.

Figure 53's QLab: There is a free version you can start with, though it is limited in features. Whilst funds are limited you can rent the full version of the software on a day-by-day basis until you can justify buying a full licence.

Novation Launchkey Mini: This is a mini two-octave keyboard with Launchpad-style buttons and some assignable knobs to give you more hands-on control. Even better, it comes with a version

The Zoom H4NPro is a reasonably high quality handheld recorder. Whilst you can record with the built-in mics, the XLR inputs allow much higher quality mics to be used.

of Ableton Live Lite to get you started with that software.

Headphones: A pair of Sennheiser HD25s will be suitable for most applications.

Sound effects: A general sound effects library will be financially out of reach for many people starting off, but have a look at Pro Sound Effects Hybrid Library. You can buy individual sound effects from www.prosoundeffects.com, or smaller

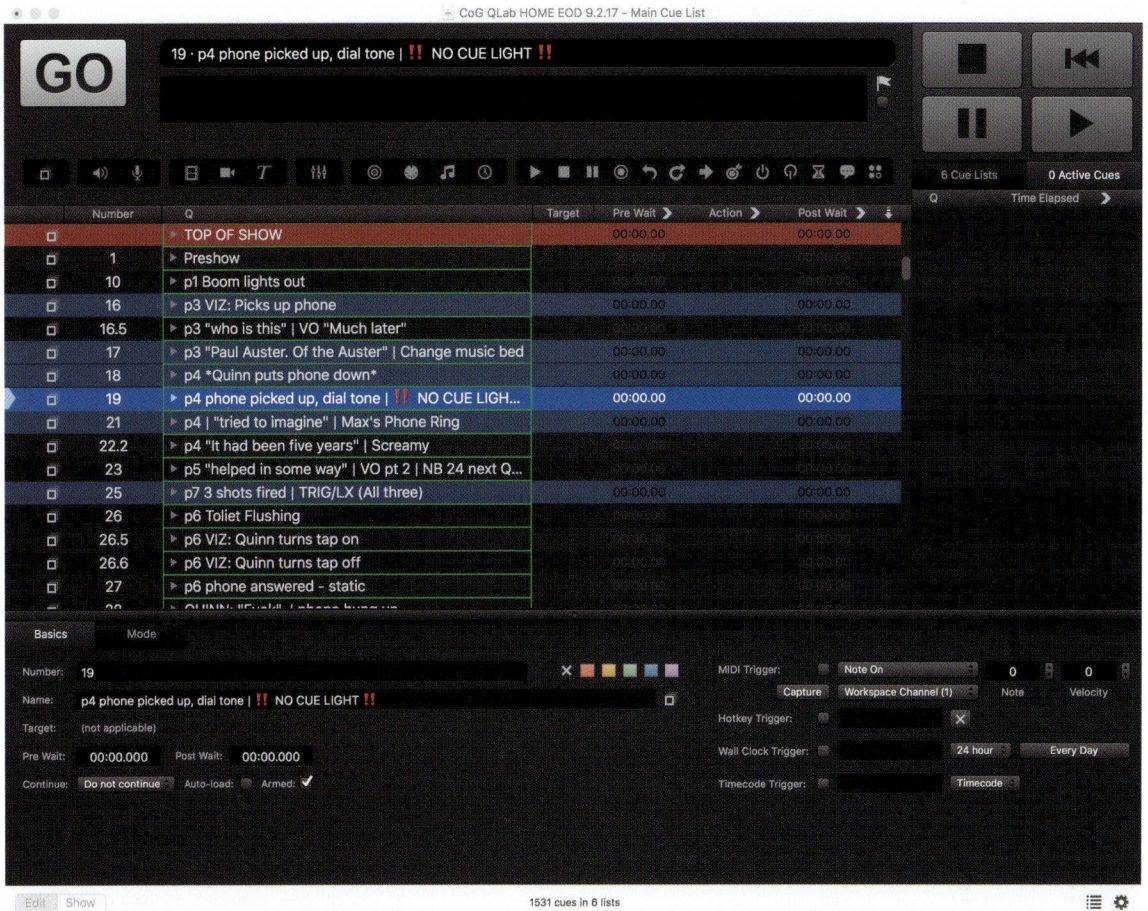

Figure 53's QLab is the industry standard for theatre sound playback.

collections of sounds from www.asoundeffect.com

There are many plug-ins compatible with Logic and Ableton that you can download for free, such as TDR Lab's Proximity, Izotope's Vinyl, and others you can find with a quick web search.

Keep your computer backed up. A service such as Dropbox Pro allows you to continuously back up your files to the cloud for a relatively small amount of money per year. Whilst this cost is not inconsequential, it is nothing compared to the potential disaster of losing the show you're designing in the middle of tech week.

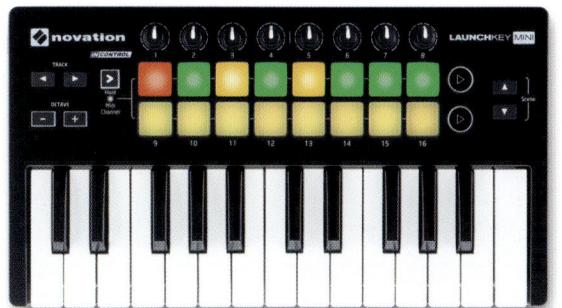

The Novation Launchpad Mini provides a small keyboard, Launchpad triggers for hotkeys, and lots of controls to manipulate sound.

8
REINFORCEMENT AND AMPLIFICATION

One of the key decisions to make in the early stages of the design process is whether you want, or need, to reinforce or amplify the show. This could be for the performers' voices, or for live musicians, or both. Sometimes we do this because we want to, for how it sounds, and sometimes because we need to, and that's usually to make the show audible when otherwise it wouldn't be.

Sometimes it is a borderline decision as to whether we need to or not, and in these circumstances there are a number of measures we can take to avoid reinforcing a show if we don't want, or can't afford, to do so.

INTELLIGIBILITY AND ACOUSTICS

Perversely, many theatres do not have great acoustics. Whilst you can happily sit in the stalls and hear everything that's being said on stage, if you wander off to the side or to the back of the stalls (under the balcony overhang), or perhaps to the top level of the theatre, it may be that very quickly you won't be able to hear what is being said.

Obviously, volume drops off over distance, so for the audience members who are furthest away, the actors will sound quieter. Whilst this is often an important factor, there are others to consider, and they impact how intelligible the speech is – how well we can make out what is being said. Making something louder doesn't necessarily make it easier to understand, a myth we often must dispel. If someone is mumbling, we can make it a loud and perfectly clear amplification of a mumble, which still won't be understood because it's being mumbled. Equally we can make a perfectly clear voice really loud and it still won't be understood because there are other factors at play.

King's Theatre, Glasgow, from the rear of the Upper Circle.

Factors Affecting Intelligibility

The following are the key acoustic factors that affect how intelligible a performer's voice is:

The 'signal-to-noise' ratio: This is essentially the amount by which our performer's voice (or any other signal we are interested in hearing) carries above the noise (anything we don't want to hear) .

The 'direct-to-reverberant' ratio: How much do we hear the performer's direct voice, and how much do we hear the acoustic of the room? We have all heard unintelligible speech in churches and train stations, where the volume of the speech is perfectly loud, but the speech is bouncing off all the walls and creating a reverberant sound that makes it hard to understand the speech.

The reverb time of the room: This is how long it takes for a sound (a starting pistol is often used to measure this) to reverberate around the room and die away. Most theatres have a useful reverb time for voice intelligibility.

We will look at these factors in more detail below.

The Signal-to-Noise Ratio

Typical 'noises' include the following:

- Whirring fans on moving lights, projectors, smoke machines
- Air-conditioning noise
- Footsteps and other sounds of movement, such as scenery moving across a stage
- Audience noise, such as coughing, unwrapping sweets. At Christmas shows, children's shows, or anything with audience interaction, the audience will probably be noisier, so the performers will be harder to hear over them

FAMILIARITY AND INTELLIGIBILITY

When judging how intelligible something is, bear in mind that you probably already know what they're going to say – you've read the script, you know the plot, you've seen the rehearsals. It's important to make provision for a lack of familiarity from our audience, which means it has to be more intelligible than it needs to be for us.

This can be an issue on long-running musicals, where the vocals are mixed slightly lower in the mix than the audience members need them to be. The show probably opened with the vocals at a good volume, but as the person mixing the sound has become so familiarized with the show, and it is they who judge how loud each microphone must be on a night-by-night basis, slowly the vocals drop in the mix, ever so slightly.

There may also be sound that we *do* want to hear, such as sound and music, live or recorded, and whilst we may want to hear them, it can make it harder to hear the performers.

There are many ways we can reduce noise to help intelligibility. Work with the lighting designer and electrics department to ensure all lights and smoke machines are on their quietest setting, or only go to a louder setting during loud moments of the show or during the preshow and interval. Hazers and smoke machines can be moved away from the stage, with pipes installed to vent in the smoke and haze. Some models are louder than others. Video projectors can be put in ventilated cases to make them silent.

Check that offstage areas are carpeted wherever possible, to minimize offstage shuffle. Can you avoid scenery changes during quiet dialogue? I have in the past discussed with the theatre management about the types of sweets they sell front of house, to encourage them to sell sweets in plastic tubs rather than in plastic bags, for example.

With our wanted 'noises', we can keep underscoring music low under dialogue, and position it upstage of the performers so there is not a wall of sound between the performer and the audience. This does place a limit on how we underscore a scene.

The Direct-to-Reverberant Ratio

This is a more complex set of factors, involving the performer's voice, helpful reflections and unhelpful reflections. The acoustics of the set design can also help or hinder.

It can be seen in the first drawing that a lot of the performer's voice goes out to the audience, but a significant part of it dissipates upstage, into

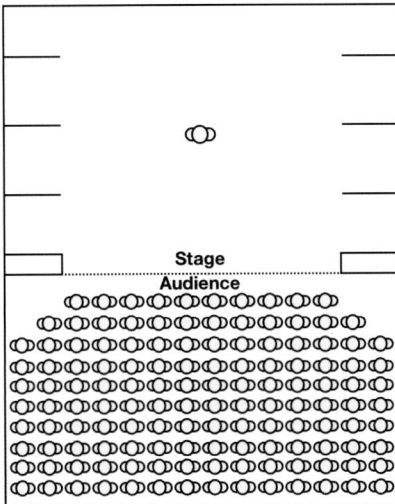

An empty stage, where a proportion of the performer's voice will dissipate into the wings and the fly tower.

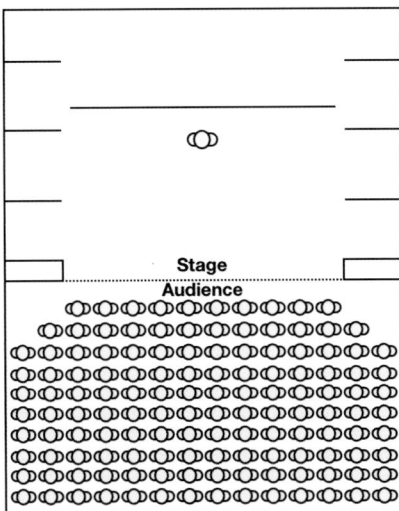

A wall upstage will reflect some of the performer's voice into the auditorium, making them louder and easier to hear.

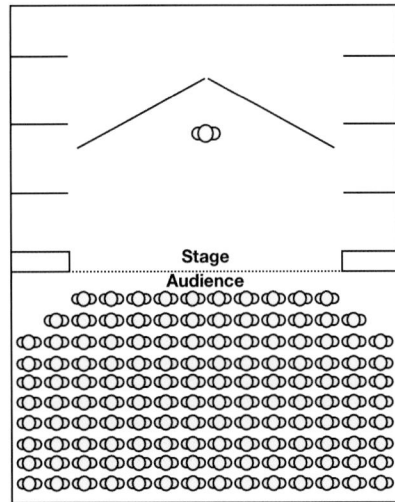

A wall that reduces the amount of vocal energy disappearing into the wings, and reflects the performer's voice into the auditorium, will make them even louder and easier to hear.

the wings and into the fly tower above. Only about 70 per cent of the voice gets to the audience – the rest of that vocal energy is wasted.

In the second drawing, there is a hard reflective surface upstage of the performer, so the voice that would have dissipated upstage instead reflects off the wall, and heads back downstage. About 80 per cent of the voice gets to the audience.

In the third drawing, the walls catch the sounds that head off into the wings as well and reflect them back into the auditorium, so we get about 90 per cent of the performer's voice heading into the auditorium.

The Olivier Theatre is a classic example of a theatre that has tricky acoustics. It has suffered regularly in the past from the audience complaining they are unable to hear dialogue. This is particularly the case when it is used in an open stage format, as illustrated.

Much of the performer's voice disappears upstage, into the wings and the fly tower. There are walls upstage, but they are so far away that the reflections that come off them hinder intelligibility rather than helping it. Sound travels slowly, so distance is significant. The further a sound travels, the longer it takes to do so. We wish the reflected

The open, empty stage of the National Theatre's Olivier Theatre. This photo from *Fram* is of a scene set in the Olivier itself. Directed by Tony Harrison. Set design by Bob Crowley. Costume design by Fotini Dimou. Lighting design by Mark Henderson. PHILIP CARTER

voice to arrive at approximately the same time as the voice coming directly from the performer's mouth. Consequently, the distance the reflected voice travels needs to be as short as possible.

Our brains can process these reflections and use them to help our understanding of the voice. They are known as 'early reflections'. Late reflections – ones that travel a greater distance and arrive more than thirty milliseconds after the voice directly from the performer – confuse our hearing and hinder our understanding of what is being said. The longer the journey these reflections take as they bounce around the auditorium, the more they may resemble echoes, which confuse our hearing even more.

In these photos from *Othello*, designed by Vicki Mortimer, the set design provides a great acoustic to push the performer's voice into the auditorium. The walls form similar patterns to those in our earlier illustrations. Here the aesthetic of the set design is in harmony with aiding the performer's voice. But the set design aesthetic isn't always

conveniently aligned in this way, and what might be helpful to telling the story, might not be helpful for the acoustics.

The Reverb Time of a Space

The reverb time of a space is a measure of how long it takes for a sound to die away (to drop by 60dB from its peak level – hence you may also see it written as RT60). This is rarely a characteristic of a space that we have a lot of control over, as it is often defined by how acoustically reflective the walls, floors and ceiling are. Generally speaking a hard surface will reflect sounds (for example, a painted brick or concrete wall), whereas a softer surface will absorb it. For smaller spaces, heavy black drapes are often used to deaden a space, to reduce the reflections. But it is not just the surface of the wall that affects how absorbent it is, but the internal construction, too. Specialist acoustic absorption panels and diffusers are often installed in

Othello, the National Theatre. Directed by Nick Hytner. Designed by Vicki Mortimer. Lighting designed by John Clark. These photos shows the set design creating strong reflective surfaces, helpfully reflecting the performer's voice into the auditorium, aiding intelligibility, and avoiding the need to use radio mics on this production. PHILIP CARTER

Othello, the National Theatre. Directed by Nick Hytner. Designed by Vicki Mortimer. Lighting designed by John Clark.

theatres (when they are built) to control the acoustics, to make it favourable to speech.

Audience members are also strong acoustic absorbers, which means that an empty auditorium can sound vastly different from a full auditorium, especially if there are plastic (reflective) seats rather than fabric (absorbing) seats. It is a relatively common phenomenon that we find we have to turn everything up 3db when we go from rehearsing in an empty theatre, to when the audience come in, to counter all those human bodies absorbing our sound. A full auditorium may mean that less sound is bouncing around, reflecting off the walls, so the reverb time shortens as well. For speech, a shorter reverb time is usually better than a long reverb space, but if it's too short, those helpful early reflections could be absent and the overall sound reaching our ears will be quieter and therefore less intelligible.

ACOUSTIC REFLECTORS

A theatre may be permanently equipped with acoustic reflectors in the auditorium, to reflect the performer's voice down from the roof. Why do we install these so low down when we could just make the ceiling reflective? We are trying to make the path of the reflections as short as possible, so they will arrive at roughly the same time as the direct sound and hence aid our understanding of the words. If they bounced off the ceiling, they would arrive later and make the words less intelligible. The acoustics of a theatre are mostly not changeable on a production basis as these solutions are vastly expensive, heavy, and require complex rigging in the auditorium.

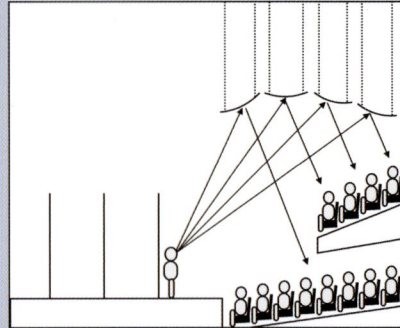

Acoustic reflectors reduce the time it takes for a reflection to reach the audience, and the amount of volume it drops off by, thus aiding intelligibility.

However, good acoustics for speech are not the same as good acoustics for music, as most houses of worship prove. Generally, music benefits from a slightly longer reverb time. Fortunately, whilst it's difficult to reduce the reverb time of an auditorium, we can increase it by adding an electronic simulation of reverb to our sound, so we can get the best of both worlds.

Blocking Affecting Intelligibility

The human voice is directional, that is to say most of the sound comes from the front of our body, from our mouth. Where our actors are facing is significant. When an actor is facing downstage, most of their vocal energy is going out front to the audience. When two actors are talking to

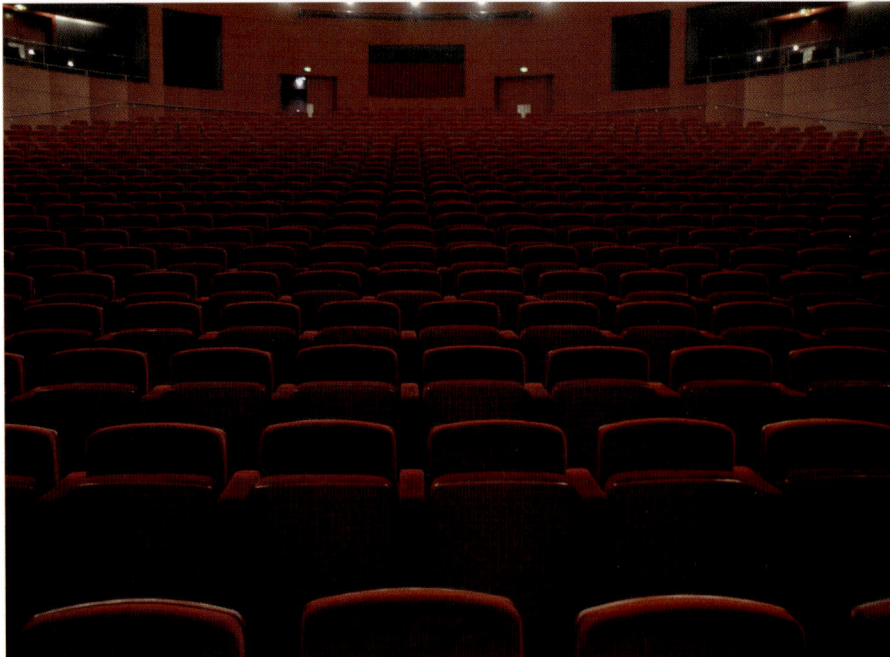

LEFT: The seats in this venue are designed to be as acoustically absorbent as a human being, so that an empty auditorium sounds similar to a full auditorium.

OPPOSITE BOTTOM LEFT: A performer facing downstage.

OPPOSITE BOTTOM RIGHT: Two performers talking to each other. Most people will hear them quite adequately, but people on the edges will find it harder to understand what is said by people who are facing away from them by a small degree.

PARABOLIC AND PARALLEL WALLS – ACOUSTIC TRIP HAZARDS

When a shallow parabola is placed behind a performer in the right position, it can help to boost their voice out front considerably. But if you are not in the focal point of the parabola (Google how satellite dishes work to understand these), then you will get much less acoustic amplification, which means one performer might be boosted in level, whilst another is less so, depending on where they're standing.

Many theatres have a shallow circle front, often in a semi-parabolic shape, and this creates a weird acoustic phenomenon when an actor stands downstage centre, which can throw them off as they walk into it. If I see anything resembling a parabolic surface on a set design, I'll assess what it might do for the acoustics.

Parallel surfaces can create 'flutter echo', where a sound will just bounce repeatedly back and forth between two opposite parallel surfaces. Changing the angle of one surface even by a degree or two can prevent this. Set designers love symmetry, but symmetry is no friend to acoustics. Any cube-like spaces will have tricky acoustic properties.

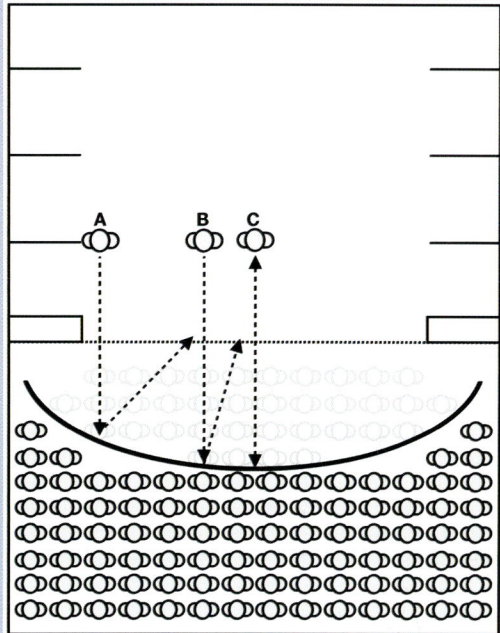

ABOVE RIGHT: The front edge of the circle can bounce the performer's voice back onstage. Performers generally like hearing a little of their voice coming back at them. Often there can be a weird hotspot downstage centre that can throw them off when they walk into it. The reflection of the voice of a performer in positions A and B bounces off to one side, so the performer doesn't get a strong reflection of themselves coming back, until they step into position C, where the reflection of their voice comes straight back at them.

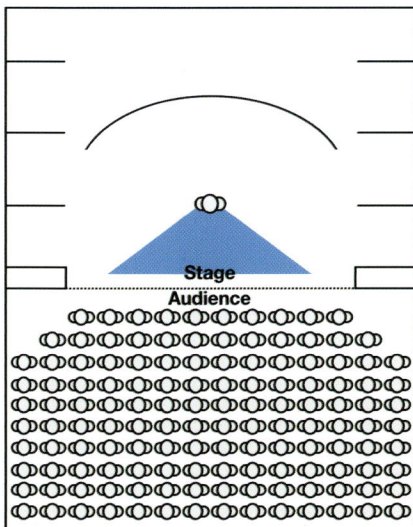

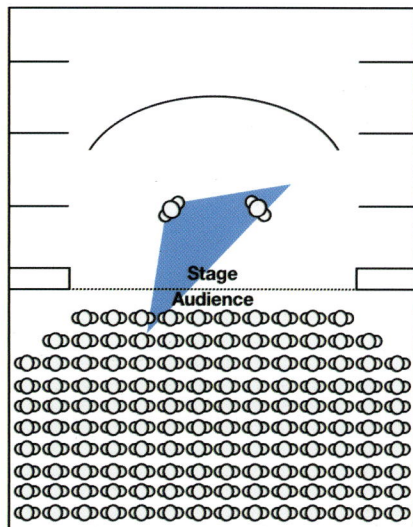

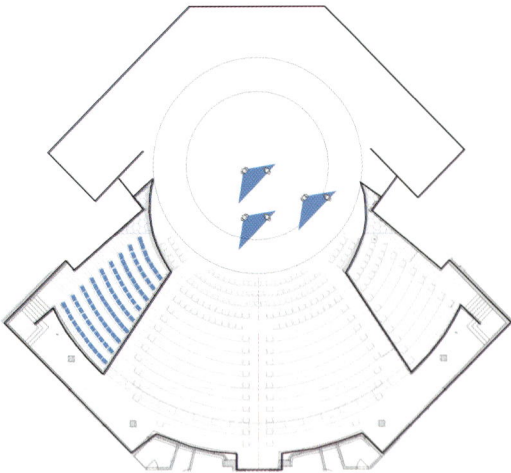

Performers in various positions on the Olivier stage. Audiences in the far left and right will struggle to make out what is being said by those facing away from them.

stage of the Olivier, as in the third drawing, we can see immediately that the seats marked in blue will struggle to hear one of our actors in a large number of positions on the stage.

Other Factors Affecting Intelligibility

Not all performers have strong voices or have vocal stamina, and it is taxing to do a big part in eight shows a week. Film and television actors often find this the most difficult part of moving into theatre, and it can often lead to cancelled shows, or to understudies going on. If the show does more than the regular eight shows a week, that will place extra strain on a performer's vocal cords.

Another factor that will affect intelligibility is a show where the audience is likely to sing along. As soon as they do, we'll be unable to hear our performers acoustically.

Accents can have an effect on intelligibility, too: if your audience is trying to understand a dialect

each other, even though they are not directly facing each other, a large section of the audience is not going to hear one actor as well as they hear the other. And if we place our two actors on the

TEMPORARY AND NON-THEATRE SPACES

If we are working in a temporary theatre, or a non-theatre space, the acoustics may not have been designed with speech intelligibility in mind. You may be asked to offer advice on how to make the space usable. Installing specialist acoustic treatment to a large space is extremely expensive. It is also not the sort of thing that can be hired in, but has to be purchased. One of the easiest, most effective and cheaper solutions is the application of a lot of heavy drapes, but these can then block the view of our lovely derelict warehouse.

Noise from the outside world can be a problem in these spaces – theatres are often sound-proofed to a large degree – whereas in a temporary space you may often find yourself competing with planes, helicopters, and the general cacophony of urban life. If you find yourself in a multi-venue temporary space, often the show in the adjacent venue can be the most prominent source of noise.

We may find that fixtures and fittings rattle excessively when the sub-bass is played, and we might cause a noise nuisance to our neighbours. Temporary seating systems often rattle, and the large volume of space below them can make the sound of someone going to the toilet in the middle of the show resonate loudly. It can be useful to add padding and insulation under stair treads, and to store empty flight cases under the seating to reduce the volume beneath it.

We may also face other issues in temporary spaces, such as unreliable mains supplies, or where there may not be enough power to go around, and it has to be shared across departments. Rain ingress can be an issue in older venues, requiring all kit to be lifted up on palettes in case of flooding, and a waterproof cover for your mixing desk is essential. The structural integrity and load capacity of any part of a temporary space is often unknown, making it difficult to hang or rig equipment safely. There will be a general lack of infrastructure across the building, from paging, show relay, assistive listening systems, infrared and normal cameras, IR light sources and cue-light systems, and there may not be easy routes to run cables around the venue.

that is not their own, they will need to hear it more clearly to pick out the unfamiliar sounds.

The speed of delivery of a line also affects how intelligible it is. Sometimes we can slow down the delivery of a specific line to make it more understandable. Obviously, slowing down the show for clarity may also make it boring!

These factors all determine how intelligible elements of our show can be.

Most set designers do not know anything about acoustics, and will rarely make decisions based on making good acoustics. Whilst we can advise them if they are designing something that may create an issue, they won't necessarily listen!

REINFORCEMENT AND AMPLIFICATION

In the early stages of a show's development sometimes we won't know precisely all the factors affecting whether we need to reinforce a show or not. We often have to take an educated guess based on our past experiences, and on what has been done in previous similar shows in the same venue. We often need to make this decision early on, before rehearsals start, because it can have a large impact on our sound budget, perhaps requiring extra equipment (unless the venue has all the equipment to do this in-house), or extra staff to be hired in.

If we decide we need to amplify the actors' voices, there are a few methods of doing it, and there are a few styles in which we can do it. We can choose how much we amplify the voices: thus we could amplify them the tiniest amount, just enough to make them audible, but not so much that the audience are aware that they are amplified. This can take skill to achieve. We tend to refer to this as 'reinforcing' their voices – an actor's acoustic voice is still the dominant source, but we are gently reinforcing it with the speaker system.

For some shows the auditorium nearer the stage may not need any reinforcement, but areas further away might. So we could mic the actors

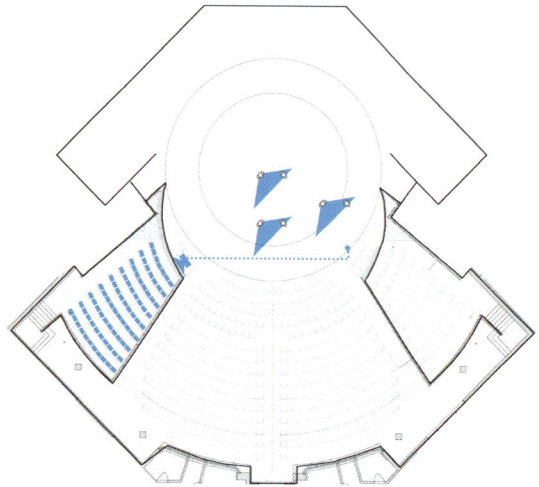

The Olivier Theatre, with a microphone on the right of the auditorium, feeding a speaker on the left of the auditorium. A matching system would be installed for the right audience members, with a microphone on the left of the stage.

but only send that sound to speakers covering those problem areas.

At the other extreme we may want to declare that we are using microphones, so the actors' voices are distinctly coming from the sound system, and perhaps we won't hear much of their acoustic voice at all. This can be useful for creative reasons, or if we want to achieve a concert-like sound.

The Use of Microphones

As well as the times we need to microphone the actors, there are also times when we may want to microphone the show:

- We may be doing a musical that we want to be loud, whether to get the energy of that, to emulate being at a concert, or to sound like one of the many musical genres that have emerged over the years that use microphones, or to create a new way for our show to sound altogether
- We may want a more cinematic, louder level of musical and sound underscoring

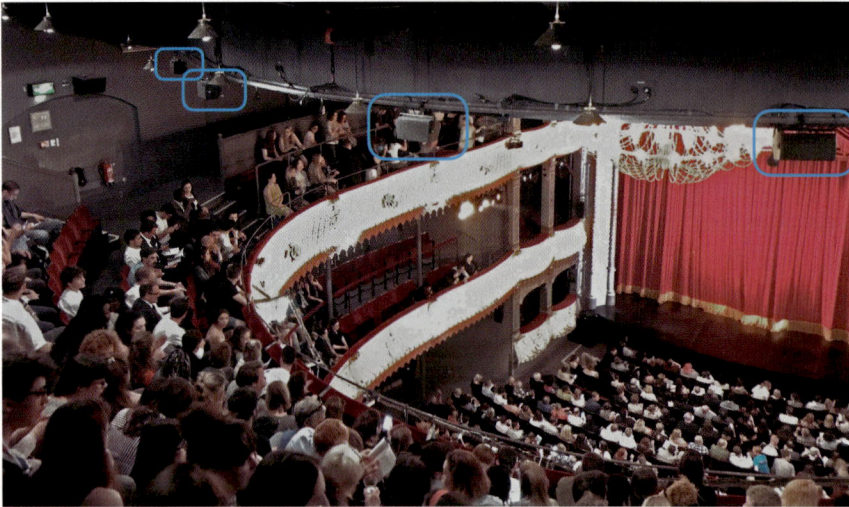

Reinforcement may not be needed for all areas of the theatre. Here, speakers are installed in the upper level of an auditorium to help boost the intelligibility for that level.

- We may want the performers to speak at a more natural level, to not project, and yet still be heard. This is often a request from directors, after a more realistic style of acting, but is tricky to achieve as we still need a certain amount of volume to come out of their mouths in order to be able to amplify it. As previously mentioned, we can only make a mumble louder, we can't make it intelligible
- We may want to use microphones to add effects to voices: for example, to give the impression of talking through a telephone, or to pitch them up and down
- We may want to give the sense that the performers are in different acoustics, in a bathroom, or a church, for example, by adding electronic reverb to their voices
- We may want to distinguish between narration and dialogue. Speaking close up into a microphone conveys an intimacy
- Microphones can also be used in the same way that performers can use a mask, in that they allow us to dislocate the voice from the actor, for example, by moving their voice into the surround speakers, or up to a projection screen –

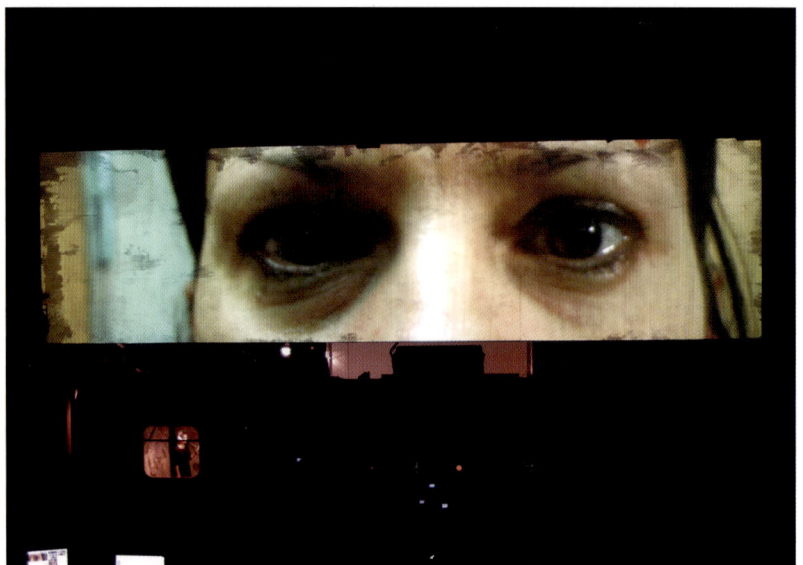

Reise Durch Die Nacht (*Night Train*), the Schauspiel Köln. Directed by Katie Mitchell. Designed by Alex Eales. Lighting design by Jack Knowles. Video design by Leo Warner and Grant Gee.

In working light, the far left compartment of our train is a voice-over booth, where an actor voices the stream of consciousness of our protagonist, whose face is seen on the overhead projection screen. The VO is routed to the four speakers above the projection screen so we better associate the sound to the image. It is also routed to the four front fill speakers for audience members in the front rows.

BELOW: *The Master and Margarita*, Complicité. Directed by Simon McBurney. Designed by Es Devlin. Costume design by Christina Cunningham. Lighting design by Paul Anderson. Puppet design by Blind Summit. HUGO GENDINNING

THE CAT IN *THE MASTER AND MARGARITA*

The story of *The Master and Margarita* features the character of a walking, talking cat. We had a puppet cat. One solution to the cat talking would have been for one of the puppeteers to also be the voice of the cat. However, the director wanted to explore a different route, so we had an SM58 on a stand offstage, into which an actor spoke the cat's dialogue, and we attached a Timax tracker to the puppet. The Timax system allows a computer to track the position of anyone wearing a tracker tag around the stage and pan their voice accordingly – in this case it panned the signal from the SM58 according to where the cat was onstage, so that the offstage voice appeared to come from the position of the cat puppet.

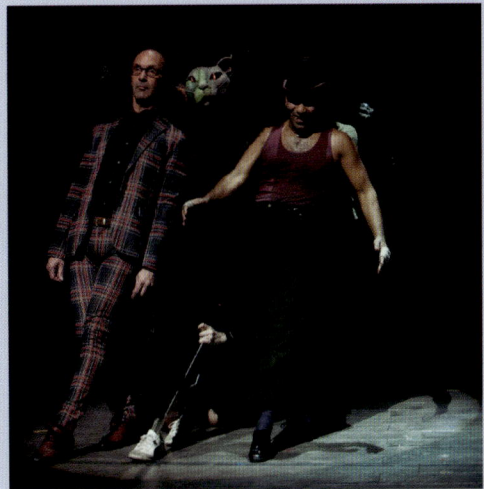

though we may need to take care their acoustic voice isn't also heard

Microphones in Sound Design

A point that is important to understand, and to convey to others, when we are discussing microphoning a show, is that we don't just 'turn the mics on' and away we go. There is in fact an incredible amount of thought, planning and artistry that has to go into making our sources sound the way we want them to sound, not just in terms of intelligibility, which is a scientifically measurable quantity, but also, less definably, in the 'sound of the show'. Here we get back into the murkier world of art again.

OFFSTAGE VO AND CHORUS

It is not uncommon for a musical number to feel somewhat thin with the available voices onstage. Sometimes we may bolster that with a pre-recorded track, or we may have additional cast members singing in the wings. We may also have voice-over for narration. These may be recorded, or they may be performed live by an actor in the wings.

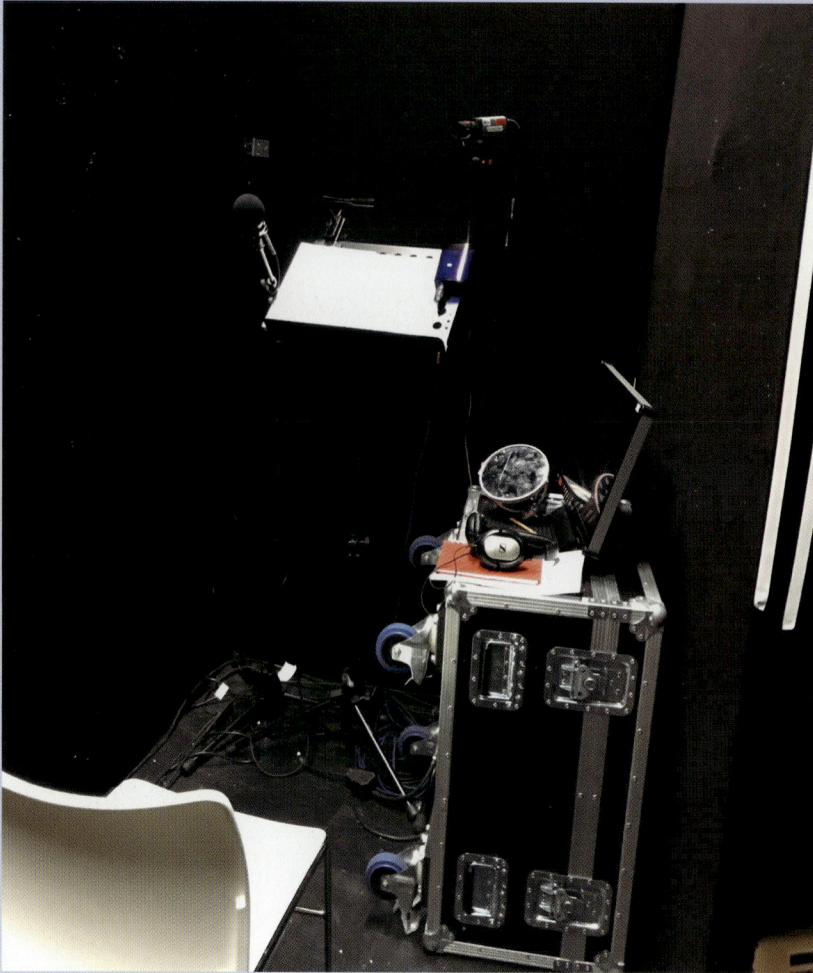

An offstage VO booth, with a microphone, a music stand for a script with a light, headphones, a monitor displaying what is happening on stage, and a camera so the DSM can see them.

An analogy I like to use, to explain this to others, is to talk about record producers, which is a job title most people have heard of, even if they don't know too much about what they actually do. In the world of music, the world of artists writing and recording albums, a record producer (also known as a music producer) generally works with the musicians to develop their music, whether into a song or an album. Obviously, the song writers, the musicians are incredibly instrumental, if you'll excuse the pun, in how a song sounds, but in the music industry it is often the record producer who guides this sound into being, who will bring it from a demo track or an idea into its fully formed state.

We are probably aware of a few record producers' names from their work, whether it is George

It's important to have a defined physical space for this backstage, otherwise you will pick up the sounds of crew and bits of scenery moving around. This can be achieved easily using drapes. We want to ensure that whoever is there can see everything they need, hear everything they need, and be cued by the DSM.

The operator has two video monitors to show the two offstage VO booths, so they can safely turn these offstage microphones on and off. Also visible in this photo are a Yamaha LS9 mixing desk, Figure 53's QLab, and Yamaha MRX Designer.

Martin's work with The Beatles at Abbey Road, Phil Spector's Wall of Sound, Joe Meek, Quincy Jones' work with Michael Jackson, Flood, Dr Dre, and so on. Most record producers' work goes unnoticed beyond the confines of the recording industry.

The record producer will often work to shape a piece of music to sound a certain way through a combination of orchestration, the relationship with the performers, and the careful use of technology. For this analogy I'll focus on the latter element, though the others are as important. In using technology, there are hundreds of parameters that can be adjusted, which can radically change the sound of each individual instrument. The placement of a microphone a centimetre closer to an instrument dramatically changes how it sounds on the recording. Alter the brand or type of mic, and the sound of the instrument is different again. Add some compression and a gate to it, and again you get a completely different sound. Similarly a delay effect, or some reverb, or any of hundreds of available effects.

These choices, often made from experience, careful experimentation or just plain luck, and the subsequent mix and processing of all those microphones, are often what define the sound of a piece of music. Much of the work of the music producer can be viewed very functionally, and many of their choices can be assessed very pragmatically. However, we can look at the end result and say, yes, George Martin's work with the Beatles was a creative act, and with them he created a work of art.

The theatre sound designer makes similar choices, when working on anything of a musical nature, choosing or trying hundreds of different permutations of parameters and equipment. They may be trying to evoke the sound of an existing genre, or they may be creating something bespoke for the show. As well as choosing how everything will be mic'd, processed and mixed, they will also design a sound system to amplify it, the choice of which also considerably affects the sound of the show. They will work with the person mixing the show each night to define the mix of the show.

Their work may not be obvious to the casual theatre visitor, in the same way that the work of a particular music producer won't necessarily be obvious when listening to an album, but it's still very much there. Ideally, it will just sound 'right' to the average audience member.

An interesting exercise is to go and watch a few different musicals on consecutive nights, and you'll clearly hear the difference between them. Whether that's the concert-type experience of a show such as *We Will Rock You*; the blurred lines between sung dialogue and the big numbers in a musical such as *Les Misérables*; the difference between an American show and a British show, the gently

reinforced cinematic *War Horse*; the lyrical foregrounding of a Sondheim or Lin-Manuel Miranda production, to list just a few. Try to imagine one of those shows with the sound design of the other, and you begin to see how much the sound design and the sound designer is contributing to the sound of the show. We are *not* just turning on the mics!

STYLES OF MICROPHONING

The sound we choose for our show often depends a lot on the style of the production. A big choice is how we will mic the performers. There will be aesthetic considerations to bear in mind of how different the microphones look compared to the visual look of the production, and generally how visible they are.

A key concept here is 'gain before feedback': how much we can amplify a microphone before we start getting feedback. This is a complex thing to calculate and depends on a number of factors. For our immediate interest, a lot depends on how close we can get a microphone to the performer's mouth. Other significant factors relate to the loudspeaker system, foldback, and room acoustics, which we'll discuss later.

If we have a mic far away from the performer's mouth, then it may start to pick up the sound from the sound system as much as the performer's voice. This is how feedback starts – the mic is amplified and sent to the speaker, which the mic picks up, amplifies and sends to the speaker, which the mic picks up again, amplifies more and sends to the speaker, which the mic picks up again… This loop can take a fraction of a second to get to the familiar horrible squealing sound.

To avoid this, we want to simultaneously make the mic as close to the mouth as possible, so we pick up as much of them as possible, and to get as little sound from the speakers as possible, so we pick up as little of that as possible. The same goes for anything we want to amplify.

By having each microphone close to each performer's mouth we can also adjust the volume of one performer versus another: so if one person is quieter than everyone else, we can amplify them more than the others; and if we want to feature one voice against many – a lead singer versus a choir – we can.

In terms of gain before feedback, the following order gives us the loudest, most direct sound from a performer. The best options are also the most visually obtrusive.

First: a handheld microphone (or on a stand) being sung or talked directly into
Second: a headset microphone
Third: a microphone in the hairline of the performer
Fourth: a microphone on the lapel of the performer
Fifth: a float or rifle microphone near the performer

The Handheld Microphone

A stand or handheld mic is often off limits for aesthetic or practical reasons. If it's on a stand then you can't move around. If it's handheld, then the performer only has one hand left for whatever else they have to do.

The Headset Microphone

Headset microphones give us almost as much direct sound as a handheld mic. A thin cable runs from the headset mic to a transmitter pack hidden on the performer's body. Whilst small they are still quite obvious, especially in a smaller venue – we can't hide the fact that we are mic'ing the performers if they're wearing these. A headset mic can interfere with costume changes, as it is difficult to get a costume over your head without the mic getting in the way.

The Hairline Microphone

A microphone in the hairline may only be about 15cm further away from the mouth, but this results in a significant reduction in level compared to the handheld and headset mic positions, so we have to amplify them more to get an equivalent level. In doing so we are also amplifying more of other signals getting into the mic, such as other performers' voices, foldback, and the acoustic sounds of the venue. A hairline mic might even be getting more sound from a performer nearby, than the person it is attached to.

A handheld microphone, positioned right in front of the mouth, gives us the most amount of volume to work with. Visually and choreographically, this won't be suitable for many theatre shows. © Sennheiser electronic GmbH & Co. KG www.sennheiser.com

ABOVE LEFT: A Countryman E6 headset microphone puts the mic closer to the mouth, allowing more gain before feedback, and more separation with other microphones.

ABOVE RIGHT: A DPA4061 microphone mounted in the hairline. The mic will often be painted to be as invisible as possible. Occasionally you'll see these dropping down a few inches below the hairline, which is often an attempt to make the mic a bit louder, to increase the amount of gain before feedback. This mic has been quickly mounted in place with a black elastic loop, or halo, but more commonly wig or hair clips will be used.

Black Watch, the National Theatre of Scotland. Directed by John Tiffany. Designed by Laura Hopkins. Lighting design by Colin Grenfell. The actor in the centre, Ryan Fletcher, has a microphone over his ear, on our left. If the actor on the left, Nabil Stewart, speaks at the same time as Ryan, Ryan's mic will pick up more of Nabil than of Ryan. Nabil's mic could pick up more of Ryan than it could of Nabil. This makes mixing the microphones quite tricky. Normally the mic cables, visible on the backs of their necks, would be painted to better match the hair colour of the actors, but this may not happen until the middle of previews, when everything is settling down.
MANUEL HARLAN

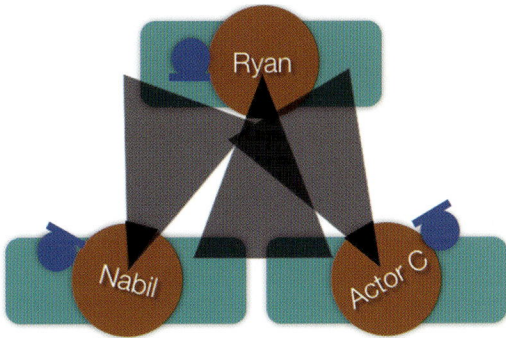

Nabil and Actor C's microphones are deliberately positioned to pick up as little of Ryan's speech as possible.

A hairline microphone is less visually obtrusive than headset microphones, particularly as the capsule and cables can be painted to colour match where they are situated.

Despite not being ideal, the hairline is the most commonly used position, as, done well, the microphones can be almost invisible, and we can often get a good sound out of them in many circumstances. Starting a conversation with the costume designer early in the process can help steer the costume design towards supporting hiding the radio microphones. If the performer is wearing a hat or doesn't have enough hair in which to conceal the microphone, we might put it over one ear.

The Lapel Microphone

A microphone on the lapel is often found in television, particularly for news presenters. This position works well in television because the presenter is normally static and looking at the camera, so the distance between their mouth and the microphone doesn't really change.

In theatre the relationship between the performer's body and their head is often very dynamic, as they turn their head around a lot, to look at each other and the audience.

The volume of the voice hitting a lapel-mounted microphone varies significantly when the performer turns their head, making it impossible to

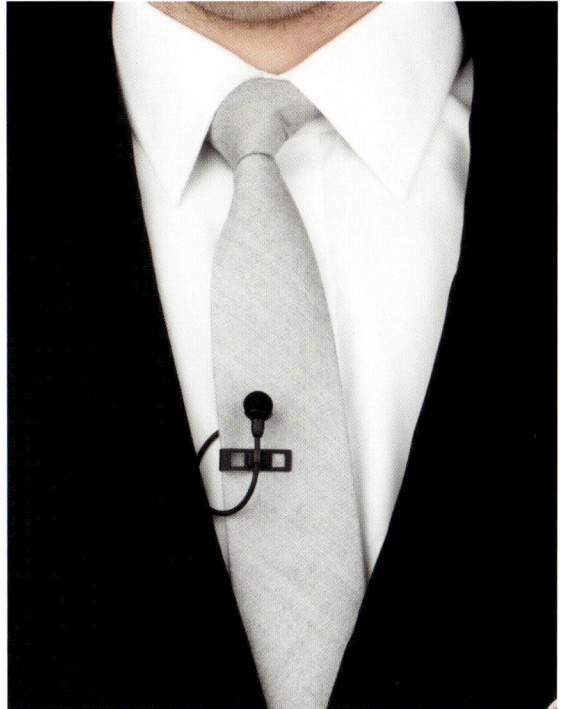

A lapel-mounted microphone, whilst common in television, is very rarely used in theatre. Pictured here, a Sennheiser MKE-2. © Sennheiser electronic GmbH & Co. KG www.sennheiser.com

get a consistent volume from them. This makes lapel mounts virtually useless for theatre except in very specific circumstances. A microphone on a performer's head will stay the same distance from their mouth no matter where they turn their head, providing a more consistent volume.

The Float Microphone

The final (and often worst) position for a microphone is when we can't actually get it on the performer; instead we try to get it as close to them as possible. This may be one mic, or a number of them, to account for the performer moving around. One common technique is to place microphones along the front edge of the stage. These might be float mics – sometimes a small, flat, panel-shaped mic, or a short condenser mic – or rifle mics, which are long and cylindrical like the barrel of a rifle. A float mic

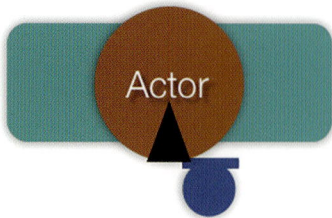

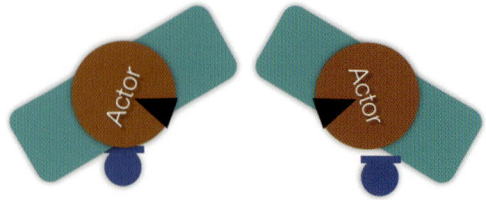

Instead, actors move their heads around, and so the distance between their mouth and the microphone is constantly varying, which means the volume of their speech arriving at the microphone is also constantly varying.

With a hairline, or ear-mounted microphone, no matter where the actor's head is facing, there is a fixed distance between the microphone and their mouth, making the volume more consistent.

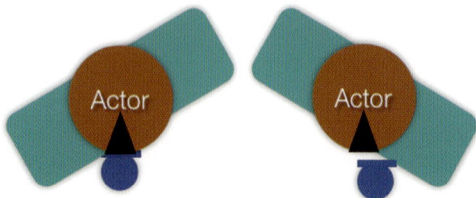

Lapel microphones are common in television, because often the presenter stays looking at the camera, and rarely moves around.

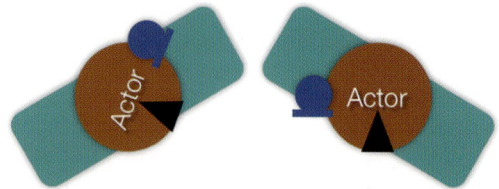

A lapel microphone would work in theatre if the actors kept looking out at the audience the whole time, and didn't move around… But that wouldn't make for very compelling theatre.

often has a cardioid pick-up pattern so will pick up sounds from onstage and slightly attenuate sounds from the auditorium. They are often effective for picking up performers on the downstage edge of the stage. Rifle mics are more directional and are good for picking up performers further upstage.

Float microphones pick up all sound on stage – footsteps, scenery movement, air conditioning, and any music that is playing. They don't allow us much ability to mix or focus on the performers, so if someone is standing near the mic and another person is five metres upstage of them, the mic will pick up the close person loudly and the distant

person quietly. That said, float microphones can provide a gentle lift in volume to everything happening onstage, and can have a more natural sound than radio microphones. However, it is difficult to get a lot of gain out of a float microphone system – you can only amplify a small amount before you start getting feedback.

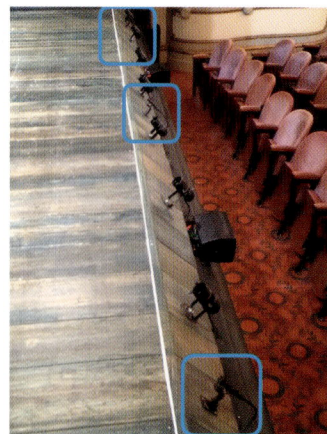

Float microphones placed along the downstage edge of a stage can provide a small amount of amplification, however, they don't just pick up the voices, they pick up everything.

In some circumstances, a regular float microphone may be too obtrusive. We can also use lapel-style mics to more discreetly mic an area of the stage. In this photo, the microphone is hidden in some carpet and is invisible in show lighting.

A DPA 4060 lapel-style microphone to amplify dialogue in this area of the stage.

OFF-STAGE AREAS

I learnt how to deal with off-stage areas from sound designer Matt McKenzie. Often performers may walk on and off stage whilst saying their lines. Sometimes that's fine and we can hear what they say, but sometimes as soon as they go offstage the volume plummets and we can't make out what they're saying. We can put small speakers near doors where we think this may be a problem, and disguise them as heating or air-conditioning vents. We then have a float microphone backstage, which is routed to that speaker. As soon as the actor goes offstage we turn on that mic, and their offstage vocals are piped back into the space via our small speaker.

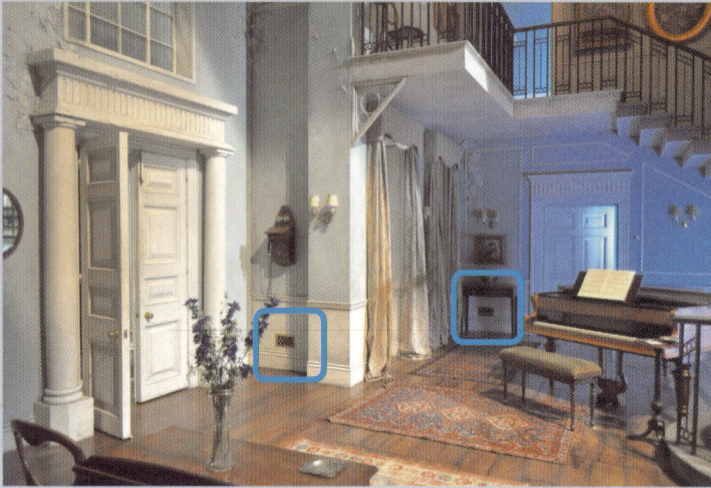

A Woman Killed With Kindness, the National Theatre. Directed by Katie Mitchell. Designed by Lizzie Clachan. Speakers are hidden behind what look like heating vents, to relay sound from an offstage microphone, to boost the volume of offstage dialogue.

Float microphoning can be more successful in an outdoor venue where the lack of a sealed auditorium means that less sound bounces back on to the stage. If float mic'ing is the best way to achieve what you're after, it is worth talking to the director to ensure that scenes are blocked as close to the float microphones as possible.

THE POLITICS OF RADIO MICROPHONES

There are a number of issues that must be appreciated when deciding to use radio microphones, or not, as described below.

They may cause offence: Performers may feel offended by being asked to wear a radio microphone, feeling it is an affront to their ability to project.

Performers often do not like wearing them: The transmitter packs are bulky, and the microphone cable restricts their movement, particularly if they have choreography or fight scenes. The transmitters often have to go into intimate parts of their body to avoid creating a noticeable bulge in tight-fitting costumes – doubly so if they are double mic'd. They can feel uncomfortable going to the toilet when they're wearing one. They can feel as if the sound team can listen in on their personal conversations backstage. Having sticky tape applied to them and peeled off every show can lead to skin irritations.

They break a lot: They will go through whatever physical duress the performer wearing the microphone goes through, whether that's dancing around the place, rolling over, singing in the rain, or whatever. These delicate boxes of equipment will have a hard, brutal life. In theatre, we consider

As You Like It, Regent's Park Theatre. Directed by Max Webster. Designed by Naomi Dawson. Lighting design by Lee Curran. Wearing radio microphones can be tricky for some physical sequences, and dummy wooden transmitters can be used in rehearsals to find ideal positions.

radio microphone capsules (the microphone and cable that attaches to the transmitter pack) a consumable because they will only last for a limited amount of time before we have to replace them. The most common cause of failure is sweat getting into the capsule, and whilst this can usually be cleaned off, a build-up over time can cause it to sound dull. The cable may get crushed, or the connector damaged. Due to their high failure rate, we often 'double mic' principal performers – we put two transmitters and two mic capsules on them, so if one fails, we can use the other.

They are expensive: Good radio microphone systems can easily cost £1,000 to £4,000 per system, and that's just for the transmitter/receiver element of it, and doesn't include the mic capsule itself, which is often around £250 for each one. We will need to bulk purchase a set of new mic capsules at the start of each show, plus spares, for our entire cast. We'll also need to allocate a running budget to buy more mic capsules as they get broken during the life of the show.

They require batteries: The typical life of a battery is about six to seven hours, so they might not last a full day of tech. Virtually the whole of the West End and Broadway have moved to using rechargeable battery systems now, which is much more environmentally friendly than a few years ago, when a show with sixteen radio microphones could easily go through over 250 batteries each week.

They fall off a lot: The microphone capsules are often attached either directly to the skin, or to hair, neither of which is the most secure of fixing places. Some performers sweat profusely, which can make it difficult to stick the microphones to them. Performers who have been drinking heavily the night before leach the toxins through their pores, making this task harder still.

Extra staff: Microphones require extra staff to deal with the maintenance, re-battering and testing. Staff may need to take part in costume changes to move the mic position according to the effect that a different hair style, wig, hat, mask might have on the sound of the mic.

Different expectations: Different audiences have different expectations of what they have come to watch. Most Broadway plays are radio mic'd for reinforcement, whilst most West End plays in the UK are not. We expect some genres to be mic'd, and others not – but often the venue will dictate the terms as much as the show.

International venues: If you are touring internationally, different countries have different (and often incompatible) radio frequencies assigned to use with radio microphones. We may have to source systems locally in each international venue.

Increasingly, actors are trained in using radio microphones, but many don't know how to perform with them. Whilst actors don't have to give such a projected performance, it doesn't mean they can sit back and give a mumbled television performance – they still need to give energy, clarity and diction. There will be times when you get a note from the director about somebody not being loud enough, and we can turn them up. Sometimes this will be because we need to turn them up, but sometimes it's because the actor isn't being loud enough. If you have a good voice coach on the

show, they can help identify and work with the performers on these moments, too.

We have to balance out the necessity, or desire, for radio microphones with the financial and political aspects.

I always make the decision about whether to use radio microphones in collaboration with the director. Sometimes it will be obvious to everyone that radio mics are necessary, but sometimes it is less clear cut. If you're going ahead, it's useful to take five minutes during rehearsals to talk to the cast about it. It's important never to assume that an actor has worn a radio microphone before and knows what it's like, and what it means to wear one. I'm always keen to explain that it doesn't have anything to do with their ability to project – which is the conclusion they often jump to first – and to explain why we think it is the right decision.

THE PRESS AND RADIO MICROPHONES

In 1999 the National Theatre made the front page of several national newspapers because it was using radio microphones on actors in several plays, including, to the horror of many, a production of Shakespeare's *Troilus and Cressida*. There then followed much outcry and disdain about microphones resulting in lazy projection from actors, about their offering 'television performances', and the state of actor training. What wasn't noted was that radio microphones had been used for about six months by the time it was reported, and several shows had opened, with the major theatre reviewers having attended all of these, and no one had noticed that radio microphones were being used! The only reason the newspapers became aware of it was because a staff member at the NT leaked the information to them.

The microphones were being used to feed the difficult areas of the auditorium where intelligibility was poor, by gently lifting the volume of the performers' voices in those areas. Whilst no one had noticed that radio microphones were being used, complaints from the audience sitting in the problematic areas about not being able to hear were significantly reduced.

To help circumvent any resistance I often explain that we are doing this to better support them – to help them overcome the tricky acoustics of the venue, or to be heard above the underscoring.

For example, for Christmas shows I might explain that they will be doing more shows per week than would be normal, with a louder than normal audience, so the microphones will help their vocal stamina over the course of the run. I often explain that I do not make the decision lightly to mic people up, as it makes my life considerably more difficult – I only do it if I think the show needs it. By talking them through the decision we can persuade them to see the advantage of using radio microphones, to see them as an aid rather than as an encumbrance.

Where possible, I'll take in a radio mic transmitter and mic capsule to demonstrate to the cast what they'll wear, and ask them to think about their physical track through the show and where the best place might be to mount the transmitter on them (for example, in a belt around their waist, in a wig, in a bra, inner thigh, around the ankle). We often look to place the transmitter and cable below any base layer of costume that they might wear so that costume changes interfere as little as possible.

If we're doing a small play and can't afford a dedicated No. 2 on board (see The Sound Department section in Chapter 11), I will endeavour to have a radio microphone specialist come in for the start of tech at least, to get the mics set up and make the cast feel as comfortable as possible.

I have had a few occasions when it has not been possible to convince anyone that we'll need radio microphones. I once worked for a first time with a director who was adamant that radio microphones wouldn't be needed in what was a notoriously tricky venue. The director had worked in a lot of outdoor venues – where the problem is often about lack of volume, rather than a lack of intelligibility – and thought we'd be fine. Rather than fight a losing battle, I said fine, and got on with designing the rest of the show. Fortunately the production manager was aware of the difficult acoustics of the venue, and understood we would need them, so we budgeted accordingly, prepared radio mic belts to hold the transmitters, worked out radio mic plots for who would need them when, what costume and wigs the cast would be wearing in each scene, dedicating spare inputs on the mixing desk, and so on.

It was also fortunate that the venue had a stock of radio mic systems we could use without much hassle, and some old microphone capsules we could prepare, so we were able to have a full radio mic system ready to deploy without any significant cost. We got approximately three minutes into the technical rehearsals before the director conceded we did in fact need radio microphones. Because all the prep work was done, we were able to deploy them and start using them almost straightaway.

There have also been occasions when I've been wrong. I did a production that opened in a large venue, which had a lot of underscoring music that required the cast to be fully radio mic'd. Our next venue, the Royal Court, where we would play for six weeks, was only about 75 per cent as big as our original venue, and typically doesn't need vocal reinforcement. However, I was cautious as we'd made the show with radio microphones, so we planned to keep using them. After our second or third preview, the director asked if I thought we really did need them, so we tried it without them, and it worked fine. Perversely, the show then moved into the West End into a bigger venue and didn't have the budget for a sound operator and radio microphones, which was a shame as it really could have been helped by having them there.

VOCAL REINFORCEMENT SYSTEMS

It's easy when we start talking about vocal reinforcement and amplification to focus on microphones, but the speaker side of it is just as important. I was once asked to help out a show where the lead performer had lost their voice: 'Can you put a radio mic on him?' they asked. And of course, that's the easy bit. The hard part was that in this case there were only a few sound effects and some scene change pieces of music in their show (which they'd done without a sound designer) so they only had a couple of speakers on the proscenium, which was also the only place to route the performer's radio mic. It sounded really bad. The volume level was loud at the front and too quiet at the back. As an audience member, the actor was standing downstage centre, but his voice was coming out of speakers on the proscenium over on the far left and right. Nevertheless, everyone was happy with this as a 'quick fix' – even though it sounded awful – because it meant they didn't have to cancel four shows whilst his voice recovered.

I'm sure that most people will at some time have been to see a show and come back thinking it sounded terrible. We'll look later at some of the more general reasons why sound systems often sound bad, but assuming that we will tweak and tune our sound system to sound as good as possible, let's look at one particular reason why a vocal reinforcement system might sound bad.

For me personally, the most common failing of a vocal reinforcement/amplification sound system is that the sound from the speakers does not match where the performers are on the stage. Directors mention this to me a lot – 'I can't tell who is talking: if I close my eyes I can't tell where anyone is standing onstage' – because the performers' amplified voices seem to resonate from the sound system, rather than a point on stage. Our ability to fix this problem usually comes down to where, how many, and the type of speakers that constitute the sound system; and the budget and the length of the production period.

Our hearing system is good at identifying where sounds are coming from in the horizontal plane – that is, on the horizon. If we sit in a theatre and the performer's voice is generally coming from directly in front of us, but the amplified sound is clearly coming from speakers on the side of the proscenium, our brain is confused. Sometimes our brain can adapt, and about twenty minutes into a show

LOCALIZING SOUND

We rarely consider how powerful and phenomenal our hearing system is, but it is able to take the simple vibrations of air that hit our ears, and then perform amazing mathematical computations and acts of perceptual determination at a subconscious level to create a very accurate narrative about the world around us.

For example, we are incredibly accurate at working out where a sound is coming from. If I hear a bang over on my left side, that sound will reach my left ear, and 0.0006 seconds later it will arrive at my right ear. As it will have travelled slightly further (about 20–25cm, depending on your head size) it will be slightly quieter (maybe by only 0.5dB), and it will sound slightly different, slightly muffled, because your head is in the way. From these minute differences your brain can calculate to within 2 or 3 degrees where that sound came from, even with your eyes closed. Your brain performs this calculation continuously on almost every sound you hear, and renders the result to your conscious brain as a three-dimensional auditory experience of the world.

you'll notice that the sound system no longer sounds weird. But sometimes the disparity is too great, and it just sounds bad all the way through.

Ideally we want the sound to come from the same place as the performer, rather than from the side of the proscenium. In an ideal world, there would be a large speaker sat on the floor downstage centre, or next to each performer. Sadly, this is considered visually obtrusive!

Actors move around a lot, so our imaging problem is compounded by the fact that their amplified voice doesn't move when they do. Ideally they would each have a speaker next to them on a trolley that they could drag around as they moved around. Needless to say, directors aren't keen on speakers on trolleys, either, so we have to find alternative speaker positions. The proscenium is often the natural home for these speakers. But rather than moving them off to the side, which we know will sound bad, we move them upwards. The human hearing system is not so good

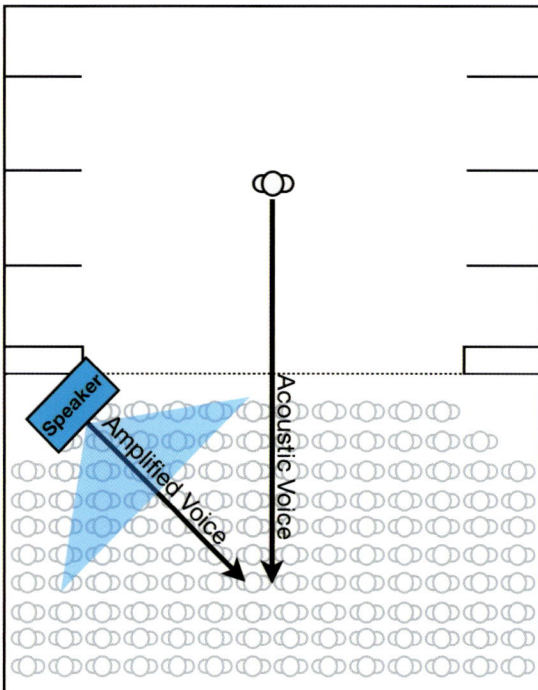

Amplified voice often sounds bad when there is a disconnect between the acoustic voice of the performer and the amplified sound. Here, the voice of the performer comes from straight ahead of us, whilst the amplified voice comes from a speaker on the proscenium, off to one side. The human brain is very sensitive to the direction of sound.

If we can get the amplified voice to come from roughly the right direction on the horizontal plane, there will be less of a disconnect from the acoustic voice. The human brain is less sensitive to the direction of sound on the vertical axis, so having the amplified voice come out of a speaker above the proscenium often sounds much better than from the side of the proscenium.

at locating sounds vertically as it is horizontally (if we had one ear on the top of our head, and one on our chin, we'd be good at locating sounds vertically, but that would make eating quite unpleasant). We can put a speaker centre stage, on the top of the proscenium, and the disparity between the performer's voice being directly in front of us, and the amplified sound coming from above us, is less confusing for us, and doesn't sound so 'bad'.

A cluster of speakers may be used rather than a single speaker, so that the sound reaches every seat in the auditorium. Speakers come in different types, with different angles of dispersion: some have a narrow dispersion (like a tightly focused torch) and others have a wide dispersion (like a floodlight). A wide speaker won't push sound as far as a narrow speaker. A cluster may contain a number of narrow dispersion speakers focused

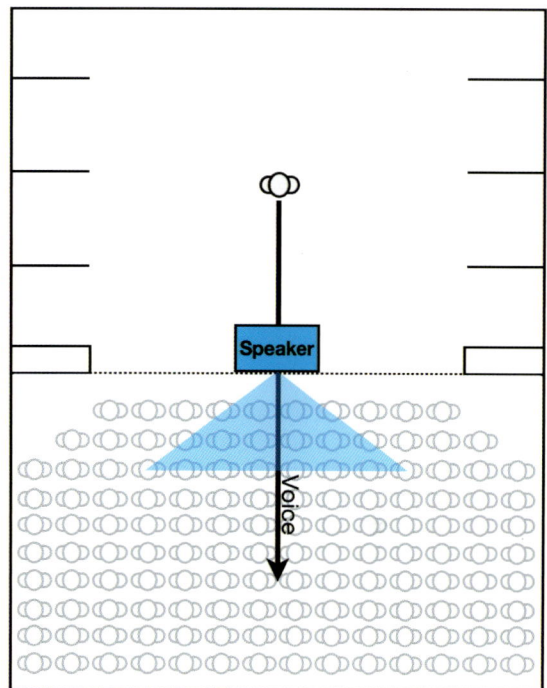

to cover the entire audience, or it may contain a single wide dispersion speaker. Or we may use line-array speakers to create something that can cover the entire space. Line-array speakers generally don't have a wide dispersion, so work better for throwing over a long distance than they do over a wide auditorium. It depends entirely on the auditorium width, depth and shape, as to which sort of speakers will work best.

The cluster, or line array, will probably be too high up for the audience in the front few rows, so a row of small 'front fill' speakers are usually placed under the front lip of the stage. 'Delay' speakers may also be added for seating at the rear that doesn't have line of sight to the cluster, perhaps because of a balcony above. We'll look at why these are called 'delay' speakers later, and how to set them up.

Richard III, the Harvey Theatre, Brooklyn Academy of Music. Directed by Sam Mendes. Designed by Tom Piper. A line array of d&b T10s hangs high above downstage centre, so amplified voices appear to come from there, rather than off to the sides, which they would, had they been routed through the proscenium speakers. Also visible are the two live music positions, with the MD and keyboards in the boxes to the left, and percussion to the right of the set. For one scene a projection screen is flown in to display a video, and speakers are also flown in for this moment, to better locate the sound to the image.

It's not uncommon for a medium-sized West End theatre to end up with between twenty and sixty speakers installed primarily for vocal re-inforcement. In most circumstances, all these speakers will need to be installed whether you are using fifty radio microphones or just one, and whether you are doing loud amplification or subtle reinforcement.

The ideal vocal reinforcement system will ensure that everyone can hear the vocals, but this alone doesn't give us any sense of where the performers are on the stage. With all the voices coming out of this central cluster there is no way for the audience to tell where anyone is. If a character walks onstage left and everyone is looking at something happening on the right-hand side, when this new character talks, their voice will come from the centre cluster just like everyone else's – we won't be able to identify where they are standing onstage, or even notice that they've come onstage.

Localizing the Amplified Sound

There are techniques that allow us to move the amplified sound around to match the location of the person speaking. They are not always used because they are either time consuming to implement, more expensive, or require additional speaker positions. Rather than having just one cluster or line-array above the proscenium, we might have three sets, so we can pan performers' voices between them. This is often known as an

Our vocal clusters are visible from the centre of the stalls.

'LCR' (left, centre, right) system. There are other ways to produce the effect, too.

Manual Zoning

To create some sense of imaging, we can program the performers' movements into the mixing desk, such that when a performer stands on the left side of the stage the sound is routed to a mix of the centre and left cluster speakers, or as we have speakers available to us. This creates the effect that the amplified sound is coming from the left, where the performer is. We might do this by having plenty of mix outputs from our mixing desk: for example Mix 1 could be Vox L; Mix 2, Vox C; Mix 3, Vox R; Mix 4, US Vox L, and so on. We would route each performer's radio microphone to the mix output corresponding to where they are onstage. We'd then route each mix output – Vox L, Vox C, and so on – to a delay matrix (either built in to the mixing desk, or an external unit), which would route the signal to the correct mix of loudspeakers.

This technique can be effective, but has limitations: it takes a long time to program the performers blocking into the desk, particularly if they move

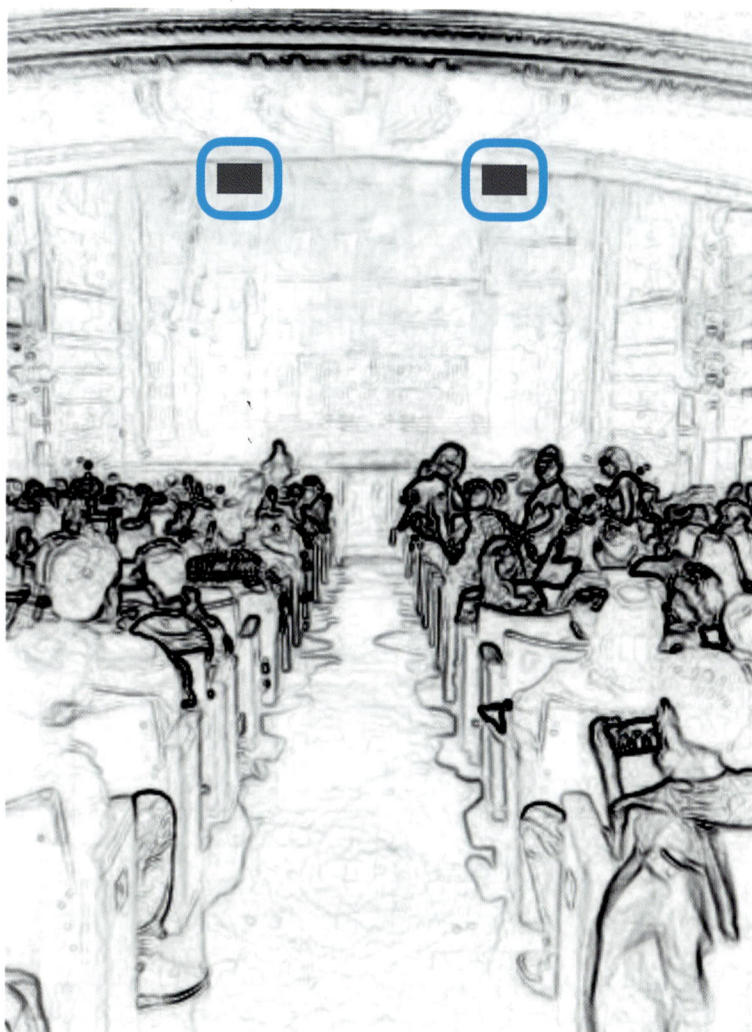

As we move to the rear of the stalls, our sightline to the vocal clusters (and hence our ability to hear them) is cut off by the balcony underhand from the audience level above. So we add small speakers, delayed back to the vocal clusters, to fill in this dead spot.

around a lot; also the system can only easily do discrete zones, and nothing in between, so if a performer moves from left to right, talking at the same time, the sound won't move smoothly with them. And it requires the blocking to be fixed, so it can't adapt to performers changing where they stand each night.

Automatic Zoning

The second technique involves the performers wearing small 'tracker tag' transmitters hidden in their costumes. A computer system uses aerials to track the position of every performer onstage, and then automatically re-routes their microphone according to where they are. It provides smoother crossfade transitions as people walk between different vocal zones. It doesn't require the blocking to be programmed into it, so is excellent when there is fluid blocking or choreography, but it does require some time to configure and optimize.

I prefer this type of vocal reinforcement system that tracks the performers. It really helps with the audience not noticing the sound system, because the sound comes from the performer more than it does from the speakers. I've noticed that when I

At the front of the stalls, our audience are often too close to the stage to be within the coverage of speakers on the proscenium, either off to the side, or above them. Typically, we add smaller speakers placed in, or on, the front edge of the stage. Depending on the genre of show, we may be able to boost the volume of the front fills to 'pull the image down' from the clusters. But we have to be careful not to make them so loud that they deafen the audience in the front rows.

use this type of system, I get far fewer notes about the volume and sound of the system from directors and producers. If a character walks onstage left, and everyone is looking at something happening on the right-hand side, when they talk their voice will come from the left side and our attention will be taken over to this character who has just entered. I mentioned earlier that people may take twenty minutes of listening to a sound system to acclimatize to it, but with performer-tracked systems, I think the audience acclimatize in a couple of minutes instead. The sound is closer to the real world, to how we hear naturally, so there is less disparity for our brain to deal with.

When Not To Image

Sometimes imaging is less important, particularly if we want to achieve a concert-like sound, where the voice is a layer in the music. In this case, imaging the voice can place the voice in a strange relationship to the music. Sometimes, particularly if we're using microphones in a mask-like way, or doing 'tricks' with the vocals (such as swapping between the live microphone and recordings without the audience being aware), I might not want the image to be so strictly located to the performer – here a wall-of-sound type reinforcement might serve the show better.

An LCR (left, centre, right) cluster is one of the methods that allows the amplified voice to be panned to match the position of the performer on stage. It is most effective on wider stages. In this photo it is achieved using conventional point-source speakers, but line-array speakers are also common. Meyer MM-4 front fills are also visible along the front of the stage.

Here the LCR system is covering the auditorium. In an ideal world, the left and right elements of this line array-based LCR cluster would be a little closer to the centre element, but a compromise had to be achieved with the lighting designer so that he could get positions that worked for him, too.

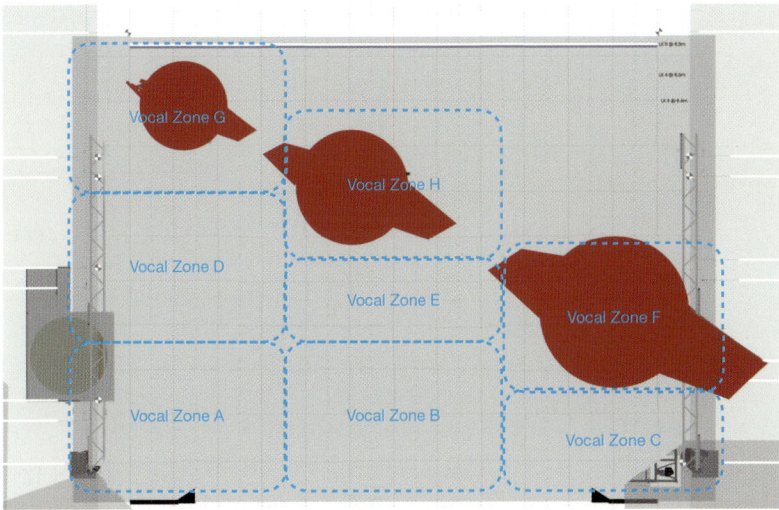

Vocal zones for a show, overlaid on the ground plan. We route the performer's microphone to a different mixer output according to which zone they are standing in. That mixer output will be sent to a different balance of speakers to make their amplified voice sound as if it is coming from where they are standing. Programming all the performers' movements into the mixing desk can involve a considerable amount of work.

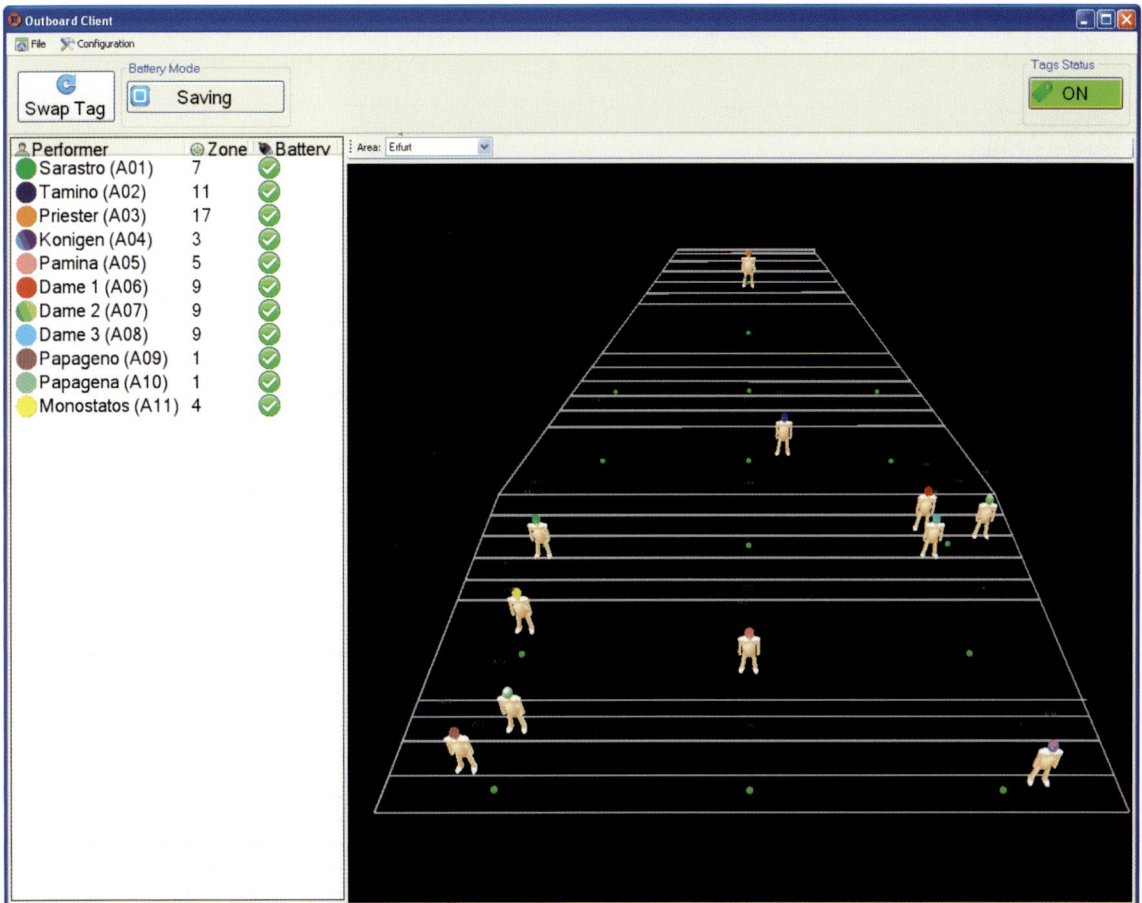

The Timax Tracker system uses a small transmitter tag on each performer to track their position on stage. The system can then automatically send each microphone to a different balance of speakers to make their amplified voice sound as if it is coming from where they are standing.

MICROPHONES FOR MUSICIANS

Independently of our need or choices for vocal reinforcement, we may need, or choose, to mic any live musicians we might have on our show. Some musical instruments don't make any significant acoustic noise, such as an electric guitar, so we can choose whether to amplify those in a small way, such as having a guitar amp local to the guitar, or whether we want to patch it into the main sound system.

We have similar choices to make about whether we want our band to sound unamplified, or definitely amplified. And as with vocal reinforcement, sounding unamplified is not the same as not being amplified. Different musical instruments produce radically different volume levels, so perhaps we might only need to reinforce the quieter instruments. Perhaps a drum kit will sound too loud, even without any amplification, and we will decide to put it in a drum booth or isolation room so we can better control its volume. Perhaps a band will be off to one side of the stage, making for a lopsided sound, so we might send an amplified version to speakers on the other side of the stage to make it sound more balanced.

Whereas we only have a few choices to mic up an actor onstage, we have many more choices about how to mic up the huge variety of musical instruments we might encounter. In my earlier record producer analogy, I discussed how much we can influence the sound of the music with our choice of microphones, the EQ, the dynamics, the effects, the mix and the speakers. To go far into this topic would require a book twice the length of this one, and even then, would fail to describe all the possible decisions you can make, and the implications of those decisions. Whilst this might seem to be avoiding the issue, there are copious resources online about the ways to mic up a drum kit and other musical instruments. We often need to get our microphones as close to the instruments as possible, sometimes to give us more gain before feedback, but more often because the

musicians are close together, and the closeness gives us more of what we want on each microphone, and less of the other instruments.

Depending on the set design, our musicians are often not visible. They may be in the pit, or in a booth or room elsewhere in the theatre, and this makes localization of the sound less of an issue. When we have musicians playing onstage, we may choose whether localization is important to us or not. If we are mixing together onstage musicians with offstage musicians, we may not to want to localize so much.

The best sound system for music amplification (or playback) often differs from the best sound system for vocal reinforcement. Musical instruments can create lower and higher frequencies than the human voice, requiring larger speakers that can reproduce a greater number of lower frequencies. We may need music to go louder than we need vocal reinforcement to go. And if we're not trying to localize the band to the stage, we may want our music loudspeakers in different places to a vocal reinforcement system.

If vocal intelligibility is very important, having the vocals coming out of a physically separate set of speakers can help our brain distinguish them from the music, to better interpret the lyrics. On the other hand, if your music is more concert-like, where the lyrics are one of many layers of the music – especially if it's a well-known track – you might want to meld the vocals and music together more.

Different designers have different tastes about how much to split their sound systems into music and vocal systems, and whether to keep them exclusive of each other, or to mix them together.

WORKING WITH LIVE MUSIC

What I find most exciting about having a live band is that the musicians can respond with their performance to the actor's performance. However, here we get into the question of whether we are creating a show where the performers, the musicians or actors are allowed or encouraged to vary their performance for each show – or are we aiming for repeatability, for consistency? I work on both kinds of show, the ones where the performers improvise off each other and the audience; and shows where consistency is the aim (and I see show reports where the actors are told off for 'deviating'). Neither approach is necessarily right or wrong. Even if we are aiming for consistency, live musicians bring a certain excitement: as audience members we appreciate hearing live music, and the skill of performing it, and the proximity to the musician, just as we do to the actor.

It is increasingly common for a band to play along to a 'click' track, a metronome being played in the MD's ear, inaudible to everyone else. Whilst this forces the band to the pre-recorded tempo, and often means they can't improvise or respond to the performance so much, it means that other elements, such as backing tracks, automated scenery, video projection and so on, can be synchronized perfectly to the live music. Whilst this can feel detrimental for some musical styles, others, such as hip hop, can benefit from the musical structure, or may have already.

Often we want music to underscore a scene, but we don't necessarily want the musicians to be playing quietly. The sound of a violin being played quietly is different in tone to one that is playing at a normal level but is being reproduced quietly. It's difficult for a violin player to hit the notes accurately whilst playing quietly, or even for it to be physically possible to play as quietly as we might want it under quiet dialogue. Having the band in the space is great if the dynamics work, or if we can mic the cast to sit above the music when we want to. But sometimes we can't get the volume balance we want if they are in the space.

The location of the band is often decided between the director, designer, yourself and the music team. It's a conversation that happens early on, and is critical to how the music will sound, so it is important to take part in it.

When we work with live music we'll often find ourselves working not just alongside musicians, but also with musical directors, arrangers, composers and a few others. Building strong relationships with these people is invaluable to the success of how the show will sound. Of course, that is also a raft of extra opinions to take on board, but they are usually well-informed opinions.

In the same way that I may have performance notes for the actors that I will only ever discuss with the director, the musical director is usually the person to talk to about the performance of the band. And the arranger and composer are our equivalents of the playwright. Often, particularly if we are struggling with vocal intelligibility, a chat with the arranger can prove constructive in discussing how dense the music is in any particular section. Thinning out the arrangement, or changing the orchestration, can solve many intelligibility problems.

Any discussion nowadays about live music inevitably rolls into one about money – namely, how many musicians can you afford? On most shows there are fewer live musicians than the music department would like. To mitigate this, keyboard players often play many different sampled instruments to expand the sound of the band, or we'll have more instruments recorded on the click track.

The Lyric Theatre, Broadway: *Harry Potter and the Cursed Child*. Directed by John Tiffany, designed by Christine Jones, lighting design by Neil Austin. Visible are an L-C-R hang of d&b Y8s above the proscenium, smaller Y8 arrays on the proscenium sides, along with d&b B22 subs in the middle-level boxes. Just visible are the four sets of Y8s behind grilles in the upstage wall of the set, just below the clock, and the two d&b Vsubs also hidden behind grilles. DOROTHY HONG

9

SYSTEM DESIGN

When deciding on how your show will sound, it is important to consider the scale of the work you are making. What may work well in a studio theatre may not in a large-scale theatre, and vice versa.

In a large-scale space, such as a large proscenium venue, the majority of the audience will be a fair distance from the stage and the performers. This distance can often create a sense that you are separated from the performance, that you are more of a voyeur on something happening over there, on the stage. Equally, the proportion that the performance takes up of your entire vision is relatively small. Sometimes we may want to use the sound design to reduce this sense of distance, for example by making the performers' voices feel closer by amplifying them. We must consider whether the sound wants to match the distance and scale of the performance from the audience, or not.

In a smaller space you are a lot closer, and indeed if there isn't a proscenium it may well feel as if you are together with the performers, in the same space. You may feel more immersed in the show, and have more of a sense that it is happening around you.

DESIGNING TO SCALE

These different relationships with the audience mean that the way we tell our story has to be considered accordingly. In a studio space every audience member can see the way an actor arches

The Gate Theatre, London, with the show *The Trojan Women*, designed by Jason Southgate. Lighting designed by Mark Howland.

an eyebrow, and what that might infer. In a larger space, that level of detail will be lost on most of the audience. From a sound perspective, I find I have to paint with broader brushstrokes in a larger venue to make things register. That is not to say that we work without subtlety, but that we have to work harder to sculpt the focus of which details we might want to be noticed.

Imaging of sound becomes more difficult the larger the scale we are working at. Even stereo sound is difficult to achieve, because to achieve it, every single audience member must be receiving sound at roughly equal volume from two speakers. This in itself can be difficult, sometimes impossible, to achieve in many large-scale venues. Having two sets of speakers covering the entire audience is twice as expensive as having one set of speakers covering the entire audience.

If we look at the illustration, we see that audience members in seats A, B, C and D will all primarily hear sound from the left speaker, while audience members in seats I, J, K and L will all primarily hear sound from the right speaker. Only

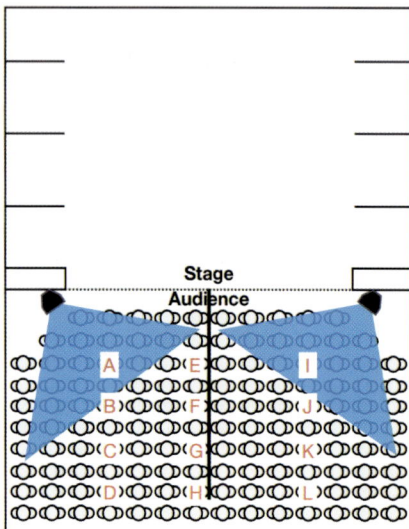

Stereo sound is difficult to achieve: audience members in seats A, B, C and D will all primarily hear sound from the left speaker. Audience members in seats I, J, K and L will all primarily hear sound from the right speaker. Only audience members in seats E, F, G and H will hear sound equally from both the left and right speakers.

audience members in seats E, F, G and H will hear sound equally from both the left and right speakers – and to complicate matters more, as they are hearing sound from two sets of speakers rather than one, it will be noticeably louder for them. This problem is not unique to theatre, as most large-scale concerts are also effectively presented in mono.

In a smaller, shallower theatre we might angle our right speaker towards seat B, and our left speaker towards seat J, such that at seat B you are hearing the right speaker on axis, but you are hearing the left speaker off axis, hence a bit quieter, so they will balance out in volume to a degree. However, for larger spaces this is a more challenging problem to solve. Instead, we will ensure that everything that we need to hear is in both the left and right speakers. We can have stereo content playing through these speakers, but we want to avoid panning things so extremely that people on the edges of the auditorium don't miss out on content that is played through the opposite side speakers.

We should also consider how we use surround sound speakers. In a smaller space, where perhaps the audience feel they are in the same space as the performance is taking place in, the sounds from these speakers can be used to create that sense of space. This can also work for in-the-round configurations.

In a larger end-on space, the surround sound system can feel quite disconnected: imagine you are sat in the upper level of an auditorium, and you are fifty metres away from the stage, and you hear sounds coming from a surround speaker that is only five metres away, behind you. The surround speakers can easily pull you out of what you are watching in front of you. In a larger space it is often quite challenging to get consistent volume coverage from the surround speakers across the auditorium – they will often be louder at the edges of the auditorium, because that's where the speakers are, and quieter in the middle, which might be a more challenging place to rig surround speakers. We can add more speakers to make it more

King's Theatre, Glasgow.

consistent if that is a priority, and budget and rigging positions are available.

In cinema, the surround speakers are quite often used as the 'offstage world' – someone or something may disappear from the shot, and travel into the surround speakers. In a proscenium theatre, we have an actual offstage world, but one that is upstage of the proscenium. If we want to create a sense of people or things happening in the offstage world, we might play it through a speaker located in the wings, rather than through the surround sound system.

So if that's our offstage world, what do we use the surround system for? For a larger auditorium

I rarely put naturalistic sound effects into the surround as they can often pull focus from the stage, and the disconnection with the stage can make those effects feel fake. Some sounds work, maybe a gentle wind or cicadas, but passing cars and the like may not. There are no rules to this. Music and abstract sounds often still work well through the surround speakers, as these are often less of the world of the play, and more a comment on it. For in-the-round I may use surround speakers a lot in the absence of anywhere to have upstage speakers.

In a more immersive venue, where the walls of the world are the walls of the theatre, it is more difficult to create a sense of the offstage world. In the past I've had speakers outside the venue playing loudly to create a sense of something happening outside, or I've played sounds through the surround system, on the edges of the studio space to create this offstage world.

In a large venue, we often have to split our surround system into side surrounds and rear surrounds, and feed different sound into these accordingly. We can delay our side speakers to the main speakers pretty easily – though we should be careful how many surround speakers we pair on an amplifier to allow us the possibility to delay them separately. (If we don't delay our surround speakers at all, if we route the sound to the stage and the surrounds, then the sound will get to the audience first, pulling the image of the sound to the surrounds.) However, the rear speakers are more difficult to find a useful delay time for, as they are facing in the opposite direction to every other speaker in our system.

It is not uncommon to add a second row of rear surrounds on the front edge of the circle fronts to cover the areas of the auditorium closer to the stage. I often avoid putting musical content into the rear surrounds because it often muddies the image unless you're in a shallow auditorium.

One of the main sacrifices we have to make when we move into a larger space is the degree to which we can image the sound to a specific place on stage. In a small theatre we can often use small speakers to locate a mobile phone ring, or similar, to the exact place on stage it's supposed to originate from, but in a larger space that small speaker may just not have enough power to register to the back of the house. We may end up having a small speaker still, and then adding the sound into a bigger speaker placed as near as possible. We may delay the larger speaker a bit to give the impression that the sound is coming from the small speaker, but this isn't always effective.

In a smaller space, for me, imaging of sound is everything. If you get that wrong, everything feels fake. In a larger space, imaging is less critical than making everything audible to the furthest reaches of the auditorium. In fact, the more that any one sound is coming from just one speaker, the more of a hot-spot of sound we will have, where it may sound very good in the middle of the stalls, but too quiet in the upper levels or at the back.

It is reasonably common practice to have a line of under-balcony fill speakers at the rear of some auditorium levels – primarily for vocal reinforcement, but we can use these for sound effects too, particularly if our upstage speakers aren't quite making it to the back of the auditorium. I allocate myself a specific QLab output to feed these speakers, so I can send some sound effects to them and not others.

For an unreinforced play in a large auditorium, we may be struggling at the limits of vocal intelligibility. Adding atmospheric sound effects may be all it takes to push the dialogue into being unintelligible. Or in the noisy conditions of an open-air theatre atmospheric effects might just not register at a 'realistic' level against the background noise. In these circumstances we might consider the 'establish and fade' technique, where we might present the atmospheric effects, possibly at a higher level than normal, or by emphasizing bold elements over a few seconds – to set up the location – and then we'll fade out the sound altogether. This technique was prevalent in the mid to late twentieth century when a theatre might have had only two stereo playback devices, making it difficult to have long-running sound effects playing, as this didn't leave enough capacity for spot cues and transition cues. Without this limitation we're more likely to 'establish and dip', where we'll slowly reduce the level by 5dB or so, rather than fading it out.

SOUND SYSTEM DESIGN

Having established what we want to achieve with sound effects, with music, with abstract sounds, with vocal reinforcement and with music reinforcement, we can begin to design the potentially epic sound system that will make our show sound its best to every single member of the audience. The success of our content – our sound effects, music, microphones – depends on how it is integrated into the performance. The best sound effect can sound fake if it is played out of a speaker too far away from what it is associated with – and equally the most expensive microphone will not sound good at all if the speaker is in the wrong place.

Theatre sound systems can often be some of the most complex you'll come across in any medium, simultaneously handling hundreds of different types of input, to hundreds of speakers and zones. The system will also handle many other functional duties that will be inaudible to the audience.

Assessing the Venue

The sound system design will often be bespoke to the venue(s) you will perform in. And whereas the set, video and lighting designer will primarily be planning what is going on onstage, your focus will be almost entirely on the auditorium. Therefore in tandem with developing our design for the show and how we want it to sound, we also have to assess the venue, and what we think we are capable of doing in there, given the time and money available.

Conducting a site visit is often invaluable, as only so much information can be discerned from plans and photos – and nothing about the acoustics. It's invaluable to talk to the local crew, who can tell you the challenges you will face in the venue, and how people have found a solution to them in the past. They will know their venue intimately, and often know the best way to achieve most things – they will have seen many shows come in and out, with different types of system and different approaches, and will have a good idea of what works and what doesn't. I'll be looking at existing rigging positions for loudspeakers, and whether these will work for us. If, for example, our set extends beyond the proscenium and covers the front six rows of the auditorium, then the

existing speaker positions may be too far upstage for us. I want to find out where the operating position might go, and how well they can hear and see the stage from that location.

Whenever we use microphones, our sound operator should be operating them from a place where they can hear them in the same way as the audience will hear them. The performers talk at different volumes each night, and their mic position may move around. The operator will have to adjust the volume of the mic each night, for almost every line they speak, to get the volume we desire to come out of the speakers, which they can only do if they can hear the speakers.

Auditoriums are often designed to fit as many audience members into them as possible, so we often need to remove seats in order to find space for the operating position. This may be only a couple of seats, or fourteen seats, depending on how much equipment the operator needs to use. This is always contentious, as the seats taken off sale are lost revenue for the producer (assuming they would sell them). If we estimate a theatre ticket selling for £50, multiplied by eight shows per week, multiplied by fifty-two weeks a year, that is £20,800 lost potential revenue *per seat*. This is why we endeavour to keep the mix position as small as possible. However, we must remember this is only potential lost revenue – if the show isn't going to sell out they would never make that money anyway. And whilst the notion of lost revenue is far from ideal, having a mix position is an absolute necessity on shows with reinforcement or amplification.

I will be assessing the location and state of any in-house equipment they might have. Many touring venues have a basic proscenium sound system that can be put up for straightforward shows – some of them are old but well looked after, some are new and lovely, and some have been utterly trashed. Do we need to install a proscenium system in its place? How well resourced does the theatre seem? Do they have equipment shared between multiple venues, and what of that can we use? Do they charge for using some of

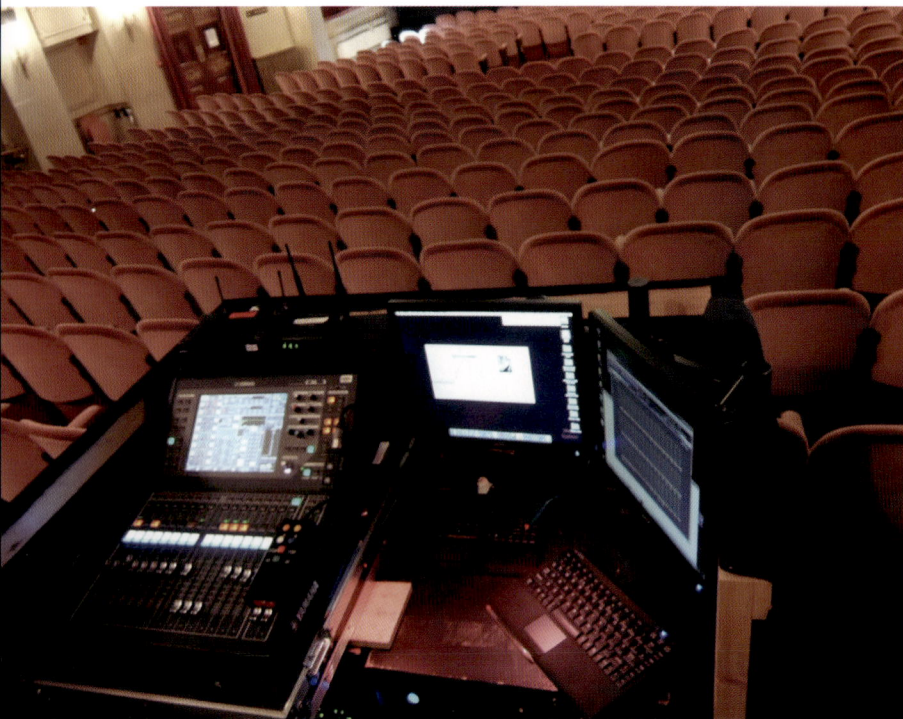

LEFT: Quite a small mix position, taking up only four seats. There are only a few radio microphones on this show, so we can utilize a smaller mixing desk, here a Yamaha QL1. In addition to this we have a Mac to run QLab, and a PC running DME Designer, to control and monitor the sound system.

BELOW: A particularly large mix position, for a show requiring two operators (one for sound effects and music, another for microphones). Here there is a Yamaha CL5 mixer, with Apple Mainstage running on the left, a main and back-up Ableton system, a QLab system, controlled by a 'Go' button and Novation Launchpad, then a DiGiCo SD10-T mixer, MultiMon wireless microphone monitoring software, and Timax2 and Timax tracker software.

that equipment? How enthusiastic and helpful are their staff?

I will often come away from a site visit with a sketch, or some idea in my head of the sound system that we'll need to cover that auditorium.

Designing for Different Requirements

A common approach when thinking about designing the sound system is to divide up its responsibilities, to design for each of those, and then see if there is a way to merge those needs together. For example, what is the best configuration to achieve the sound effects playback, what is the best for the music, what is best for vocal reinforcement? What other functional aspects do we need to include, such as foldback or backup systems?

A vocal system might focus on localizing the performer's voice to the stage, using many small cabinets to ensure that the amplified sound is conveyed to every part of the auditorium for maximum intelligibility. A music system needs speakers that reproduce a wider range of frequencies, particularly in the low end, so often requires larger cabinets and sub-bass cabinets.

There may be areas of the theatre that won't have line-of-sight to our 'main' sound systems, and a 'fill' speaker (because it 'fills in' an area) may be needed to deliver vocal, music and sound effects to that area.

The sound effects system may have different requirements again. Let's have a look at a common sound effect: a ringing mobile phone. For a play in a small- to medium-sized theatre we might have a mini speaker hooked into an IEM receiver in the actor's pocket, which we can transmit our sound effect to. Or we could send it to a small speaker hidden within nearby furniture. We could also use a system to make the actual mobile phone ring, but these aren't super reliable. In a larger venue these solutions might not be loud

enough at the rear or upper levels of the auditorium, so we might add a delayed version of this sound into other speakers. These are ways of making the phone ring sit naturally within the world of the play.

Sometimes we want to be more abstract – which frankly means we can do what we like with it! Or we might want it to cut across the world of the play. Or if our phone ring happened in the middle of a musical number, we might want it to cut across the music, which it couldn't do at a naturalistic level. In these cases, we might want to play it through the proscenium speakers. For every sound you're thinking of playing, you should consider where you want it to be heard from.

For the work I do, most of my sound effects end up being imaged to the stage, and I spend a lot of time finding places to hide speakers onstage. But often we end up with speaker positions that perhaps aren't as ideal as we'd like. Sometimes this can be for aesthetic reasons, sometimes it can be a lack of rigging positions – an open-air theatre, for example, will not have a ceiling to hang anything from.

You can also consider your system design by looking at each area of the auditorium and imagining what you would like to hear in it in each area – what would be the best combination of speaker positions for each area to convey the music, voice and sound effects.

Sketching Out the Sound System

In designing our sound system, it's useful to start by sketching it out on paper. I might start by sketching out a plan of where things might go, and a simple

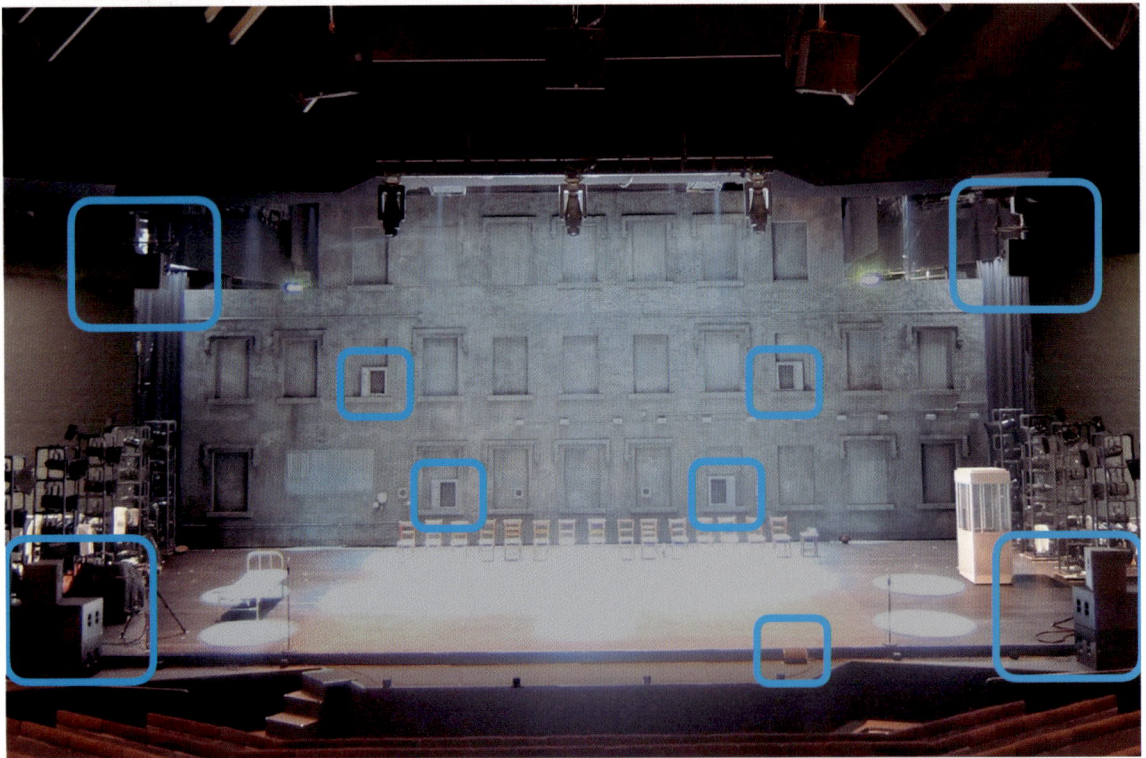

Four speakers have been worked into the back wall of the set, semi-disguised as heating/air-conditioning units on the wall. Under normal show lighting they are a lot less visible. There is also a small speaker downstage right for a more localized sound effect, and the sub-bass and proscenium speakers (one set for the stalls, and another flown set for the circle level).

The Master and Margarita, Complicité. Directed by Simon McBurney. Designed by Es Devlin. Lighting design by Paul Anderson. Video design by Finn Ross. Under normal show conditions, the speakers are a lot less visible.

flowchart of my system. As ideas solidify, these will develop into more complex, detailed drawings. With all drawings and paperwork, it is worth bearing in mind who it is for, what information it is meant to convey, and in how much detail. Paperwork can often be divided up into the schematic, which only the sound department will be interested in; the plan, its physical location and layout – which will be for us, and other departments; and paperwork for your own records.

In the analogue and early digital era, it was quite easy to do a schematic showing what would be connected to where. Audio flowed in a simple fashion from one piece of kit to another, in a chain. In the audio-over-network era everything connects to a network switch and is routed in software to many places. Whilst the next schematic shows more accurately how the sound system is connected together, it shows relatively little detail about how it will be configured.

If I'm working in a fringe venue, and maybe having to move all the speakers around myself, there is rarely no one to share any paperwork with. I might draw a simple schematic for myself to look at the system and check where I might be missing a cable, or perhaps the mixer doesn't have enough outputs to do what I'd envisaged.

If I'm working in a venue with a fixed in-house system, they may only need a few specific documents from me, such as which microphones and speakers go where, and the routings for the different outputs of QLab.

If I'm working with a production sound engineer, I may give them sketches that show what I'm wanting to achieve, and let them work out the detail of how best to achieve it. In the USA, some of this paperwork may be done by the assistant or associate sound designer.

The plan for the touring production of Let The Right One In (see diagram on p.121) shows the

QLab System (main) — DANTE — DANTE MAIN-BACKUP SWITCHER — DANTE (32CH) — DANTE (64CH) — YAMAHA MRX7-D — DANTE (64CH) — DANTE TO AES CONVERTER — AES TO AMPS

QLab System (backup) — DANTE

Ableton System (main) — DANTE — DANTE (32CH) — YAMAHA CL5 MIXER

DANTE MAIN-BACKUP SWITCHER

Ableton System (backup) — DANTE

8x RADIO MICS

AES CARD

PCM92   PCM92

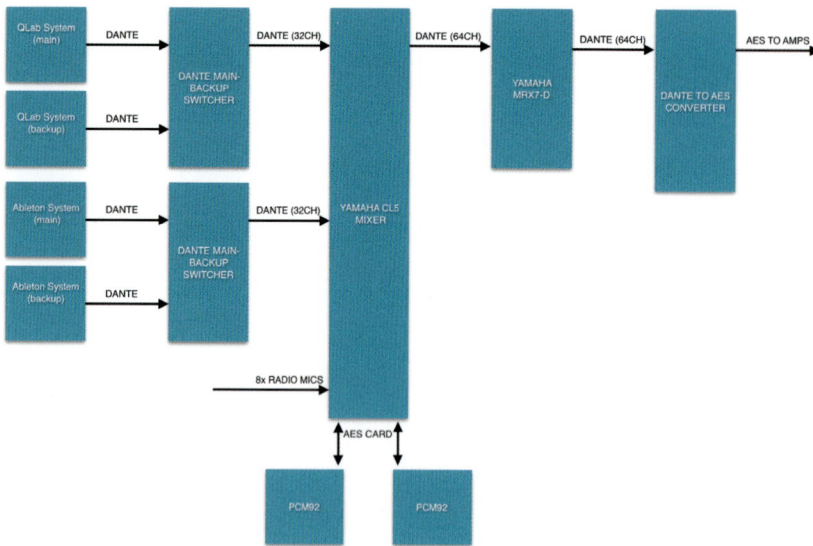

A flowchart schematic should demonstrate the basic intent of your system without necessarily showing the detail.

BELOW LEFT: This schematic is a more accurate drawing of how our previous flowchart schematic is actually wired up, but it shows relatively little information about how the system will be configured.

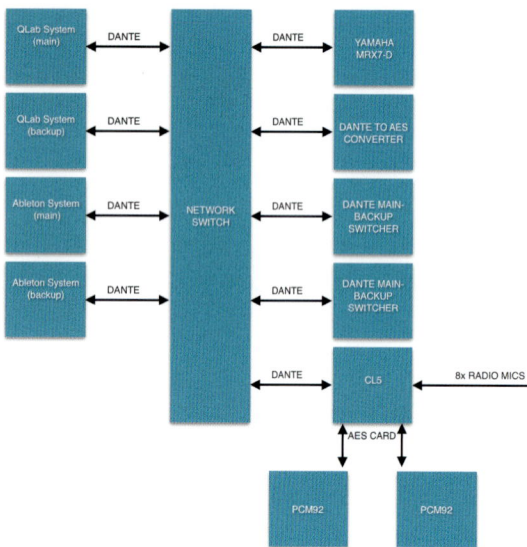

QLab System (main) — DANTE — DANTE — YAMAHA MRX7-D

QLab System (backup) — DANTE — DANTE — DANTE TO AES CONVERTER

Ableton System (main) — DANTE — NETWORK SWITCH — DANTE — DANTE MAIN-BACKUP SWITCHER

Ableton System (backup) — DANTE — DANTE — DANTE MAIN-BACKUP SWITCHER

DANTE — CL5 — 8x RADIO MICS

AES CARD

PCM92   PCM92

not to matters of structural integrity and/or safety.' The safe rigging of heavy speakers above our peers and audiences is crucially important, and if we don't possess the knowledge about whether and how it can be done safely, we should ensure that someone checks this. This may be the production sound engineer, the production manager, or someone with knowledge about the venue or materials involved.

Co-Existing with Lighting

There can often be hotspot areas where both I and the lighting designer might want to place equipment. The two most discussed areas are the central position above the proscenium, where I might want a centre cluster, and the LD might want a light to hit downstage centre; and the proscenium booms, where I might want speakers to cover the stalls auditorium, and the LD wants to hit downstage from the side.

It's important to work together to find a compromise that enables both departments to get what they need. Occasionally I may pull out the 'frequency of use' argument: the centre cluster position will be used continuously for vocal

location of the speakers in relationship to the venue and the set design. Consequently it can often be passed back and forth between multiple departments, as a way of negotiating the positions of everything. This can involve a lot of coordination and negotiation with the lighting and set design team.

I generally include a caveat on my plans: 'This drawing and the specification therein relate only to aural and visual aspects of the production, and

An early flowchart for *Let The Right One In*.

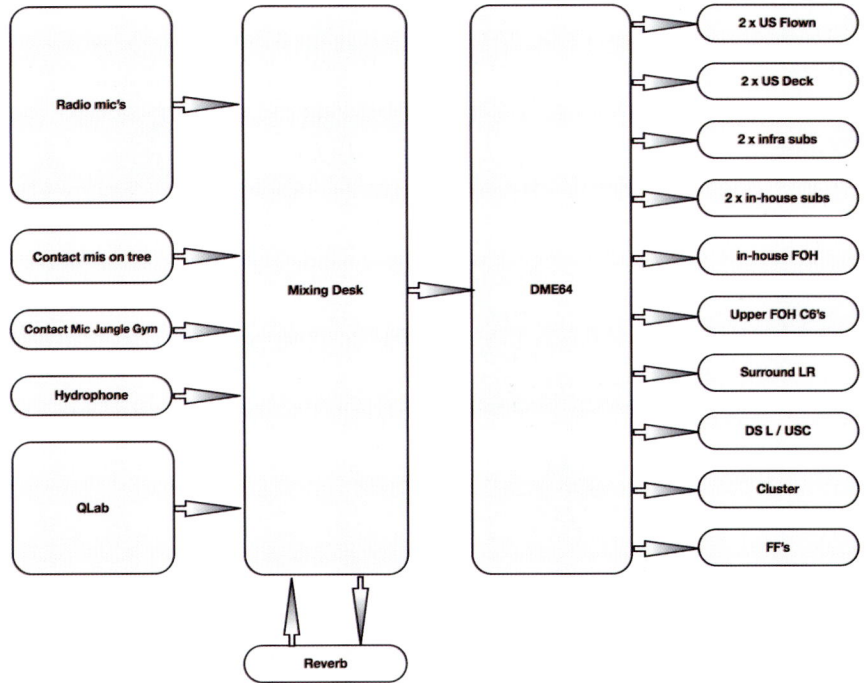

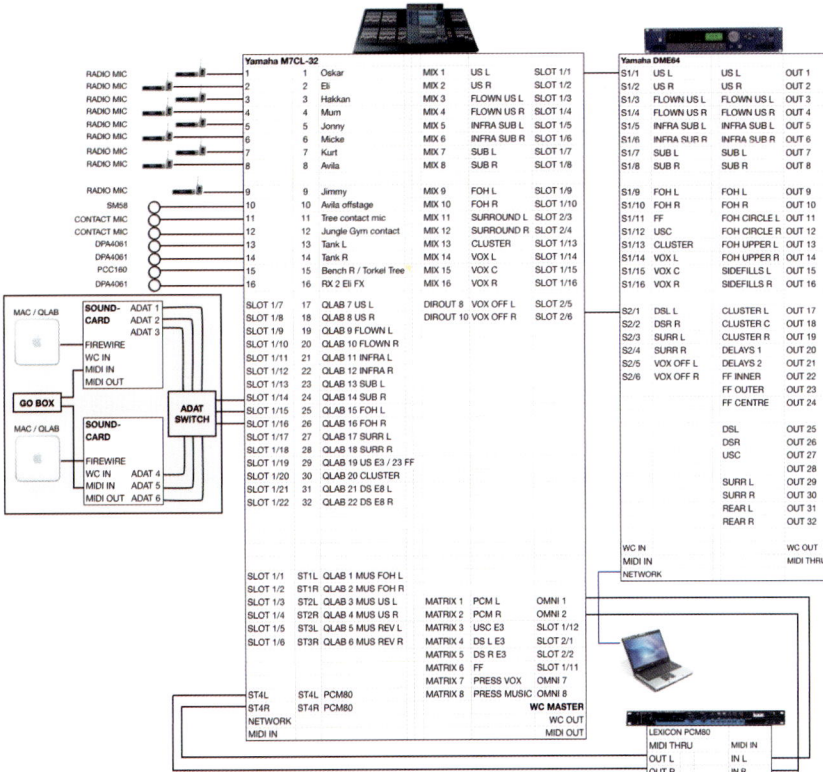

Flowchart

Inputs: Radio mic's · Contact mis on tree · Contact Mic Jungle Gym · Hydrophone · QLab → **Mixing Desk** → **DME64**

Mixing Desk ↔ **Reverb**

Outputs: 2 x US Flown · 2 x US Deck · 2 x infra subs · 2 x in-house subs · in-house FOH · Upper FOH C6's · Surround LR · DS L / USC · Cluster · FF's

Detailed schematic

Yamaha M7CL-32

Input	Ch	#	Name	Mix	Label	Slot
RADIO MIC	1	1	Oskar	MIX 1	US L	SLOT 1/1
RADIO MIC	2	2	Eli	MIX 2	US R	SLOT 1/2
RADIO MIC	3	3	Hakkan	MIX 3	FLOWN US L	SLOT 1/3
RADIO MIC	4	4	Murn	MIX 4	FLOWN US R	SLOT 1/4
RADIO MIC	5	5	Jonny	MIX 5	INFRA SUB L	SLOT 1/5
RADIO MIC	6	6	Micke	MIX 6	INFRA SUB R	SLOT 1/6
RADIO MIC	7	7	Kurt	MIX 7	SUB L	SLOT 1/7
RADIO MIC	8	8	Avila	MIX 8	SUB R	SLOT 1/8
RADIO MIC	9	9	Jimmy	MIX 9	FOH L	SLOT 1/9
SM58	10	10	Avila offstage	MIX 10	FOH R	SLOT 1/10
CONTACT MIC	11	11	Tree contact mic	MIX 11	SURROUND L	SLOT 2/3
CONTACT MIC	12	12	Jungle Gym contact	MIX 12	SURROUND R	SLOT 2/4
DPA4061	13	13	Tank L	MIX 13	CLUSTER	SLOT 1/13
DPA4061	14	14	Tank R	MIX 14	VOX L	SLOT 1/14
PCC160	15	15	Bench R / Torkel Tree	MIX 15	VOX C	SLOT 1/15
DPA4061	16	16	RX 2 Eli FX	MIX 16	VOX R	SLOT 1/16
SLOT 1/7	17	17	QLAB 7 US L	DIROUT 8	VOX OFF L	SLOT 2/5
SLOT 1/8	18	18	QLAB 8 US R	DIROUT 10	VOX OFF R	SLOT 2/6
SLOT 1/9	19	19	QLAB 9 FLOWN L			
SLOT 1/10	20	20	QLAB 10 FLOWN R			
SLOT 1/11	21	21	QLAB 11 INFRA L			
SLOT 1/12	22	22	QLAB 12 INFRA R			
SLOT 1/13	23	23	QLAB 13 SUB L			
SLOT 1/14	24	24	QLAB 14 SUB R			
SLOT 1/15	25	25	QLAB 15 FOH L			
SLOT 1/16	26	26	QLAB 16 FOH R			
SLOT 1/17	27	27	QLAB 17 SURR L			
SLOT 1/18	28	28	QLAB 18 SURR R			
SLOT 1/19	29	29	QLAB 19 US E3 / 23 FF			
SLOT 1/20	30	30	QLAB 20 CLUSTER			
SLOT 1/21	31	31	QLAB 21 DS E8 L			
SLOT 1/22	32	32	QLAB 22 DS E8 R			

Slot	ST	QLAB	Matrix	Name	Out
SLOT 1/1	ST1L	QLAB 1 MUS FOH L			
SLOT 1/2	ST1R	QLAB 2 MUS FOH R			
SLOT 1/3	ST2L	QLAB 3 MUS US L	MATRIX 1	PCM L	OMNI 1
SLOT 1/4	ST2R	QLAB 4 MUS US R	MATRIX 2	PCM R	OMNI 2
SLOT 1/5	ST3L	QLAB 5 MUS REV L	MATRIX 3	USC E3	SLOT 1/12
SLOT 1/6	ST3R	QLAB 6 MUS REV R	MATRIX 4	DS L E3	SLOT 2/1
			MATRIX 5	DS R E3	SLOT 2/2
			MATRIX 6	FF	SLOT 1/11
			MATRIX 7	PRESS VOX	OMNI 7
			MATRIX 8	PRESS MUSIC	OMNI 8
ST4L	ST4L	PCM80			WC MASTER
ST4R	ST4R	PCM80			WC OUT
NETWORK					WC OUT
MIDI IN					MIDI OUT

Yamaha DME64

In	Label	Out label	Out
S1/1	US L	US L	OUT 1
S1/2	US R	US R	OUT 2
S1/3	FLOWN US L	FLOWN US L	OUT 3
S1/4	FLOWN US R	FLOWN US R	OUT 4
S1/5	INFRA SUB L	INFRA SUB L	OUT 5
S1/6	INFRA SUB R	INFRA SUB R	OUT 6
S1/7	SUB L	SUB L	OUT 7
S1/8	SUB R	SUB R	OUT 8
S1/9	FOH L	FOH L	OUT 9
S1/10	FOH R	FOH R	OUT 10
S1/11	FF	FOH CIRCLE L	OUT 11
S1/12	USC	FOH CIRCLE R	OUT 12
S1/13	CLUSTER	FOH UPPER L	OUT 13
S1/14	VOX L	FOH UPPER R	OUT 14
S1/15	VOX C	SIDEFILLS L	OUT 15
S1/16	VOX R	SIDEFILLS R	OUT 16
S2/1	DSL L	CLUSTER L	OUT 17
S2/2	DSR R	CLUSTER C	OUT 18
S2/3	SURR L	CLUSTER R	OUT 19
S2/4	SURR R	DELAYS 1	OUT 20
S2/5	VOX OFF L	DELAYS 2	OUT 21
S2/6	VOX OFF R	FF INNER	OUT 22
		FF OUTER	OUT 23
		FF CENTRE	OUT 24
		DSL	OUT 25
		DSR	OUT 26
		USC	OUT 27
			OUT 28
		SURR L	OUT 29
		SURR R	OUT 30
		REAR L	OUT 31
		REAR R	OUT 32
WC IN		WC OUT	
MIDI IN		MIDI THRU	
NETWORK			

LEXICON PCM80

MIDI THRU	MIDI IN
OUT L	IN L
OUT R	IN R

Left device chain: MAC / QLAB · SOUND-CARD (ADAT 1, ADAT 2, ADAT 3) · FIREWIRE · WC IN · MIDI IN · MIDI OUT · GO BOX · ADAT SWITCH · MAC / QLAB · SOUND-CARD · FIREWIRE · WC IN · MIDI IN · MIDI OUT · ADAT 4, ADAT 5, ADAT 6

A more detailed schematic for the touring production of *Let The Right One In*. Whilst more detailed, this schematic doesn't detail how microphones will get from the stage to the mixing desk, or the outputs to the speakers, which would be variable for each venue the show toured into.

Schematic for the touring production of *The Encounter* showing part of the system, with audio, audio-over-ethernet and MIDI, but excluding mains power, monitors, keyboards and mice, and ethernet for file sharing, amongst others. Often a system is too complicated to show all aspects of it on one plan.

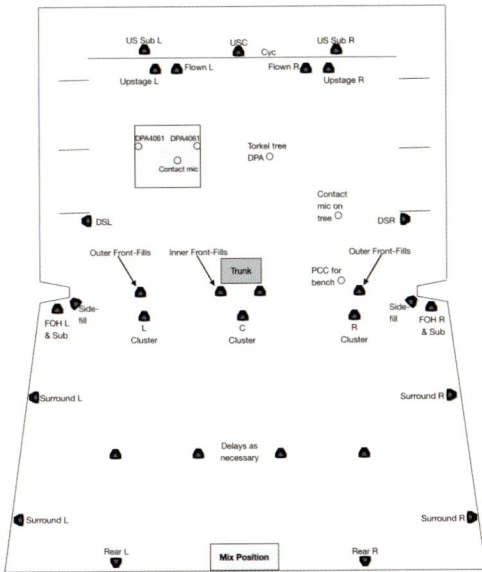

Sketch plan for the touring production of *Let The Right One In* showing a generic ground plan for speakers, where the exact detail will be worked out for each venue.

reinforcement throughout the show, and to significantly compromise its position will be to compromise the listening experience of 500 people for the entire duration of the show. By comparison, if the light has to move, how much effect will it have, and for how long?

Co-Existing with the Set

I often need to place multiple speakers onstage, which will often need a sightline to the audience. This can be tricky if the set design is a pristine, unbroken surface. I work with the set designer to find ways to hide speakers in their set. They can, understandably, be protective of their creations, so I will be sensitive, by going through all the possible options for having speakers onstage, whether disguising them as different objects, bouncing the sound off walls, or changing set materials to be

Woyzeck, at the Old Vic Theatre. Directed by Joe Murphy. Designed by Tom Scutt. Lighting design by Neil Austin. Within each of the paper-fronted scenic element is a small speaker. Each of the elements could fly in and out independently, so this meant there was always a speaker audible for whenever we might need sound. There are also some Meyer UPAs hidden in the darkness upstage. MANUEL HARLAN

Let The Right One In, Abbey Theatre, Dublin. Directed by John Tiffany. Designed by Christine Jones. Lighting design by Chahine Yavroyan. Can you spot the speakers?

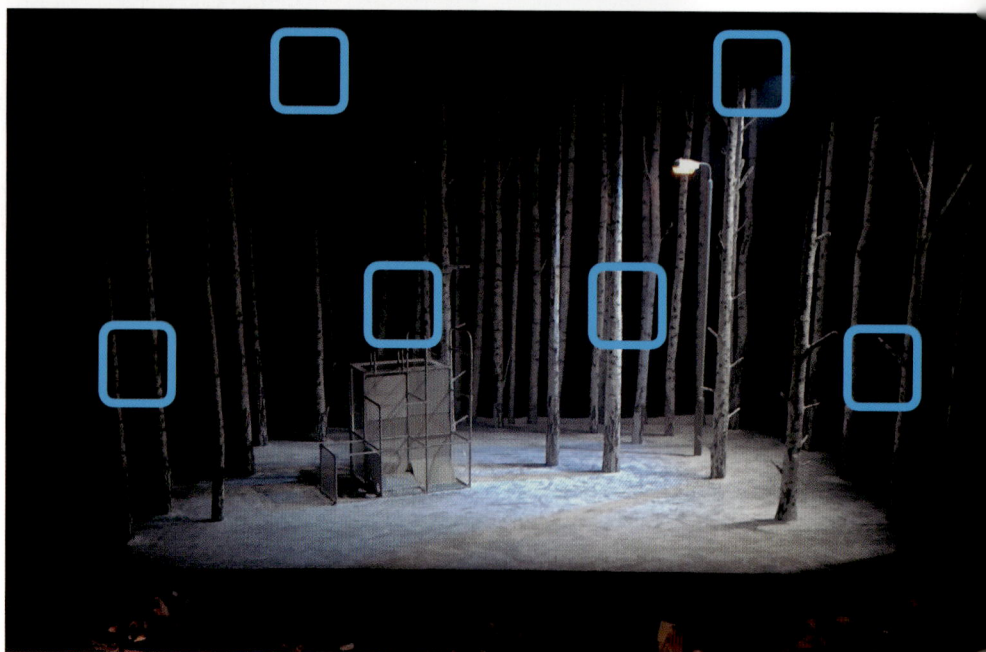

Let The Right One In, Abbey Theatre, Dublin. Directed by John Tiffany. Designed by Christine Jones. Lighting design by Chahine Yavroyan. There are two speakers flown up high, then another two hidden behind the backcloth, and another two smaller speakers just in the offstage wings. There are also six microphones hidden on the stage.

more acoustically transparent. But it's important to be assertive: we have real needs, and the set design has to be functional as well as artistic. Ultimately, we're all in this together, so sometimes everyone has to accept compromises.

The construction of the set may begin around the same time as rehearsals begin, so ideally you will have agreed upon, and drawn up, details of where the speakers will go, so that any grilles or holes can be incorporated into the construction

This speaker is firing through the gauze in the backcloth. As there is a black drape upstage of the speaker, the speaker is completely invisible from the front. At the end of the show, the backcloth is flown out and the gauze is backlit, and for this moment we fly the speakers out.

drawings. It is possible (and common) to do these later, but often the results are not so good, and you may face limitations that could have been avoided had they been planned earlier. You also need to consider what equipment you (or the composer) will need in rehearsals.

SOUND BUDGETS

It's important to consider the system design at an early stage, partly because it influences how your sound design will sound, but also because you need to ensure you have enough budget or resources allocated to achieve your design.

Are there in-house dedicated sound staff, or multi-skilled technicians? Is there a full-time sound operator? Do they rota who operates sound? Are there staff available to run radio microphones onstage? Do you need to hire staff in? When do staff need to start – when do they need to attend rehearsals?

Is there equipment available in-house? Is there kit available for rehearsals? What will you need to hire in?

The sound budget is often set months before rehearsals begin, so you need to start that conversation as soon as possible. Most budgets have flexibility, or contingencies built into them early on, but as time goes by, the budget becomes less flexible as departments spend (or over-spend) their allocation, and contingencies disappear. The earlier you cost up what you need, the more likely you are to get it.

Sound budgets are divided into up-front and running costs. Up-front costs include purchases (such as a bulk purchase of radio microphone capsules), and running costs will be hires or replacement radio microphone capsules.

Budgets vary widely, so find out what's been allocated early on. Will you be able to deliver what has been discussed with the director if there aren't the resources available to do it?

As rehearsals happen, discoveries will be made, and the capabilities of your sound system will change. For example, speaker positions may need to move, be cut, or added. Your initial system design needs to include spare inputs and outputs to incorporate these developments.

You also need to include spare inputs and outputs for backup systems.

CHOOSING THE KIT YOU WANT

Having a preference for certain types of kit will come from the experience of using it, and learning what sounds best to your own subjective senses in different scenarios. Everyone has different preferences. Whilst you learn your preferences you can start by reading the industry magazines, the showcases explaining what different people have used for different shows, and why. You will notice that in few articles will you find people criticizing certain bits of kit – there is a complex relationship between manufacturers and a trade press that is almost entirely funded by the manufacturers who advertise in them. This is not to say that what you read is without merit – far from it – but you will mostly only read about the positive aspects of equipment in them.

You will notice that certain manufacturers are mentioned time and again, and often this is because some make products specifically for the theatre market, whereas others focus on other markets. Some companies focus on certain regions at the expense of others, so you'll see that one manufacturer's products are more popular in certain countries or areas than others. Also, some products are more appropriate to theatre scenarios, which draws people to use them repeatedly.

You can learn a lot about what kit to spec by looking through a hire company's inventory on their website, and the prices that different items are available for.

Below I've listed some of the models I use, or see other people use a lot in UK and US theatre currently. Other equally good products are often available from other manufacturers, or may be prevalent in other territories, so please view this as somewhere to start your internet searches from. Many of these will probably have been superseded by new models by the time you read this.

Radio Microphones

Sennheiser and Shure wireless mic systems are most prevalent in UK/US theatre, with the Sennheiser 5212 and Shure UR1-M being favourite small analogue transmitters. Sennheiser Evolution systems are popular at the lower end of the market. Avoid anything cheaper than that price point. Digital radio systems are maturing, and Sennheiser, Shure and Sony all offer equivalently miniaturized digital transmitters.

DPA 4061 Radio Mic capsules have long been an industry favourite, with Sennheiser's MKE-2 a close second.

DPA 4066 headset microphones are popular, as are Countryman E6 single-sided headsets.

Handheld Microphones

Neumann KMS105s are popular handheld mics when there is more money available, otherwise the Shure SM58 and Beta 58 can be found in almost any theatre.

A DPA d:screet CORE 4061 microphone. CALEB HILL/SOUND NETWORK LTD

A Sennheiser 6212 digital transmitter – in theatre this might more often be held within a cloth pouch. © Sennheiser electronic GmbH & Co. KG www.sennheiser.com

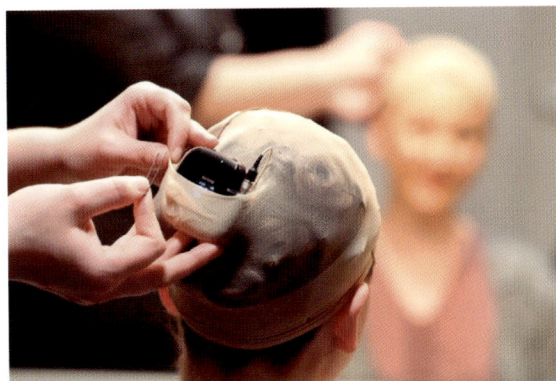

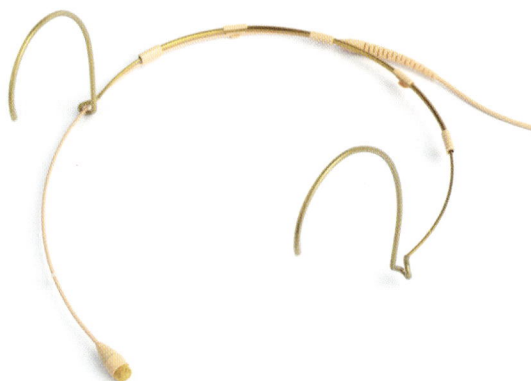

A DPA d:fine 4066 microphone. CALEB HILL/SOUND NETWORK LTD

A Shure ADXIM transmitter being mounted into a wig cap, allowing the radio microphone to be concealed within a wig or headpiece.

Instrument Microphones

There is a huge array of microphones used from a variety of manufacturers, so I won't mention any specific ones. DPA 4060 and 4061 mics are popular for when we have to wirelessly mic an instrument.

Mixing Desks

DiGiCo mixers are fairly standard across most mid- to large-scale theatre shows – they have developed theatre-centric software for us to deal with problems, such as having to reprogram the

A Shure SM58 vocal microphone – a simple, robust design icon.

Neumann KMS105 vocal microphone, with a more directional supercardioid pick-up pattern.
© Neumann.Berlin www.neumann.com

mixing desk at each performance to deal with numerous understudies and covers going on. Increasingly, mixing desks sound similar and have flexible network/audio inputs and outputs, so it's the desk software that most determines the choice of desk.

Avid, Soundcraft, SSL, Studer, Yamaha and others all make large-format desks that can be found in some venues, but not all have the flexibility needed for a large show.

Yamaha QL and CL desks are popular at the lower end of the market and are known for their reliability and value for money.

However, mixing desk software evolves fast, so who knows what the future holds.

Reverb Units

Lexicon and TC electronics are popular hardware reverbs, as most reverbs built into mixing desks are poor in comparison. Increasingly effects are being hosted on computers, with Waves Soundgrid, Apple Mainstage and Ableton Live offering popular platforms.

Playback

Figure 53's QLab and Ableton Live have already been frequently mentioned. They are both popular, with QLab predominant in the UK and USA. Prior to QLab, Stage Research's SFX was the UK/USA industry standard. Alternative platforms are in use, such as CSC, SCS and Merging's Ovation.

Processors DSP

Yamaha DMEs, and latterly MRX7-Ds, are an easy and flexible way to matrix out, and control, a complex sound system. Its accompanying software allows you to drag and drop various components, EQs, delays, delay matrices, dynamics,

A DiGiCo SD7-T mixing desk. Increasingly what makes one manufacturer's mixing desk better than the others is whether the software has been designed for our specific application. DiGiCo's -T console software was developed in collaboration with sound designer Andrew Bruce with the specific demands of theatre in mind.

Yamaha CL5 mixing desk.

Yamaha QL1 mixing desk.

and so on, into the software and draw cables between them, and the many inputs and outputs, so you can configure it to do exactly what you want.

A number of manufacturers provide fixed architecture Processors with delay-matrixes and EQs, such as Meyer's Galileo system. Outboard's Timax system also has a fixed architecture but is more theatre-optimized, allowing complex imaging and localization to be achieved. Timax has a performer tracking system, where the performers wear a

small transmitter that allows Timax to track their position on the stage and delay-pan their voice to appropriate loudspeakers to make it sound as if the amplified voice is coming from their physical location. Other manufacturers have recently moved into this area with d&b's Soundscape system (alongside the existing TTA tracking system) and L'Acoustics LiSA.

Whilst other systems exist, they are often optimized towards installation solutions such as restaurants and shops.

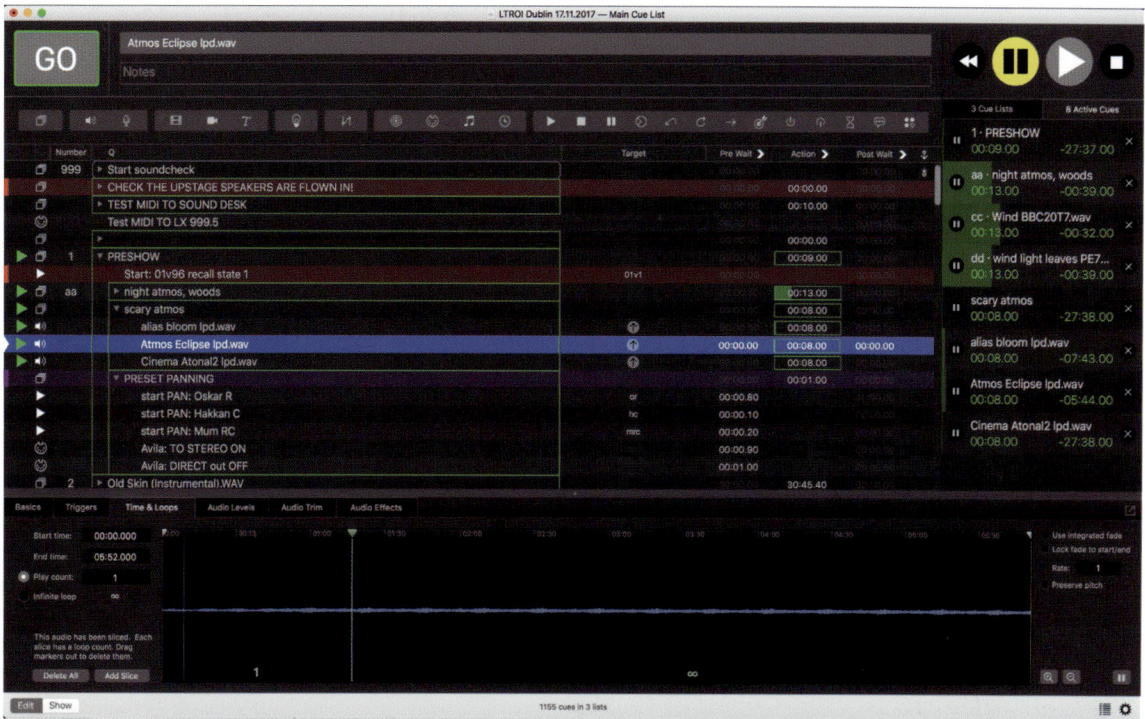

Figure 53's QLab is the industry standard for theatre playback in the UK and the USA, allowing complex designs to be built from a simple but powerful set of tools.

Amplifiers and Speakers

Loudspeakers – and their interaction with room acoustics – requires some knowledge of the physics of sound. Whilst many of us get around this by using kit that we know works well in most scenarios, or copying what other people use, sooner or later you will find yourself in a situation where you need to know more than you do.

One of the key aspects of speaker design relates to dispersion, which can be considered analogous to how closely a speaker resembles a floodlight, or a narrow beam of light. Generally, smaller boxes have a wider dispersion, as a loudspeaker needs a certain physical size to control dispersion in the lower frequencies. The tighter the dispersion (the narrower the focus of the light), the more you can point it at the audience, and the less it points at reflective surfaces, avoiding creating excessive reverb or echoes. This can be

beneficial in rooms with poor acoustics, or where you are not getting enough gain before feedback, but more loudspeakers may be required to accomplish coverage.

Dispersion and good coverage is not always intuitive, with some large venues being covered spectacularly well with only a couple of high-power speakers, whereas some smaller venues may require a great many smaller cabinets to get good coverage. Our audience location and stage configuration will determine which speakers may best cover our audience, with an in-the-round configuration often requiring different types of speaker configurations compared to a proscenium configuration.

Many loudspeaker manufacturers provide software tools to allow you to draw in your venue and seating areas, and experiment with different placements of different types of virtual speakers to help you choose the best configuration and locations

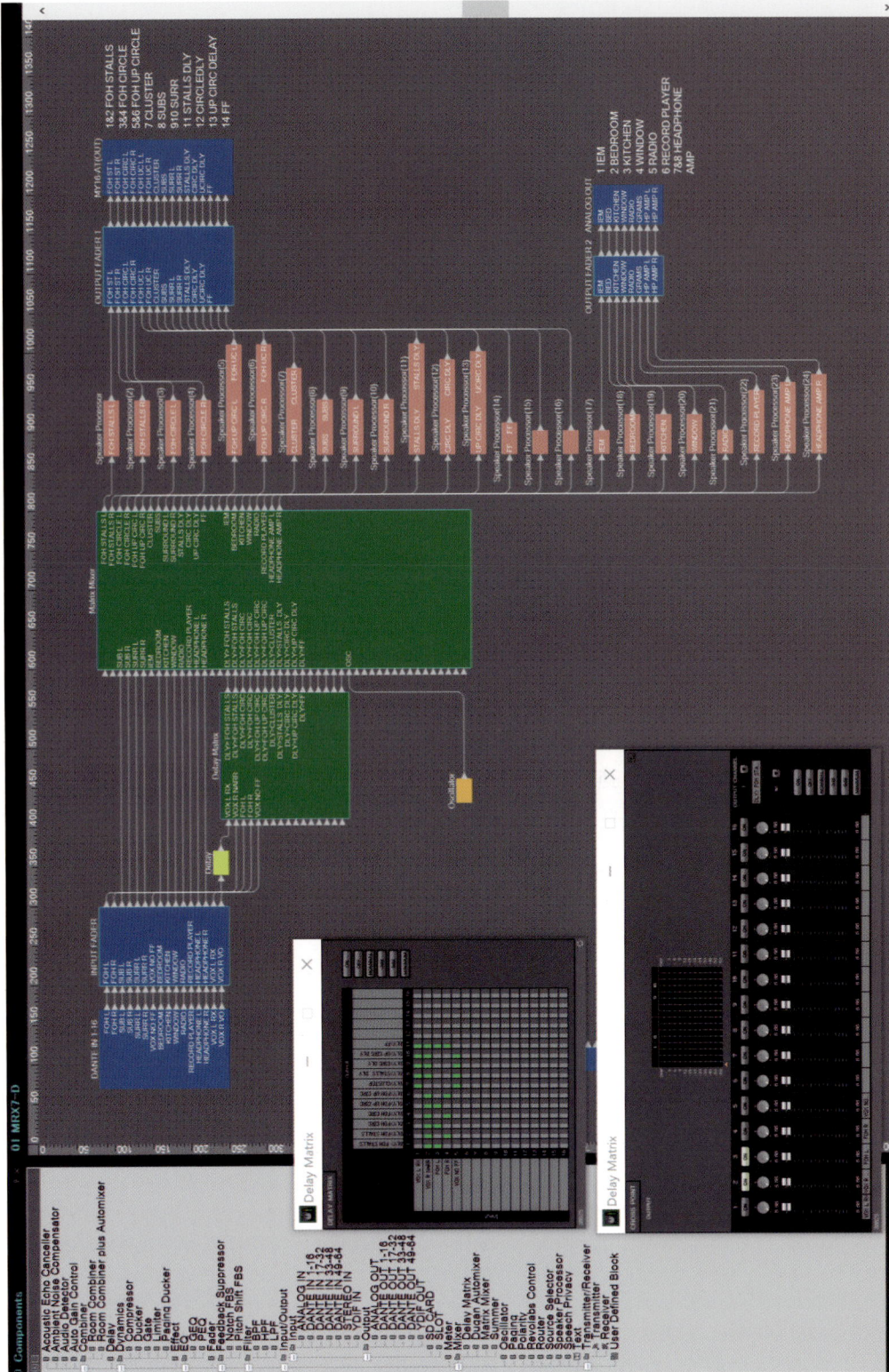

Yamaha's MRX Designer software provides a drag-and-drop configurable set-up that can be changed to what the user needs for their show.

Timax software combines multiple audio inputs alongside playback software, with advanced delay panning and matrixing. It can be combined with their Tracker system to track the location of performers onstage automatically, and delay-pan them to appropriate outputs.

of speakers for that venue. Many manufacturers provide training in how to use this software.

For many years, amplifiers were simple but often unreliable devices. However, they are now fairly reliable devices. Whilst cheaper amps are still simple, with little more than a volume control on them, higher end amps increasingly include EQ, delay and other features.

Some speakers are available as a powered speaker (where the amplifier is built into the speaker enclosure), and some may have individual amplifiers optimized for each speaker driver. No space is required for racks of amplifiers, and signal can be sent to the speakers from anywhere convenient, rather than from an amp room. However, powered speakers are heavier than passive speakers, potentially limiting rigging options, and you have to replace the entire unit, or fly in a whole line array if an amp channel fails. Also, both power and audio must be run to each cabinet,

and care must be taken if it is to be used outside (as rainwater and mains electricity can be a lethal combination).

A design that uses passive speakers allows easy access, control and replacement of amp channels. Speaker arrays will be lighter, smaller and more weatherproof, and only require speaker cable to be run to them. Both methods have advantages and disadvantages, depending on the circumstance.

Sub-Bass Speakers

Sub-bass speakers can be divided into two types of speaker: the type that provides the lower bass frequencies that the normal loudspeaker can't reproduce well, typically below 180Hz; and the type that provides really low bass frequencies, often (but inaccurately) called

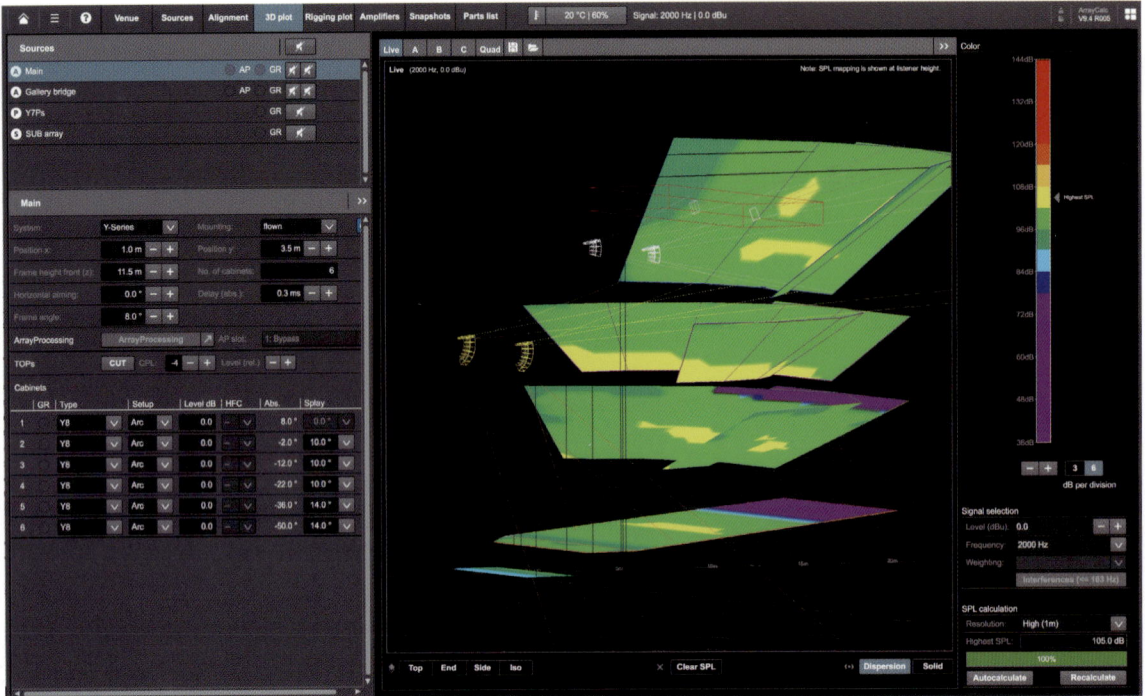

d&b ArrayCalc allows the user to experiment with different speaker positions and types within your venue, and to calculate the level of direct sound at various audience positions.

infrasonic frequencies. A normal sub-bass speaker might be a single 15" speaker to accompany a couple of regular speakers. An infra-sub might be multiple 18" cabinets in a large cabinet, of which only a few may be needed for the entire venue.

Foldback

Sennheiser HD25 headphones have long been popular with their DJ-style folding earphone, which allows the user to wear them comfortably with only one earphone on and the other off.

Genelec monitors and Galaxy Hotspots are popular with an easy-to-access volume control. (Hint: set the input level such that with the volume control at 'full' it's not outputting a problematic level for us. The musician should have the power to turn it down at will, but not louder than the level we've set.)

A d&b Y-Sub subwoofer speaker, containing an 18" driver at the front, and a 12" driver at the rear, to create a more directional sound, covering 39Hz to 110Hz.

We have seen a shift to musicians having personal monitoring systems, where they can set their own foldback levels per number, or as they see fit. This gives them control, which they like,

A d&b B22 subwoofer speaker, with two 18" speakers. When operated in 'infra' mode this will cover 32Hz to 68Hz.

Aviom A16 personal monitoring station, with a custom-moulded ear piece in the foreground.

and they don't have to keep requesting different levels from us. Aviom was the pioneer in this area, though other manufacturers are moving in on it.

IN-HOUSE EQUIPMENT

Venues with plenty of in-house equipment may only allocate a small sound budget, on the assumption that you can use everything in-house. If you need to use additional equipment or resources, this needs to be flagged up as early as possible.

For example, I designed a show in a small, well-known, well-equipped venue. However, they didn't have any radio microphones. For a cast of six people, we had to buy eight radio microphone capsules (two spares): at £230 each, times eight came to £1,840. Plus there was a weekly running cost of hiring six radio microphone systems at £60 each, so times six amounted to £360 per week – plus, a staff member to look after them, at £800 per week. For the eight-week run, this was £11,120. The standard budget allocation there was £300. I managed to get in our request early, and so the money was allocated from the budget. If I'd done that at the start of rehearsals, there wouldn't have been any money left to allocate. Sometimes in these sorts of venues, equipment may be available to borrow from other spaces, or staff can be reallocated. But that also needs careful planning and time.

HIRING EQUIPMENT

We often hire in equipment for a production. So why doesn't the company buy it? Firstly, the way a company accounts, and can tax deduct, a capital purchase works differently from how they can deal with a weekly hire cost, with the capital purchase working less favourably in the short term. And then at the end of the run they'd have to dispose of that asset, or store it.

Secondly, if we purchase a piece of equipment and it breaks down, it is our responsibility to replace it. What do we replace it with, and how do we get it to the theatre in time if we only discover something is broken at 6pm and we have a 7.30pm show? Retailers don't have that fast a delivery network. We could hire a replacement whilst the original is repaired, but that takes time to organize, and there is no guarantee that a hire company will have what we need in stock. Hire companies offer a support network for their equipment, either to come to your theatre and fix it, or to send you a replacement that can arrive before your show starts. If you are touring or hiring from a company that is a long way away from you, it's sensible to tour some spares.

Hire companies have different methods of pricing their goods. They might take their set weekly cost for each piece of equipment, multiply this by the quantity, and then again by the number of weeks it is required. You're unlikely to get a discount on a one-week hire, but you might get around 30 per cent for four weeks, or even 60 per cent for a long hire. Some companies provide discounts for paying a percentage in advance, some not. If you get a quote that is out of your budget you can discuss substituting equipment on the list for cheaper models, or fewer of them. If they are keen for your business, or you have built up a good relationship with them, the hire company may just ask what your budget is and make it work for that.

The majority of a hire company's running costs are associated with getting jobs in and out the door, and equipment isn't earning money if it's sat on the shelves. Hire companies prefer longer hires, and earning something, rather than not getting anything. Building a relationship is useful so hire companies value your business, so may be able to make a small budget show work for you, knowing they will be able to offset that potential loss against future work when you've got a better budget.

There are different types of hire companies – some specialize in broadcast sound, some in concert audio, some in conferences and events, and some in theatre. Each have different lines of kit, priced using different models. A broadcast-focused company will predominantly do one-day hires and might not have many speakers. A theatre-specialist hire company is likely to provide equipment more suitably configured and at a better price.

The interaction with a hire company might start with you emailing them with a request for a quote for your project, with the start and end dates of the hire, where kit will be delivered to and collected from, whether you want the hire company to transport it, or alternative arrangements; and a list of what you want. You would also introduce them to who will pay for the hire, probably the producer or venue. On no account should *you* be paying for the hire and charging that cost on – if the producers have money issues, this will leave you owing the hire company a *lot* of money, and your relationship in tatters.

Some producers or a government-run venue may require a process where multiple hire companies are asked to quote, to find the cheapest. This is less typical on smaller shows, where your relationship with the hire company can be more valuable than attempts to play companies off against each other. The lowest bidder won't necessarily be the company who can best support the show, which should also be considered.

Most companies are receptive to working with new designers and can support you in choosing the equipment you might need. If you are unsure about what you need for a specific purpose, rather than asking for a specific microphone model, you can ask them to quote for a mic suitable to clip on a violin, and they will be able to suggest something from their available stock. Hire companies can provide support to you and your team, helping to set things up and get them working, as well as when things break down. Larger companies may have product specialists, for radio microphones or computer networking.

Different hire companies have relationships with different manufacturers, so some may stock certain brands and not others. If you have something specific they may be able to source it from another hire company, called sub-hiring, but you're unlikely to get any discount on those items.

Most companies won't hire out radio microphone capsules due to the amount of wear and tear they receive on most jobs. It is typical to purchase radio microphone capsules from the hire company, or from elsewhere, instead of hiring them.

Different companies have different approaches to how they prepare their equipment before sending it out. If you have specific requirements regarding how the equipment is racked, you can provide drawings or information to illustrate this. On medium to large shows it's typical for the production sound engineer to spend time at the hire company configuring the equipment to the way we want it.

Rehearsals for Complicité's *The Encounter*. SARAH AINSLIE

10
REHEARSALS

WORKSHOPS

Before rehearsals begin there may be a work-shop. This could be some months before rehearsals begin, and often fulfils one of two functions: first, it can be to explore a few different possible approaches or ideas of how to stage the show, particularly if it's a complex or unusual piece. As this may define the entire style of the production, it can be important to be a part of it.

The second reason for a workshop is to attract funding, or venues for the show to tour to. A few scenes, or perhaps the whole show may be roughly rehearsed, and at the end of the workshop there'll be a 'showing' for potential producers, or representatives from potential touring venues, to decide if they want to invest in it, or book it in. This is common for new musicals, and we may be brought in to radio mic everyone through a small PA system, perhaps alongside a piano or small band, and to record the showing.

NON-DEVISED REHEARSALS

A typical non-devised rehearsal schedule for the cast will involve the following few stages:

The first day: This may involve a 'meet and greet' with the cast, creatives, producers, venue team, marketing, education and other departments. There may be a showing of the set design modelbox, talking through the journey of the set, led by the set designer and director. There may be a read-through of the script, round a table. These can happen in any order. After this everyone apart from cast and creatives will leave, and rehearsals will commence.

Table work: It's common to start work around a table, talking through the themes of the script, the context, talking through the historical context, discussing the characters and their 'back story' (the characters' personal history prior to the start of the play). It may involve going through the script in minute detail, clarifying the exact events that happen, and the intention that each character has when they say each of their lines. This ensures everyone is 'on the same page'. With a large cast, the table work might happen with just the principal performers the week before rehearsals officially begin.

'Putting it on its feet': This phrase comes from getting up from the table and rehearsing the scene whilst moving around. Depending on the style of rehearsals, only the cast members who appear in the scenes may be called into these rehearsals. If there's a scene with only two people in it, but a cast of twenty, it can be distracting to have eighteen people hanging around. In more ensemble work, the entire company may be present all the time. Or there may be a second rehearsal room, where the choreographer or associate director might work with a group. This first pass at rehearsing the script can be when the performers feel most anxious or vulnerable.

The second pass: After getting to the end of the script, it's typical to circle back to the start and revisit each scene. By now everyone will have bodily experienced the arc of their character through the show. The second pass usually takes less time, and will offer culminate with a run-through of each act, or the whole show. After this, rehearsals will focus on the scenes that aren't quite working.

Complete runs: Some directors like to do a few complete runs of the show as they enter the last week of rehearsals. Some will only do one, some don't do any. These are when you get your first proper sense of the arc of the show – and the last time you'll get that sense before the dress rehearsal.

THE SOUND DESIGNER'S PRESENCE IN REHEARSALS

Different shows, different genres, different directors all want, or require, different levels and types of support in rehearsals. Some require my attendance in rehearsals full time from day one, or from the moment that we start to put it on its feet. Some require me to pop in once a week. For simple shows, I may pop in a couple of times and just watch the final runs. It's essential to talk with the director in advance, to avoid a crisis mid-rehearsals, about what we want to achieve, and how much support will be needed.

A rehearsal studio should have some sound system in place, even if it's just for warm-up music. Sometimes support might be desired but isn't strictly necessary: the deputy stage manager (the person on the prompt book, who will call the show in the theatre) yelling 'ding dong' in place of installing a system to play a single doorbell sound effect is fine. However, these shows are increasingly rare, as directors are wanting more sophisticated and layered soundtracks.

In the UK, in the absence of a sound designer or sound operator, the DSM will often operate sound effects in the rehearsal room, as long as there aren't so many that it interferes with their job.

One of the easiest mistakes to make is to underestimate how much support will be needed, especially if you book yourself on another job elsewhere. The performers use rehearsals to find out how to occupy the aural realm – when to speak, when to pause, when to be loud, when to be quiet, their rhythm and arc. If sound support is missing at a critical moment, it can be like rehearsing with one of the actors missing: shows can hit crisis point if sound support is missing and needed.

If you try to add complex sound design from scratch during the tech, you may be battling against how the performers have occupied the aural landscape – potentially breaking or changing their rhythm and arc. It's not uncommon in this circumstance to find that there's no room left to put in any foreground sound, and little for background sound. A common sign of sound designs that are added in the tech is 'sound design in the gaps': finding a moment where the actors pause, and putting a sound in the pause. Clearly only being able to put sounds in the gaps you can find is not a technique that is going to result in artistically satisfying results.

As much as is possible or appropriate, I'll attend rehearsals to add in sound as the performers develop their rhythm and arc – rather than forcing them together in the theatre. The performers can also respond to and incorporate the sound into their rhythm. Rehearsals are often where problems about how to stage the play are encountered, and solved. How do we 'do' this moment in the script? If I'm there, I can offer sound solutions to these moments. If I'm not there, they'll probably find an acting solution instead. But by developing the performance and sound design together, we create something integrated. I can also suggest (to the director) about how we could tweak the performance of something so everything works together better.

First Playing Sound into Rehearsals

I choose the moment when I first play sound into rehearsals very carefully. The director may be keen to have sound in the room, but some actors may not be used to it. I introduce it quietly and carefully. I avoid playing sound if it feels as if an actor is struggling with a scene – you don't want to be shut down because you're making a difficult situation worse. I often find myself coming into rehearsals planning to start playing sound into rehearsals straightaway, but spending a few days waiting until the moment is right to do so. Choose that moment so you are supporting the director, the performers and the process, so that you and your work are welcomed as a contributor, rather than as a distraction or obstruction.

Whilst I bide my time, I'll play sounds to myself over headphones. I may play sound and music over the speakers during the coffee and lunch breaks, to start seeding bits of music and sound into people's consciousness so my work sounds familiar when I start playing it into rehearsals.

Having established myself in the room, rehearsals are normally a safe space to experiment, to fail, to try different ideas, without judgement. It is also the place to potentially re-conceive your concept of the show if it doesn't feel right for the direction the show is going. We can all have the best ideas and imaginations in the world, but it is amazing how often, when you see a script being performed, your understanding of it may change

completely – or the way a particular group of actors interprets and performs a script can change the meaning of it completely (watch David Lynch's *Mulholland Drive*).

I normally make, and improvise, content from my laptop as I create and iterate it. As it becomes more locked down, I'll transfer it on to the rehearsal room computer, which might be operated by me, the DSM, the sound operator or the associate. It's useful to have a separate computer for playback so I can be working on whatever I choose whilst rehearsals carry on with another part of the show.

Employing a Sound Operator

If it's looking like a busy show, I'll consider employing a sound operator or associate sound designer for rehearsals. My differentiation between

Rehearsal-room rig, showing Ableton Live with Behringer control surface, and Figure 53's QLab with Novation Launchpad, Yamaha CL5 mixing desk, and 4 Shure radio microphones.

Some rehearsal-room set-ups may not have quite so much space.

those two roles, in rehearsals, is that the associate would, as well as operating, also potentially create content for the show and be able to discuss and evolve the concept with the director in my absence. It can be a significant budget implication to have a sound operator in rehearsals, as theatres rarely have spare staff available. Given enough notice, some venues can reorganize their staffing to accommodate this, but more often it will require extra staff to be employed, probably coming out of the sound budget.

In the UK, on all but the larger of shows, the cost of an associate sound designer would normally come out of the sound designer's fee, so this is a potential cost that needs to be factored back at the fee negotiation stage. In the USA, associate sound designers are more commonplace,

and more likely to be employed directly by the producer.

SUPPORTING REHEARSALS

Composed Music

A composer might start rehearsals with 'demo' tracks, which they'll develop over rehearsals. It's useful to provide a means for them to play sound off their laptop, or off their keyboard, and some easy volume control so they can experiment. The sound system is your responsibility, the keyboard is theirs!

As rehearsals develop, the need for fades, dips and crossfades will develop, and so we'll start putting their files into QLab.

If the demo tracks will be replaced with real in-struments, you may find yourself getting involved in the recording session for that, effectively working as the record producer. It's often best to leave this recording session as late in rehearsals as possi-ble to allow for timings to change as run-throughs happen (which is where everything tends to speed up). Some composers have recording studios they use regularly, and may produce their music them-selves, just delivering a stack of audio files to you. Others may want you to book the studio, engineer the session, edit and mix the recordings.

Both methods have different advantages in dif-ferent scenarios. If you have an already busy show, you may not have time to produce the music alongside everything else, and I have on occasion brought in an associate solely to deal with this. Alternatively, producing the music is more collabo-rative and allows your ideas and concepts to influ-ence the music.

Found Music

Found music refers to non-composed music – music we find somewhere, whether on CD, vinyl, off the internet or wherever.

Choosing music is one of the most negotiated aspects of a performance. Everyone has an opin-ion: writer, director, cast, producer will all input, whether you want them to or not! Some people may offer terrible suggestions. Some people may be experts in a particular genre and offer amazing suggestions. I won't pretend to be an expert in a genre when I'm not, but I research as much as I can. Sometimes inviting collaboration about the music opens the door to people submitting their opinions on a range of other topics that are less welcome. Ultimately you and the director must decide how much to listen to those opinions, and how collaborative you want to be.

The director and I will normally have discussed music prior to rehearsals starting, so I'll load up the rehearsal-room computer with some material to play with.

If I'm not in rehearsals, the conventional way a director might ask for music is to ask the stage manager to put the request on the rehearsal-room notes email that is sent out at the end of each day. I would then source the music, come into rehears-als at the next available opportunity, and load it up on the computer. This is time- and resource-consuming for everyone. Often I set up Spotify or iTunes Music on the rehearsal-room computer, so ideas can be quickly tried out. However, some-times the slower process can be better, particu-larly if there are politics at play or someone in the room is proffering too many suggestions, or trying to steer things away from where myself or the di-rector want things to go.

Instant gratification and the near unlimited choices of streaming music services can be over-whelming things to have access to, in the same way that rolling news television channels are often the worst source of accurate news, compared to a news source that takes time to reflect, research and get the story correct.

We have to ensure that we can get permis-sion to use what we've found. The procedures for copyright clearance are complex, and vary incred-ibly from country to country. It may involve liaising with your producers and the copyright clearing agencies that operate in your country (in the UK it is PRS for Music and MCPS), and possibly ne-gotiating directly with the publishers of the music you want to use. If you are touring internationally then you may need to clear each piece of music with agencies or publishers in each territory you will visit.

During rehearsals we're often developing and rehearsing choreographed sequences. Some will be locked to a piece of music, some we will want to edit, or to compose the music so it matches the movement. I use Ableton Live a lot for this as it enables me to fluidly edit, vamp and react with music to what is going on. Sometimes we may eventually lock down those edits into a sequence that will always happen to the same timings and counts each time. Sometimes we may want to keep it fluid even in performance.

ASTRONAUT, THEATRE O

The director, Joseph Alford, was keen to use a specific piece of music for a scene about a family waiting for a phone call that never comes. Each day they wake up, wait and wait, getting increasingly frustrated and bored. Each day we move faster through their day, so they get bored faster and faster. The music that Joseph wanted to use had a great beginning and middle but was otherwise full of lyrics that weren't relevant to the scene. I put the music into Ableton Live and chopped the intro and middle into bar-long loops.

As we rehearsed the scene, I could play the mellow start of the track as they woke up, and progress through the track to the more aggressive parts of the track as they got frustrated. When they went to bed and woke up I could loop back to the start of the track and we'd repeat the process, but faster. When we were happy with what we'd made, I hit Record on Ableton, and we rehearsed the scene. The software recorded my performance of the loops, which I bounced out and we played back as a fixed, choreographed section from then onwards.

Ableton provides a great way to re-edit music to match a choreographed sequence.

Live Music

It is reasonably rare that musicians can be afforded in the rehearsal room. But actor musicians, where an actor will also play a musical instrument, are more affordable. There's no rule for what support will be needed here, as the range of instruments and electronica is vast. Rehearsal rooms are often small enough that no serious amplification is needed, maybe a guitar amp at most. Sometimes, some sense of what will be used in performance is needed, as often to rehearse the mechanics of getting it on and offstage. Occasionally we may need to have a full band and PA setup, but that's quite rare.

We may have the live musicians join us for the last couple of run-throughs to give them some chance to rehearse together with the performers.

Microphones

Microphones always add complexity, simply because if not supervised they can easily go into howling feedback. A microphone on a stand, or two, is something that a stage manager can often deal with in rehearsals. More than that, or as soon as you get into radio microphones, and you should look at having a sound person there to look after them. That's not a criticism of stage managers, but they have their own full-time job to be getting on with.

It's best to have a digital mixer if we use microphones, to put compressors and limiters on them to automatically suppress loud bits without anyone having to 'ride the faders' (keep their fingers on the faders to pull down shouted lines, or to boost quiet lines).

Radio Microphones

Radio microphone transmitters are bulky items, and if the performers have physical roles where they might roll over, or fall on the pack, or its presence may interfere with what they're doing, it can be useful to provide some transmitter-shaped wooden blocks in mic belts they can rehearse with. This helps them get used to the physical object, and to try the various locations the transmitter can be hidden (around the waist, front and back, in the small of the back, in their groin, round an ankle, in a wig, in a hat, and so on). This can save time later, prevent injuries, and prevent damage to the equipment.

There are a few reasons for using radio microphones in rehearsals. Sometimes we do need to amplify voices for them to be audible in a rehearsal room: if we're in a large room with bad acoustics; or if we're rehearsing a show with audience configurations that place the actors with their backs to us in the rehearsal room; or if we have a particularly loud piece of scenery or machinery (for example, wind machines) in rehearsals, or other loud sound we're creating; or to provide foldback monitoring to someone. Obviously these are not likely scenarios on the average Noël Coward play, but there are many more complex shows where we might need them. I'll avoid using them for amplification in rehearsals where possible, as it's inconvenient for all, and costly in terms of people and resources. But it can be useful to have a couple of them available for specific scenes or problems.

If we're using them for creative reasons, that's a strong reason to use them in rehearsals, too.

I tend to put cheaper radio microphones into rehearsals than those we might use in the show, as they won't receive the same level of care or attention that they'll get in the theatre. I'll use old mic capsules from a previous show and put them on elastic loops (also known as halos) so the cast can pull them on and off easily.

The West End and Broadway are using rechargeable batteries almost entirely for radio microphones, so a stock of these is useful.

It's also useful to have a table with tape marks, so people can take their packs and put them back in the same place each time. This allows us to see who has wandered off with their mic, and to have them all in one place to do battery changes.

Sound Effects and Soundscapes

A range of sound effects and elements of the soundscape can be developed in rehearsals.

It can be useful to have some of the more atmospheric sounds in rehearsals, though sometimes they can just get in the way. This is true for both naturalistic sounds and more abstract soundscapes. Sometimes the actors find them useful, to help them get 'in the zone', in the same way a performer might find that a particular item of costume helps them get into character better. But at other times they may just raise the ambient noise level of

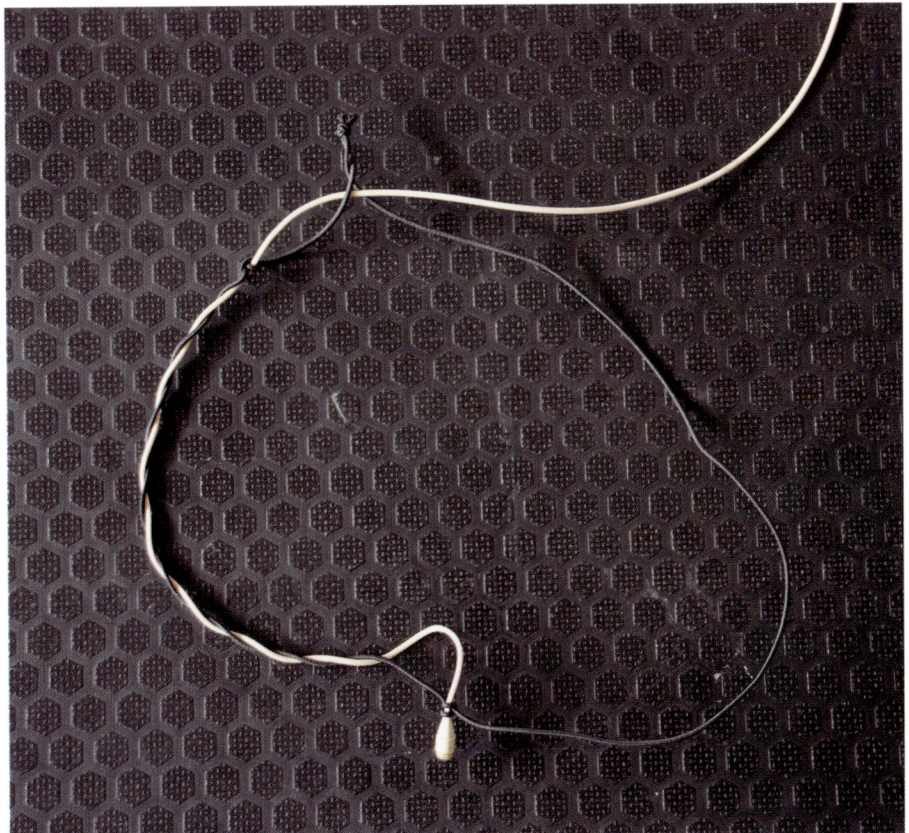

A microphone can be taken on and off quickly using a loop of elastic.

the rehearsal room, which often doesn't have ideal acoustics anyway, which can just make it difficult for everyone to hear each other.

I spend a lot of time watching the ways the performers are performing the text – the energy, the pace, the dramaturgical peaks and troughs, and I'll map my sound design to that – which may well be different to what I had originally envisaged when reading the script.

When watching rehearsals, I often get a sense of where a cue might be needed without necessarily knowing that it will be. I put empty Group cues into QLab where they'll go.

If there's a long sequence of sound, I'll look at how it might break down into different cue points, so it can best respond to the performance.

I have a large library of sound effects that I have bought, recorded or made for previous shows. I use an application called Soundminer (Basehead is a popular alternative), which creates a searchable database of all my sounds, so I can quickly find any sounds. The software is clever enough to use a thesaurus on search terms automatically, so a search for 'car', for example, will also automatically search for 'automobile'. My workflow is optimized so I can turn around an idea of a sound into something I can play into rehearsals, in seconds or minutes.

I tend to have just a pair of speakers upstage, ideally close to the position they'll be in, in the theatre. I may also have a couple of speakers to represent the front of house (FOH) proscenium system, and sometimes a couple of small speakers to represent a surround system.

Matching Sound to Action

One of the most useful aspects of attending rehearsals is being able to precisely create a sound that matches a performer's action, considering their rhythm, their élan, and the characterization they are

Soundminer software allows rapid searching and auditioning of sounds, and easy transfers into your editing software.

putting into that movement – perhaps to the way they flick their wrist, or the speed they walk. If you can make sounds to play whilst a scene is being rehearsed, we can enter into a dialogue, an interaction with the sound and the performer.

Sometimes it's useful to leave some sound effects in rehearsals for them to play with when I can't be there. I'll leave them a MIDI keyboard or a Novation Launchpad, or some other control surface, so the DSM or director can play in different sounds. This can be particularly useful early on, before our ideas can be organized into a cue-list, or where lots of sounds may be overlapping but the order hasn't been finalized. It can also be useful to let the director play with variations of one cue, to give them five versions of something to try each time they run a scene.

Occasionally I add sounds that I know will never be used in the theatre. They might lend support to scenes where there are elements missing in rehearsals. We're often rehearsing moments that will eventually have lighting, video, costume and scenic elements added to them, to make something amazing. In rehearsals these can fall flat in a dingy church hall, with everything else missing. It's not uncommon to get requests from the director to beef up those moments, to help everyone maintain their nerve through rehearsals. I'll often remove a lot of these sounds once we get into the theatre and join up with the other design elements.

If a sequence is cut, don't delete it – make a separate cue list to put cut cues in. If it gets reinstated a couple of days later, it'll save you a lot of time just being able to drag it back into place.

STARTING OFF WITH QLAB

You can save a great deal of time by developing a template, an almost-empty workspace, which is set up the way you like it. In it you can set your preferred settings for each type of cue: for example, I prefer an eight-second fade over a five-second fade. You can include your favourite music, voice and noise sound-check files, some pre-programmed MIDI cues for changing scenes on mixing desks, changing reverb patches, triggering lighting and any other things that are done regularly. There are plenty of AppleScripts you can download (search the QLab user group) to assign to keyboard hot keys.

There are three keyboard shortcuts built in to QLab that are less well known but extremely useful:

- V – Play/Go the selected item, ignoring any pre-wait times. This is very useful to hear a section of a cue in isolation from the sequence it's in
- S – Stop whatever is selected. Rather than hitting Escape, which stops absolutely everything, S allows you to selectively stop just one thing. This can be useful for rehearsals, tech, and in performance if your operator accidentally presses 'Go' twice
- If you select multiple cues, then press the keyboard shortcut to insert a group cue (by default Apple-0): it will create a group cue and put all the currently selected cues inside that group

I assign all my outputs, as many as I know, including some extra outputs for new ideas that emerge during rehearsals and the tech. I also set up gangs and default levels. Doing this in advance saves hassle later with dozens of cues with default settings. We often have an idea that we might have some speakers upstage, some on the proscenium, some subs, some surrounds. I tend always to assign outputs one to eight with these outputs. Beyond that outputs are more show specific or venue specific.

I allocate as many outputs as possible to individually route to as many different speakers as possible. I'll include a dedicated output(s) for any delay lines. I'll split surrounds into sides and rears, but I'll gang them together as default, and break the gang on individual cues as necessary. I might add four feeds for broadcast, two direct, and two via a Proximity Audio Unit, to make sounds more distant, to create a stereo mix to send to an OB truck, if I feel that's a possibility – *see* the section 'Adapting a Stage Show for Broadcast' in Chapter 15 for more details.

Audio Levels | Audio Trim | Audio Effects

master	1	2	3	4	5	6	7	8	9	10	11	12	13	14	15	16
0	0	0	0	0	0	0	0	0	0	0	0	0	0	0	0	0

inputs	crosspoints	
0 1	0	
0 2		0

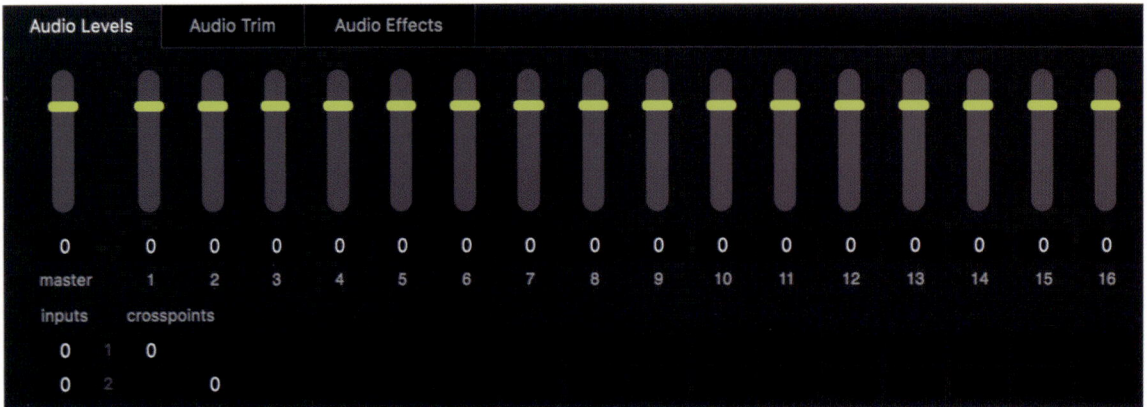

QLab's default levels route your sound to every single possible speaker connected to your system at full volume. This can be a great way to blow up your sound system! Fortunately, the cross-points aren't assigned to any outputs, so that won't happen.

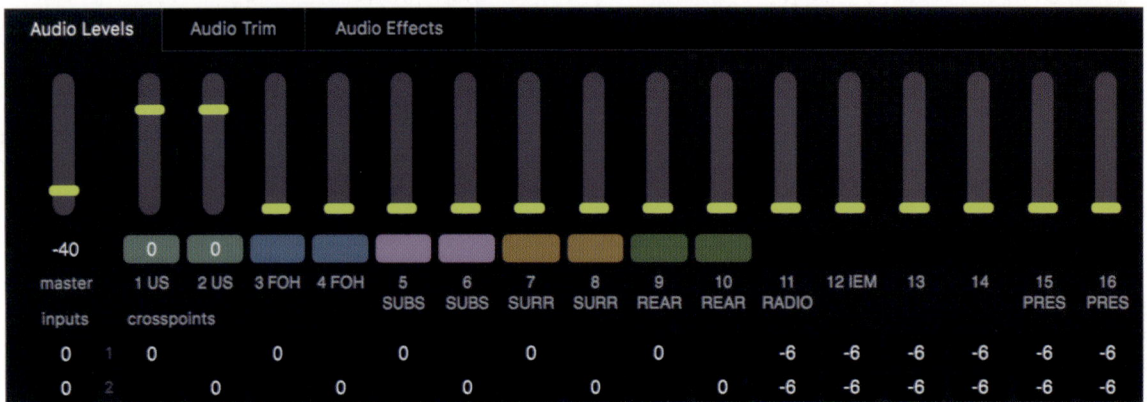

Audio Levels | Audio Trim | Audio Effects

master	1 US	2 US	3 FOH	4 FOH	5 SUBS	6 SUBS	7 SURR	8 SURR	9 REAR	10 REAR	11 RADIO	12 IEM	13	14	15 PRES	16 PRES
-40	0	0														

inputs	crosspoints											
0 1	0	0	0	0	0	-6	-6	-6	-6	-6	-6	
0 2		0	0	0	0	0	-6	-6	-6	-6	-6	-6

An example of how the author sets up QLab default levels (Workspace Preferences > Cue Templates > Audio). The sound file will be routed to a couple of speakers, so I can quickly audition it, and the Master level is turned down, so it can be started at a quiet level and slowly brought up in volume. The first ten outputs have been grouped as stereo pairs, and named for a generic sound rig. The cross-points have been set to route a stereo file to stereo outputs, and the mono outputs have the level at –6dB (if you send both the left and right channel of a normalized sound file to a single output, they will distort. By sending them both at –6dB, they will sum together to 0dB). A couple of outputs – 15 and 16 – have been assigned for press outputs.

WHAT DO WE WANT TO ACHIEVE IN REHEARSALS?

It's important to work out what you want to achieve in rehearsals, and not let too many things roll over into the technical rehearsals when time is precious. But rehearsals are rehearsals, and there are some things you can't work out until you get into the theatre.

For a conceive-and-execute process, I aim to have about 85 per cent of the playback side of the sound design in place by the end of rehearsals. Much of that will evolve in the theatre, but it's good to have something to start with. The other 15 per cent might be the elements that will integrate with lighting and scenic elements, often transitions and scene changes that are difficult to shape in the rehearsal room. The existing 85 per cent will need to

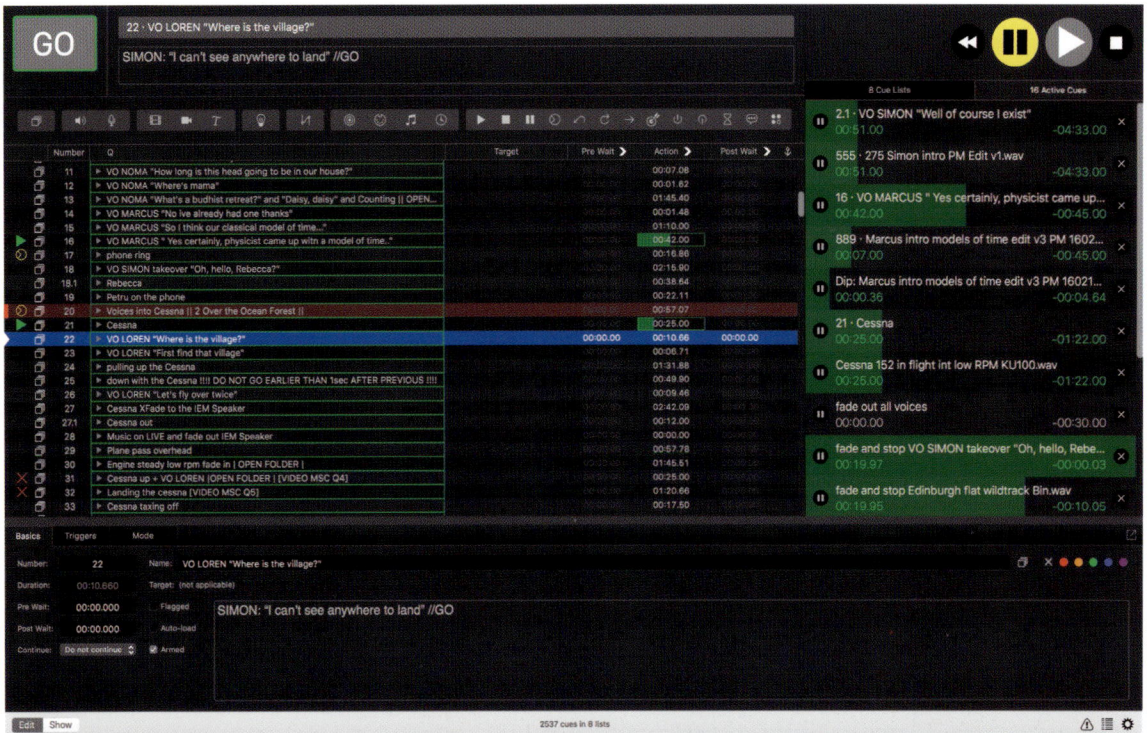

During rehearsals you can build up a cue list containing empty groups for where you think there might be a cue, even if you haven't worked out what that cue will sound like.

be re-routed and balanced for the larger speaker system in the theatre. If we have more than the average time in the theatre, or if it's feeling like a straightforward show, I may leave more to be done in the theatre.

Regardless, I usually have a cue structure programmed into QLab by the end of rehearsals, with empty groups/folders in the cue list for everywhere I think there will be a cue. I tend to write all cueing information into the Notes field of each cue, so all info is within QLab. Cue sheets are a relic of an earlier era, and don't have a use nowadays. I'll write up a script with QLab cue points, and details of any microphones going on or off, cues not tied into QLab, or other useful information, such as which musical instruments are used, and when.

I'll get the majority of the cues and cue points in the prompt copy with the DSM/show caller. Sometimes we put the cues in, but leave numbering them until the tech, or number them with gaps

DEADLINES

Aim to hit your deadlines earlier than you need. This gives you contingency time in case there is a problem. Don't leave everything until the last minute. You have an absolute unmissable deadline when the audience walks into the theatre.

I thrive off deadlines and do everything at just about the last minute. I've optimized my workflow, so I can work fast and efficiently when I finally get round to it. If there is some new or unfamiliar element to a show, whether that's working with a new director, or some new software, I'll move my schedules and deadlines earlier, so I can hit them sooner.

for other cues that might be added in the tech. It's important to go through with the DSM and sound operator to explain what each cue does, so they know why they're calling it there, and how to

VISITING REHEARSALS CHECKLIST

- Do you have a copy of the script?
- Do you have the name and contact number of the DSM? (Most rehearsal rooms have security locks)
- Do you have a USB stick or ethernet cables to transfer files on to the rehearsal room computer?
- Do you have an audio cable to plug your laptop into the rehearsal-room sound system?
- Do you have a pair of headphones to listen to material?
- Do you know what is scheduled to be rehearsed today? Is it a good day to visit?
- If you don't know the names of the cast, get a headshot sheet (photos of each cast member with their names underneath) from stage management

modify their calling as the show evolves. Explaining the intention and effect of each cue allows them to improvise intelligently when things go wrong, or to tweak the cueing as the show develops over the course of the run.

If I can't be in rehearsals as much as I'd like, I make sure I've had a chance to sit down with the director and play through all my sounds, so they get to hear, approve, and suggest changes prior to tech. I would be leaving myself exposed if the first time they hear anything at all is the tech rehearsal. I do often add caveats, such as 'It'll sound better in the theatre when we have sub-bass'.

REACT AND REFINE

The creation process of a devised show varies considerably from director to director, and according to where the source material takes you.

Many devising projects will be preceded by more comprehensive workshop weeks. These workshops typically involve research of the topic, experimenting with adapting the source material into a stage form and getting a sense of how the piece may evolve through rehearsals. The workshops allow the director to get some idea of who they might need to cast in the show. There are practical things that need to be established before rehearsals can start, so you have the cast in place and a sense of what resources you might need in rehearsals.

The Start of the Devising Process

The start of the devising process will often involve research, examination of the source materials, interviewing people, seeing what sparks off ideas, and what resonates. Some devising projects start with more source material than others. An adaptation of a novel, or material based on interviews, may offer a large amount of dialogue to experiment with in rehearsals. Others may start with nothing, or with only abstract ideas, which will require exploration to find something tangible. We can ask many of the same questions that we might use to examine a script, to help us find connections to the material, whatever that may be.

Early on, we might devise some moments or scenes to see where they take us. This merges the conventional processes of script-writing, analysis, and putting it on its feet into one fast exercise. One approach is to divide the ensemble into a few groups, each tackling a fragment of material, to see what they can make. They may have 15 to 30 minutes to do this, and as they do this I'll work with each group simultaneously to provide some rudimentary sound design for each of the scenes they make. Each group will then show what they've made to the whole company. We'll analyse that to see what works and what doesn't, what's interesting, and what isn't. We might merge the best of two groups into one, or get both groups working on one group's work to develop it further. This process iterates, developing each scene, creating more material.

As material is created, the directing team will look at how to organize and refine it, examining how to create an arc through it. What order should the material happen in? Can we find parallels between elements, how can the material be layered? Often good material has to be discarded because it doesn't work with the arc of the show. Extra scenes may be devised to bridge from one section to another.

Whilst this is a simplified explanation of one devising process, you can see that it is very different to the 'conventional' process. My react-and-refine workflow is consequently different from the conceive-and-execute workflow. With the latter approach, more preparation can be done before rehearsals start, and I might not be needed in rehearsals full time. Devised work often requires full-time support from the sound designer, or their team, as so much more work happens in the rehearsal room.

I make material as fast as possible, aiming to turn around an idea for a sound effect or music in minutes or seconds – the 'react' part of the process. The devising process is often more collaborative in where ideas may originate from. When small groups are working together they will often have ideas for sounds or music to integrate, and I always welcome these. I often walk round from group to group to see how they're developing their ideas and to discuss how we can use sound with that. But the creative process can be stymied by the fact that you may have four groups all wanting things from you in the last ten minutes of the exercise, which puts you under a lot of pressure.

It can be tricky dealing with devised material if you are alone in the rehearsal room, as you are then having to play-in already devised material whilst also designing new material, and the former can prevent you from properly concentrating on the latter. I often work with an associate sound designer or sound operator on these shows, where financially possible. Devised shows are often not the shows with the biggest of budgets, which can make for a tricky balancing act. I find devised shows the most fun to work on as a sound designer, so I often find myself doing bigger, more conventional, better paid shows, to subsidize my time working on a devised show.

A Devised Rehearsal

For a devised rehearsal, I will ensure there's a method to access a library of music and sound effects, a method to record, edit and play back voice-overs, an easy way to add effects to microphones, and often some Foley-type props to experiment with. I will have as many control surfaces as possible, so I can be hands-on creating sound: MIDI keyboards, Launchpads, Fader control surfaces. I use Ableton Live software a lot, as it allows fast and flexible playing, and recording, of sound into rehearsals. Everything can change at any moment, and does, so I bounce sounds down as lots of stems, so I can manipulate them really easily. We might not program mixing desk automation until the last moment on a devised show, as it can often get in the way when a sequence changes. I set up a video camera so I can record scenes and then refine them later.

The Refine Part of the Process

As the directing team finds arcs and layers in the devised material, I will do the same with the sound I've devised – the 'refine' part of the process. This involves looking through at the music and sounds that we've used, to see if there are threads that can be pulled across the show. This may involve changing the sound and music in one scene so it better fits within the arc of the rest of the show. I may use flip-chart sized pieces of paper to look at what we've used, and how, to guide what we might use in devising more material.

Often voice-overs will be recorded in the rehearsal room, with a large amount of background noise and often undesirable acoustics, so often these will need re-recording later on.

THE ENCOUNTER REHEARSAL PROCESS

This show was developed over a few years, with one- or two-week workshops happening every nine months or so. We started with a book, *Amazon Beaming*, the account of a *National Geographic* photographer, Loren Macintyre, who essentially got lost in the Amazon rainforest, and his experiences with an indigenous community, the Mayoruna, with whom he keeps company.

Early workshops established that the conventional method of having different actors play each part in the story wasn't the best way to tell the story, or to convey some sense of the epic and claustrophobic nature of the Amazon. We started to look at other ways of telling the story, taking us back to the basics of storytelling, of just one person telling a story, relating what happened to Loren. We looked at using microphones to allow director and performer Simon McBurney to take on different characters' voices, using techniques such as pitch changing, de-locating the amplified voice from his body, and looping. The need to find a way to distinguish between narration, dialogue and stream of consciousness led us to look at using binaural sound and headphones.

Having many months between each workshop enabled us to reflect on what we'd learnt from each workshop, and to begin the next workshop with more developed ideas, and fresh ideas to explore. Early workshops had a small amount of sound support as ideas were researched, discussed and tried. As it became clearer that sound was going to be a central part of the storytelling process, my time in workshops grew, eventually becoming full time, and the amount of sound equipment grew exponentially each workshop, starting with my laptop, an analogue mixer and a couple of SM58s, into many computers, multiple mixing desks, radio microphones, IEMs and beyond.

By the fourth workshop I'd discovered it was too complex for one person to operate and design simultaneously, and Pete Malkin joined me to work on both aspects. By the time we started formal rehearsals we had a sound team of four, myself and Pete designing the sound, and Helen Skiera and Ella Wahlström operating the show. We required two sound operators because the show is very complex, with hundreds of sound effects, music tracks and voice-overs, as well as lots of looping, pitch-changing, effecting and swapping between multiple microphones.

In the middle of this Simon and I spent a week in the Amazon rainforest making recordings that would form the base soundtrack of the show, and talking to members of a Mayorunan community.

The Encounter, workshop rig. Early workshops and rehearsals may start with a small amount of equipment. Often that equipment will be what can be easily and cheaply sourced, rather than what we might necessarily want.

The Encounter, late rehearsal rig. As rehearsals develop, the amount of equipment and staff you need in the rehearsal room may grow too. The closer you can get to the equipment you'll have in the venue, the more you can configure and program the equipment in advance of getting in the venue, saving a lot of valuable time.

Recording on location in the Amazon rainforest. CHLOE COURTNEY

DESIGNER AND OPERATOR

It is not uncommon in devising processes for the designer to be the sound operator too. The primary reason is that the sound design is often incomplete by the point where we would normally be handing it over to the sound operator.

For Complicité's production, *Shun-kin*, I was designer and operator for its initial run. The show was a co-production with the Setagaya Public Theatre in Tokyo, and was performed by a Japanese cast, in Japanese.

For this devised show, I wanted to weave a soundscape out of a number of different audio loops, each with a different mood or associated with a different story thread in the show. I had twelve audio loops playing continuously in Ableton, and two fader control surfaces, so I could make a constantly evolving soundscape by bringing up and down any of these loops at any moment. This made for a more organic sound than I could ever have achieved by looping them in QLab and having lots of fade cues.

A complex designer-operator rig, for Complicité's *Shun-kin,* with a Yamaha M7CL mixer on the left, where the radio microphones were mixed, above that Stage Research's SFX software, Ableton Live, and DME Designer. There is also a gooseneck microphone so the author could Foley in some live breathing sound effects, two MIDI keyboards, each with a range of sound effects, music stings and other abstract sounds on them, two Behringer BCF fader control surfaces to allow the levels of the loops and sound effects coming out of Ableton Live to be mixed, and the design laptop.

The refining process continues throughout the tech and preview period, with devised shows often continuing to evolve well after press night.

KEEPING IT LIVE

'Keeping it live' involves retaining fluidity whilst locking down choreographed sequences. A theatre performance is a living entity, which changes from night to night, and we have to allow for this in our design. To the audience member, what looks like a tightly choreographed track may actually be a number of smaller sections flowing together. We may break something into sections for artistic or practical reasons – for example, to allow a moment of audience interaction in the middle of a sequence that could take an undefined amount of time. Or we may have flown or automated scenery elements that we need to ensure have moved safely into place before we can move into the next part of the sequence.

There may also be more subtle variations that we want to work within the show. A few years ago, a director came up to me at a workshop I was running, and said, 'I work with a sound

I gave myself multiple MIDI keyboards and fader control surfaces, so I could respond quickly and intuitively – or as much as I could, given that I couldn't understand a word anyone was saying! It was difficult to be both designing on my laptop, on headphones, whilst also staying aware of what was happening in the rehearsal room and responding to that – and made even harder by the language barrier. We revived the show the following year, adding a separate sound operator, so we could each better focus on our roles.

Having a designer-operator is common in Europe, often because of the schedule of how rehearsals work, in that rehearsals might happen onstage over a few months, whilst other shows are performed in the evening.

Shun-kin, Complicité. Directed by Simon McBurney, designed by Merle Hensel, lighting design by Paul Anderson.

designer a lot, but I think they're lying to me. I have a piece of music underscoring a scene, which I want to start fading out at the start of the last paragraph of a monologue, and I want the fade-out to finish on the last word'. Before computerized playback, in the time of CD players, MiniDisc or reel-to-reel tape, it was common to specify the cue line on which a fade would start happening, and the cue line the fade should complete on, and the operator, who would be manually fading it using a fader, would slow down or speed up their fading to match the performer's speed of delivery, or whether they paused slightly more, or less, as they delivered their lines from night to night.

Computerized playback systems don't currently work this way: you tell it to fade out a piece of music over 'x' seconds, and it'll do that regardless of what the performer is doing. It also used to be commonplace to ask the sound operator to 'ride the music' during a scene: if a piece of music had peaks and dips, they might pull back the peak, or push it higher, using the fader, depending on the speed the performers were going at and whether they were hitting an emotional peak at the same time as the music.

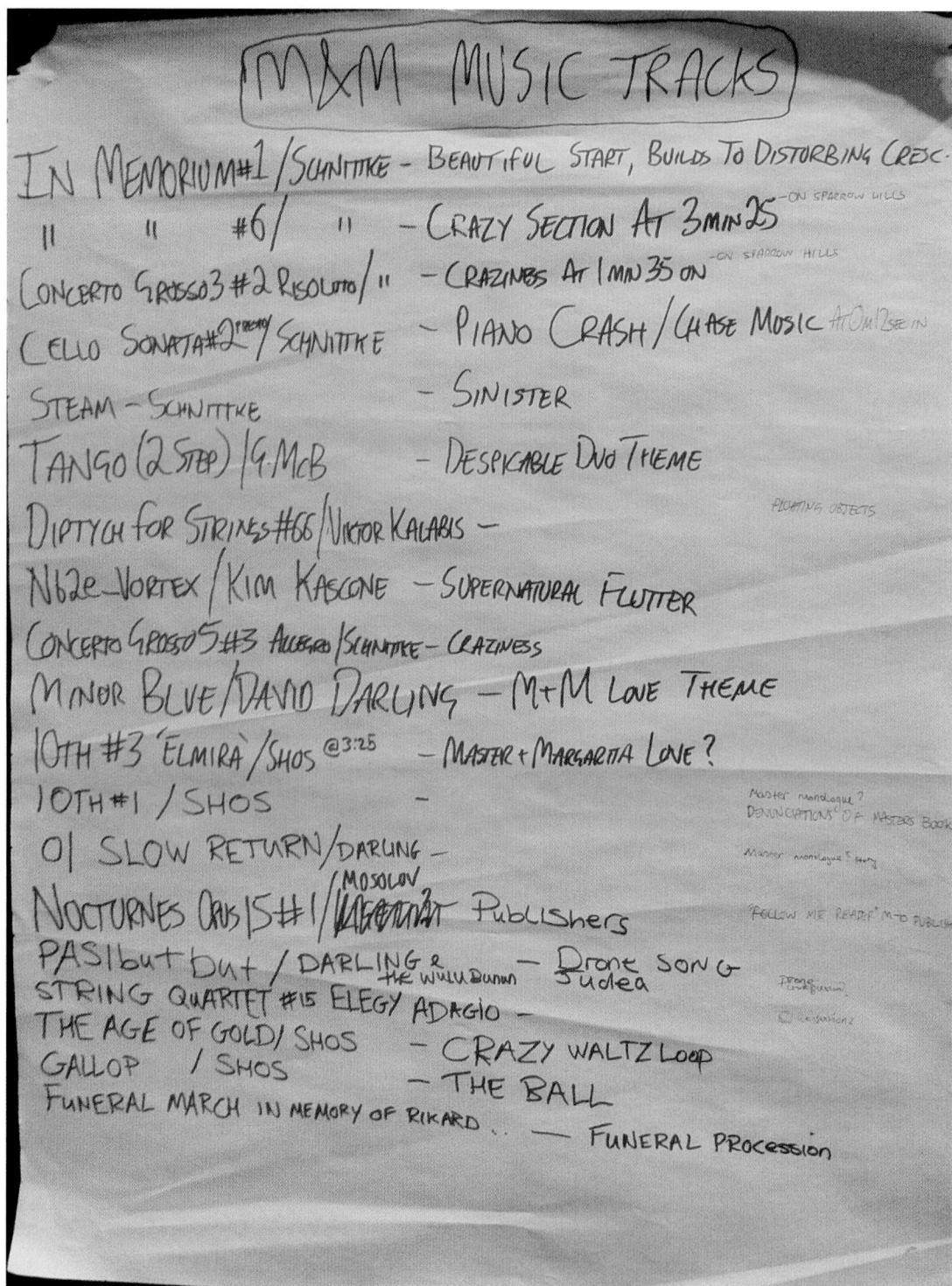

A white board or similar can be used to keep track of music, establishing a music vocabulary, where you are using it, finding themes and connections between them.

Whilst QLab, CSC, SCS, SFX and other play-back systems have brought us many advanced features, we have lost the ability to do some things, too. Whilst there are ways we can program QLab to allow a sound operator more flexibility in operating the sound if we desire, I've found that using Ableton Live in conjunction with QLab gives us the best of both worlds. Ableton is adept at vamping multiple stems of music and sound, and very responsive to hot key-triggered sound effects. It has a raft of live optimized effect plug-ins, and works with a range of control surfaces, to allow an operator to have more hands-on control, so they can fade out and ride a piece of music as desired. If we have stems of the music, for example, drums, guitar, piano, and so on, then the operator can mix those stems using a con-trol surface as if they had a live band. Well, almost.

This is also about putting the operator back in control – to have more controls than a single 'Go' button – so they can respond to each individual performance. Sometimes they may be busy mix-ing radio microphones or some such, which re-duces what they can do, and for these moments we can automate Ableton using MIDI from QLab so we get the best of both worlds.

Ableton and QLab will happily run alongside each other on the same computer, sharing the same soundcard outputs, communicating with each other using MIDI IAC. If it's a busy show, I'll use separate computers. Ableton is also one of the most stable pieces of software I've come across.

Ableton is popular in its own right for show play-back, and is probably more popular in Europe than QLab. Sometimes this is because of its musical roots, and sometimes if the sound operator is also the designer, it allows the designer to evolve the design as the performance evolves. Ableton is also very good for actions such as:

- Stopping a piece of music, in a way similar to a record player slowing down effect
- Going into slow motion, or fast forwarding
- Subtly slowing something down over a long pe-riod of time to create variation in a looped track
- Creating momentary glitches in the soundtrack

OPTIMIZING YOUR WORKFLOW

Optimizing your workflow is important because speed of creation is critical. Being able to make something fast, even if crudely, can earn your work a place in a show. Make it slowly and your place might be lost. A lot of this can be achieved through preparation.

Set up templates: Set up templates for all the applications you use, so they are set up how you like it. Having a template you can open saves you from having to start from scratch every time you use that program.

Bouncing out sound: Learn how to bounce out different sections of time, and different tracks and stems from your software, as quickly as possible. There are different techniques for different software packages. Ensure that each time you bounce it out, you are bouncing it out at a consistent level. Some software programs are set to normalize the level of the audio you bounce out. This is not helpful if you are going to be adjusting the mix and bouncing out multi-ple versions of this sound, if it randomly adjusts the level of the resulting sound file every time you bounce it out. Also, if you need to monitor the project at different volumes, make sure you are doing that externally to the project, rather than changing the master volume fader in your project.

Creating sound for theatre: A good format to bounce your sounds out is as a Wav file, at 48 kHz with 24-bit resolution. (Different media favour dif-ferent formats – for example, most VR and game audio software runs at 44.1kHz, while most broad-cast networks run at 48kHz.)

Save presets for your plug-ins: Making some-thing sound as if it's on a record, or through a wall, shouldn't be more than a couple of mouse clicks away.

CAT IN THE HAT, NATIONAL THEATRE

This show has recorded music running continuously throughout. We envisaged there could be audience interaction at any point, so any sequence could take a different amount of time each night. We worked with the composer Paul Clark to split out his music into lots of sections, with holding loops, transitions and sequences. Over the course of any five-minute section of the show we might go through fifteen sections of music, each perhaps in different tempos and time signatures, vamping as needed, all changing on the beat of the music. This is something Ableton handles easily and musically. The music was also broken out into

The Cat In the Hat, National Theatre. Directed by Katie Mitchell, designed by Vicki Mortimer, lighting design by Jon Clark. The author in discussion with the Cat.

stems, so we could remix and more easily edit the elements in tech and previews without having to bounce out files continuously every time we wanted to tweak anything.

Ableton doesn't have the best interface for an operator to use during the show – in fact we just want the operator to interact with the launchpad and the control surface. The majority of the show is operated using a Go Button connected to QLab. QLab then sends a mix of MIDI note-ons and control changes to Ableton Live to trigger audio clips and scenes, and automate the volume faders, filter sweeps, and any other parameters.

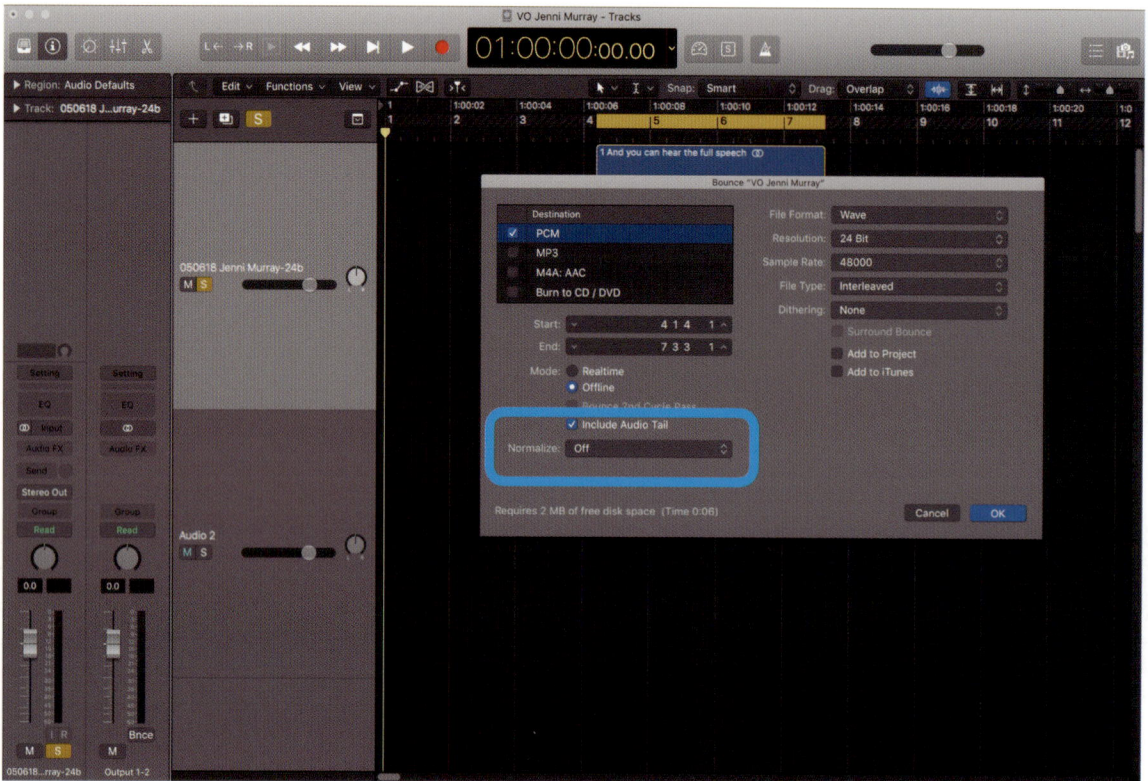

Check that any options to normalize after bouncing out are turned off. This ensures you bounce sound out of your project at a consistent level each time.

Organize your music: I have a folder with plenty of music tracks arranged by genre and era. I always have some music ready to put into a scene to act as a placeholder.

Organize your sound effects and abstract sounds: As well as my larger sound effect collection, I have a folder of easy-to-reach, commonly used sounds such as rain, birds, thunder, boomers, stings and so on. This enables me to get something into a show within sixty seconds of being asked for it, and I can then replace it with something more considered later. I use SoundMiner software as a search database for my sound effects, which allows me to search for a sound, audition the search results, and transfer them into Logic, ProTools, QLab or Ableton incredibly fast.

Learn some computer networking: You need a wired ethernet link between your computer and the show computer for fast transfer. A USB stick or WiFi will be too slow. Search online to learn how to use your computer's network settings to connect to the show computer.

FILE BACKUPS AND NAMING

It's important to maintain multiple backups of show files. Backups should be made daily from day one in the theatre, and time allowed to do this. As the show finalizes, aim to keep a backup on site but away from the sound equipment, such as with the company manager, and an off-site backup.

Backups mean you have multiple versions of all your files around the place, which can cause confusion. A naming convention I learned recently is as follows:

- At the start of each day, save it with the date appended with an A, for example MyShowFile20181225A
- At lunchtime or with a major change, save it as MyShowFile20181225B, and C, and D, etc.
- At the end of the day, add a Z

You'll end up with a folder like this:

MyShowFile20181225**A**
MyShowFile20181225**B**
MyShowFile20181225**C**
MyShowFile20181225**Z**
MyShowFile20181226**A**
MyShowFile20181226**B**
MyShowFile20181226**Z**

Your most recent file is always at the end of the list.

On my main playback machine I have a folder containing many other sub-folders – SFX, Music, VO, Tonal and sub-folders within – to make files easy to find. I make 'bundles' for the backup computer, which will only contain the audio files used, so are smaller in size (but unnavigable). For example:

VO Nancy 1 LAURA BENEDICT 20180323.wav

Name audio files with a YYYYMMDD date for versioning. The VO prefix keeps all your voice-overs together. Note how we're distinguishing between the character name, Nancy, and the actor's name. This helps when we deal with understudies and re-casts, where we'll have the same VO voiced by different actors.

I endeavour to include a hint to their origin within the file name of edited sound effects, maybe to a Logic session where I've made the sound, or to the library or source of the original sound effect. If I need to make a shorter or longer version, or to find something similar, I can use this hint to get to the source.

11

INTO THE THEATRE AND HOW TO SOUND CHECK

As rehearsals near their end, work will be ongoing in the theatre – installing the set, lighting, video and sound equipment.

Visit the fit-up to check that your imagined vision of how it all works matches reality. There are always snags encountered during a fit-up, the classic one being that part of the set doesn't fit; the most exciting one is that they want to move the entire set upstage or downstage for a better relationship with the audience. These adjustments can throw off all your plans and send you back to the drawing board – so visit early and often.

THE SOUND DEPARTMENT

Let's take a moment to look at the roles of members of the sound department; for the purposes of brevity these are rather simplified descriptions.

Production sound engineer: The PSE, or PE, will work with the sound designer to realize the sound system in the theatre. As a sound designer I'll often specify the sort of speakers I want and roughly where I want them. The PE will take those vague notions and make that into a practical and safe reality, on budget and on time. They will co-ordinate a team of sound crew for the fit-up of the show to get the sound system installed and working. The PE normally has a wide and extensive knowledge of all types of sound equipment. They often design large parts of the technical infrastructure too, which often includes all communications systems.

Sound operator: Typically this is the term used for the sound engineer who will be running a play, as opposed to a musical.

No. 1 sound (or A1, in the USA): Typically this is the term used for the sound engineer who will be running a musical. Increasingly we use radio microphones in plays, and have complex soundscapes in musicals, so the roles of the sound operator and No. 1 can often be quite similar, even if the content of the show is quite different. They will be at every performance, at the mixing desk, mixing all the microphones and playing all the cues into the show at the appropriate moments (or be cued by the DSM to do so).

No. 2 sound (or A2): The No. 2 is often responsible for the onstage side of the sound for a show. This can cover a range of responsibilities depending on the show; typically they are employed on shows where radio microphones are used, to maintain them and ensure they are fitted, and stay fitted, to the performers. They will also mix the show to provide holiday and sickness cover to the No. 1.

No. 3 sound: It is not uncommon to employ a second person onstage on shows with several costume changes, or large numbers of performers.

The fit-up crew: The crew typically employed just for the fit-up (installation) of the show: this is a team of people who can install all the various bits of equipment into the theatre.

Pit monkey: The affectionate name given to the sound engineer, who will stay in the band pit during sound checks and early band sessions to configure everything around the band.

Radio microphone technician: Radio microphones are a complex technology requiring an understanding of the mechanics of radio frequency transmission, intermodulation and interference. It also requires a sensitivity to the performers who wear them. Marrying technology with human beings results in all sorts of problems, from myriad technical issues to a variety of wigs, hair, make-up and costume-related intricacies. It is not uncommon, especially on plays, to bring in a specialist to set up the radio microphones, particularly if there are more complex issues to deal with, such as nudity, wigs, masks or prosthetics.

Whilst the sound op/No. 1 will be in the auditorium at the mixing desk, it is the No. 2, No. 3 and the radio microphone technician who will often be the face of the sound department to the cast, which requires both extreme diplomacy and people skills.

These job titles are most often found in the freelance world: if you work full time in a venue you may have to move between any, or all of these roles, on a regular basis.

Shannon Slaton's book *Mixing a Musical*, whilst being focused on the unique environment that is Broadway, contains great detailed descriptions of what each member of the sound department does throughout the production process.

HOW TO SOUND CHECK

When the fit-up schedule is running behind it is often the sound check that the production manager will try to squeeze or cut to get back on schedule. It is a horrible thing to start a technical rehearsal with a sound system that you haven't had time to check properly. It wastes everyone's time and makes the sound department look incompetent, reducing everyone's faith in you.

It is always important to give yourself the time you need to get a sound system working. A simple system might not take much time, whereas a larger system can take several days. I try to get a number of short sound checks scheduled over a couple of days, rather than in one long session. This allows time to remedy any major issues that can occur during the first sound check, such as speakers that need moving, or a fundamental flaw preventing sound from coming out of the system.

The notion of the 'sound check' is fairly well known in our cultural world – the band stroll on, play their instruments, and shout at the sound engineer. Actually, this is only the last part of the sound check, assuming you have live music, and there's a whole other set of sound checks before this. The aim of the other sound checks is to avoid us getting shouted at quite so much! Joking aside, musicians shouting during a sound check is 40 per cent 'I have to shout because it's so loud up here', and 40 per cent embarrassment because they're playing out of tune or out of rhythm. I'll leave it up to you to allocate the other 20 per cent.

Sound checks exist to give us the opportunity to make the combination of the various sound making, amplifying, mixing and emitting components sound their best in that particular acoustic environment with that particular type of content.

Occasionally you can install your sound system in a room, turn it on and it sounds great straightaway. But more often there is an issue somewhere. You can do all the planning in the world, have the best kit in the world and be the most experienced sound people in the world, and it can all still sound awful. Sometimes you can fix it, but sometimes the combination of time, money, other design choices and architecture means you have absolutely no hope at all of succeeding.

Playing sound through the system for the first time can be a nerve-racking experience – you can often tell within the first thirty seconds whether everything is fine, or is fixable, or you need to find a cupboard to hide in.

Line Check

This is usually done quietly as the system is installed by playing 'pink noise' quietly through a specific speaker once it's been installed to check it is working. Or, to check that a microphone is getting into the mixing desk. This will happen throughout the fit-up, to verify that individual elements are connected and working. Pink noise contains noise at all frequencies, from low sub-bass through to the highest audible frequencies, so it is a good test as to whether all the components within a speaker (the woofer, the tweeter, the mid-range driver) are working. Sometimes one of those components may have failed or become disconnected in transit. The line checks happen in advance, so if there is an issue, replacement units can be sourced, or long cables be re-run, all of which takes time that you won't have in the sound check.

System Check

We need to test that the system as a whole is working in the way we're expecting it to. There can be a lot of problem solving at this stage as you discover that whilst everything is working, it may not be doing quite what you want it to. Speakers might be connected to the wrong outputs of the mixing desk, or going through the wrong processor, or the mixing desk might need re-configuring. It's a common time to discover that a piece of equipment that you thought had a certain functionality, doesn't – for example: 'I thought the mixing desk inputs could route directly to the matrix outputs, but they can't, so I have eight fewer outputs than I thought. How am I going to plug everything in?'

Use this time to go through and check the system by function:

- Can all the inputs get to the relevant outputs?
- Can you do the things you need it to do, such as add an effect to a microphone?

- Is it doing it in the way you expect it to, or are there any discrepancies in level or tonality?

I will often listen to music tracks, and voice tracks through the system, tracks that I have sound checked with for many years. I know how they should sound on a decent system, so I can hear quickly if something doesn't sound right. People have different preferences for sound check tracks. It should be something you like, as you are going to hear it repeatedly. Ideally it should be well recorded – that is, not have much distortion on it, so you can hear if the system has distortion on it – and be fairly even across the track (so you can walk around and know that any variation is due to where you've moved to, not because you are in a different part of the track that has different instrumentation). Many sound engineers use Steeleye Span to sound check with, because it's well recorded and you can hear lots of instruments in different frequency ranges.

If, like me, you don't like Steeleye Span, feel free to use whatever track you like, but just keep using it time and again, and listen to it on headphones, car stereos and HiFis. The more familiar you are with it, the more you'll notice discrepancies on sound systems. I use Craig Armstrong's *Rise*, which has a pronounced bass element that I find useful to highlight bass issues, and Suzanne Vega's *Tom's Diner*. It's important to convert your track to mono so that the only differences you hear between the two sides of your system are down to the system, and not any stereo mixing in the test track. In *Tom's Diner*, I've edited down the gaps between each line. Stephen Fry reading the Harry Potter audiobooks is also a popular choice.

SOUND SYSTEM OPTIMIZATION

Once everything is working we'll optimize the system. Different people have different processes, and they all have their merits for different types of work. I tend to work by attacking a certain set of parameters at a time. I'll start by looking at the volume of each speaker, working through the whole system, then I'll look at delay time. Then I'll play some show content and look at EQ.

The first thing I'll do is have a quick listen to each speaker individually to identify that everything is working, and that there aren't any immediately obvious issues.

Next, I'll set the levels of the amplifiers, so that if I send a sound at full volume out of one output of the desk, then out of a different one, they'll be heard at approximately the same level: if I send it to my proscenium left speaker (which might be four large line-array speakers) it should come out at approximately the same volume as if I send it to surround left (which might be a few really small speakers). In this example I'd probably turn down the proscenium a little to match the lower power of those smaller boxes. I do this process so that I'm starting out with everything at an equal volume. Later on I shall adjust this, but this is a useful step in getting everything into harmony.

I'll play pink noise out of each speaker one at a time (or group, if they're physically wired together), and then stand in the centre of the area the speaker(s) is (are) covering. I'll use a sound-level meter app on my phone (set to a slow response) to measure the volume. I'll then move to the next speaker and measure the volume of just that speaker. I'll adjust the volume of the amplifier, or the output of the DSP processor or the mixer output, to adjust the speaker volume to match the first speaker I measured. And so on.

I tend to start with the smallest, furthest away speaker, for example a rear delay line of speakers, as they will often be the smallest speaker(s) that have to be turned up to maximum. I'll then move forwards towards the stage. Some people like to start with the front fill speakers and work backwards – they are also often small speakers being driven loud. It's up to you. At the end of this process, everything should be roughly matched for level, and I may have my rear delay speakers running at full, and the proscenium turned down 12dB.

Delay Time

Let's imagine you have an actor standing on a stage, wearing a microphone routed to a speaker just above your head. Assuming the speaker is at a similar volume to the sound from the actor, the sound will appear to come from the speaker nearest you. This is because the sound from the speaker will arrive at your ears noticeably before the actor's voice reaches you, because sound waves travel slowly (you'll have experienced this with thunder and lightning: you see the lightning, but it takes a few seconds for the sound to arrive because it is travelling a long distance). If we add a time delay to the speaker, we make it so the actor's voice and the sound from the speaker both arrive at our ears at exactly the same time. This is known as time-aligning the speakers.

The Haas Effect

For our purposes, the Haas effect says that time-aligning a system is not enough to shift the image from the speaker to our actor's voice. To shift our perceived image of where the sound is coming from, we need to add some extra time (from 5 milliseconds to 30ms) so that the actor's voice reaches us first. The brain then interprets the sound from the speaker as a helpful early reflection, and suppresses the direction it is coming from, making us think the sound is coming from the actor. Add more than 30ms and we hear the amplified sound more like an echo and we struggle to make sense of it. In fact, the sound from the speaker can be up to about 10dB louder than the sound from the actor, but because we hear the sound from the actor first, our brain will make us think we're hearing all the sound from the actor, and not from the speaker.

Time-Aligning a System

After I've set levels, I'll look at delay times. The goal here depends on how you want your show to

Here we want to time the sound system back to an actor standing downstage centre. We imagine a line across the stage, which we'll call t0. We can measure from our front fills back to our t0 line. If that measurement (from t1 to t0) was 1m, then we would add a delay of 2.9m to the front fill speakers. We would measure the proscenium speakers, vocal cluster and under-balcony delays back to t0 and delay those speakers accordingly. If the vocal cluster is really high up, we may find that we want to use little or no delay on it, and instead time the rest of our system to this source. Delaying a system is an imperfect process, as what may sound great for one seat may sound terrible for another, so the measuring must be followed by listening and adjusting. To make our amplified voice sound as if it is coming from t0, it's not enough to time-align the system to our t0 position: we have to add some extra delay time so that the actor's voice arrives first, and the amplified version arrives second. We might add anywhere up to 25–30m to achieve this.

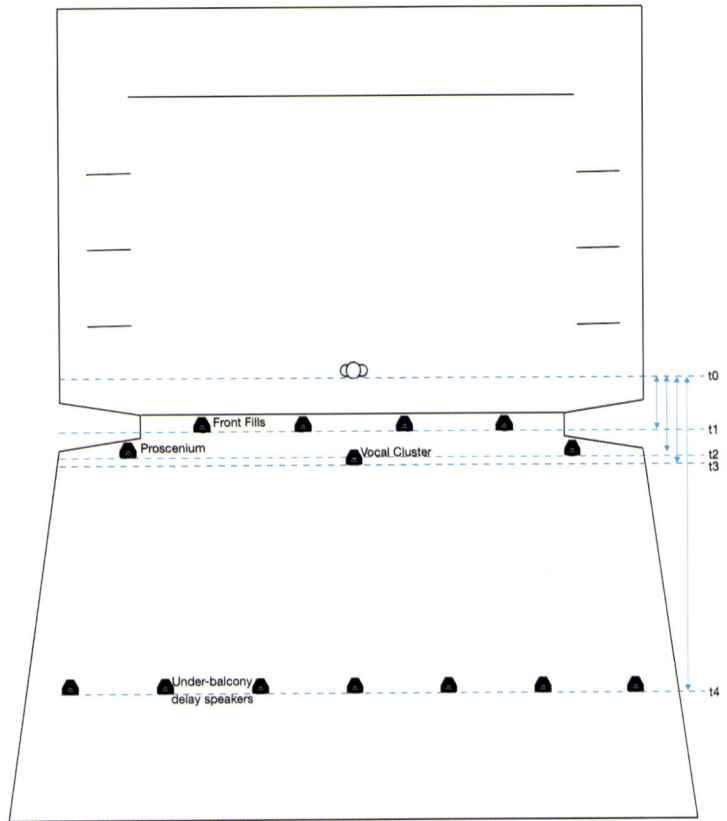

sound. For some shows I might want to create a 'wall of sound', perhaps seeming to come from the orchestra pit or the proscenium. For other shows I might want the sound to appear to be coming more from the stage, from the performers, from their world. The place we want sound to seem to emanate from, we call t0 ('tee-zero'), and rather than thinking of it as a point, we should consider it as a line running across the width of the stage.

The closest speaker to t0 covering the audience may be the front fills. I will measure the distance between the front fills and my t0 line. I will imagine a line running through my front fill, parallel to my t0 line, and measure the distance between my t0 and t1 line. This is a simplistic means of dealing with the fact that sound emanates in three dimensions in a complex manner, but we only have simple tools to deal with this.

A laser measure is useful for measuring, and we can calculate the time that sound takes to travel this distance, in milliseconds (though most delay units allow you to type in a number in metres), and type this delay time into the sound-system output feeding the front fills. Delay units may be built into mixer outputs, specialist DSP processors, or into the amplifiers themselves.

I will then move on to the next speaker, perhaps the proscenium speakers, imagining a parallel line and measuring that back to t0, and delay those speakers accordingly. I'll do this with all the speakers, including the subs.

After we've done our measuring, we need to listen. Working out a good delay time that works for a certain speaker often involves adjusting to make it sound good. I will tend to alternate between using a metronome click and the spoken word to test that my delay times sound good.

By the end of this we will have a sound system that is time-aligned. If you play some content through the system, the speakers should sound in

Upstage Speakers

Additional delay added to
microphone input if actor
moves upstage

t0

Front Fills

t1

Proscenium

Vocal Cluster

t2
t3

Under-balcony
delay speakers

t4

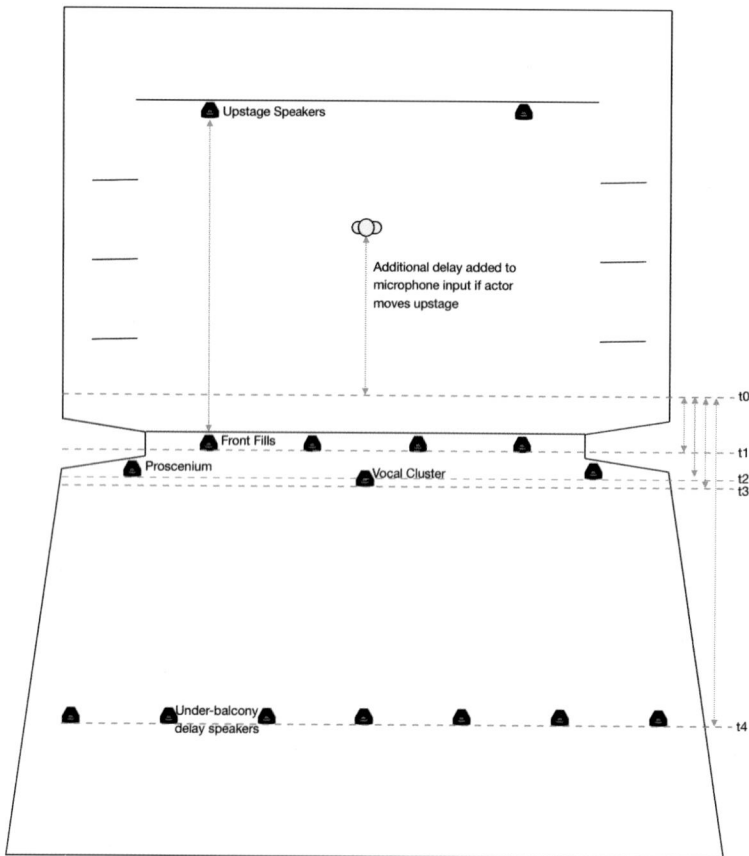

If our actor moves upstage we could add additional delay time to their specific microphone input (rather than to the loudspeaker outputs) to shift the perceived image of their voice upstage too. If we want to send music to our upstage speakers and have the rest of the system time-aligned to that, we might have an additional delay matrix to send sound to the different speaker outputs, where we imagine the upstage speakers are our t0 line, and measure and time accordingly.

Delay time = distance (in metres) divided by 0.343

Calculate the delay time between two points by measuring it, then dividing that distance in metres by 0.343, to get the answer in milliseconds. This is for somewhere with an average humidity and a temperature of 20°C.

sync with each other. This can be easier to judge if you have a sound source (someone wearing a mic, or a speaker) positioned at your t0 to compare it against.

We haven't added any delay for Haas effect yet, so it won't seem to come from our t0 location. I'll often add that extra time on individual inputs, or specific mixer outputs, so I can choose which

sounds appear to be at t0, and which further up-stage of that. For example, by adding 20ms of delay to a microphone input we shift the image of that mic about twenty feet (6m) upstage (one foot, or 30cm, of distance is approximately 1ms of time), across every speaker we are routing it to. Or we could delay the inputs from our play-back device routing to the proscenium so that they are time-aligned to the upstage speakers. Or we may have multiple delay zones according to where people are standing on stage.

I often design my sound system so that the mixing desk has a music group output and a vocal group output. These will then be routed to different speakers either using the mixing desk matrix, or a DSP processor. By having these different groups, it means I can have a different EQ, volume and delay settings for the music, another set for the voice, and another again for the sound effects.

Next, I'll see which speakers need some EQ. Small speakers often need a high pass filter (HPF) so that we don't blow up the driver by sending them low frequencies that they can't handle. It's important when EQ-ing to make sure you are EQ-ing the correct part of the system – if a mic sounds bad, but the music sounds good, then you need to be EQ-ing the microphone input, not the speakers. If one speaker sounds good, but another sounds bad, playing the same content, then you need to start looking at the EQ for that speaker.

There are no rules for how to EQ a speaker, but I tend to avoid boosting frequencies as much as possible, and will reduce the other frequencies instead. A spectrum analyser app on your phone (such as SignalScope) can be good for visualizing and identifying problematic frequencies, though they are not very accurate. Boosting the gain of one of the mid-band frequencies, with a relatively high Q, then sweeping the frequency parameter up and down ('sweeping the mid') can be helpful to find problematic frequencies.

Sometimes, even after adjusting the volume, delay and EQ parameters, something still sounds bad. At this point you have to consider whether you have the correct speaker in the correct location, and whether the acoustics are being favourable to you or not. Refer to the section 'Why Does It Sound Bad?' in Chapter 13 for more on this.

Some people like to sound check using an application called SMAART, which uses a computer and a measurement mic to analyse what is coming out of the speakers. This can be a useful tool, particularly for diagnosing problems that otherwise you may struggle to detect. However, it is easy to misinterpret the software if you don't really know how it works, which can cause more problems than it solves. It's a valuable tool if you have the time to learn how to use it.

It is important when you are sound checking to remember that you need the sound system to sound best for the *show* content, and not for your sound check music. If your show mostly features Shostakovich or Stormzy, then your Steeleye Span-balanced system won't sound very good. After you've got the system working well with your sound check tracks, move on to using the show content.

By now, you probably have a rough idea of what is going to be the loudest part of your show. I'll often start by playing this to check that the system can go loud enough to deliver it. Always allow some headroom to be able to turn it up a little louder still. If you find the proscenium speaker is too quiet, having turned it down to match it to the delay speakers, then we may need to look at turning it back up, which may compromise the imaging, or getting more powerful delay speakers, or pairing fewer of them on the amplifiers.

Plotting Session

You may need a plotting session, either alone, or with the director. This is an opportunity to listen to the show content prior to the stress of the technical rehearsals, to experiment with different routings and levels for cues. Sometimes these may be done in conjunction with the DSM and the lighting designer, to get everything working together – for example, how to start the show. These are known as 'dry techs' (to technically rehearse without the actors present). Or there may be a 'paper tech', which is where we may all go through the cues with the DSM's prompt copy, talking it through, but not actually seeing or hearing any of it.

I often find that plotting sessions are not particularly useful – so much of my work depends on interaction with the cast that without them it is difficult to set levels or timings properly. I tend to plot levels during the tech instead. That said, it can be useful to have some things prepared for the start of tech.

Sound Checking Radio Microphones

It's a good idea to get someone up onstage wearing a radio microphone – to whisper, to shout – to check that our gain settings are able to deal with those dynamics without distorting. Much of the sound of our radio microphones depend on wigs and hats, so we tend only to line test the radio mics, and do a proper check with the cast in mics at the start of the technical rehearsals, unless we're lucky to have a full sound check.

SOUND CHECKING WITH MUSICIANS AND THE CAST

If you have a band there may be two to three additional sessions that happen before tech rehearsals begin.

The Band Seating Call

The band seating call is typically where the band will visit their playing area, whether that's an orchestra pit, band room or somewhere on the set, and work out their seating arrangements. This will often be sketched out in advance by the MD, and is a key conversation to take part in, to ensure that loud instruments aren't next to quiet instruments, and in particular that loud instruments are screened off. We may also consider whether any acoustic treatment is needed around individual players – though it's not uncommon to need to change who is sitting where during the seating call.

Once we know where everyone is sitting, we can then finalize the positions of all the microphones and stands, music stands, drum screens, personal monitor stations and all the other paraphernalia. It's useful to give the MD a 'Voice of God' microphone, a mic with an on/off switch routed into all foldback speakers (including personal monitoring stations), upstage speakers, and proscenium speakers so they can talk to everyone easily.

The Band Sound Check

The next call, the band sound check, will be an opportunity to work through hearing each instrument, one at a time, to make it sound nice, by adjusting the microphone position, EQ, dynamics and so forth. Before you head into this, it's good to check in with the music department and make sure that you are up to date on which instruments are supposed to be playing in which parts of each number.

It is reasonably standard practice to start with the kick drum, snare, hi hat, toms, overheads and other percussion instruments, then on to the bass guitar, lead guitar, and so on. Once you have each instrument sounding how you like it, you can start working on making sure everyone can hear each other the way they like to. The musicians will each have particular requests for what they need to hear in order to keep rhythm, to hit their various musical cues. Increasingly we use personal monitor systems, Aviom being a popular make, to allow them to set their own foldback mixes, which makes them happier and saves a lot of time for us. Then we can start to play through some of the songs and work out the mix of how we want it to sound.

The duration of a band call is limited so we may sketch out the sound quickly and prioritize getting through every musical number rather than working in too much detail. We are often aiming for functionality above art at this stage. It is critical to be fully prepared for the band sound check – ten minutes wasted getting something to work can have bad consequences.

The musical director (MD) is often downstage centre in the orchestra pit, in view of the performers onstage. On the front edge of the stage is a camera routed to monitors on the circle front and in other areas where performers need to see the MD conduct. They have two microphones, one for singing, and one as a switched 'Voice of God' mic so they can communicate with the cast and the sound team. A float microphone can also be seen next to the camera, lifted up on some foam to reduce the amount of foot noise it picks up; in the far left is a drum kit behind a Perspex shield to reduce the drum sound spilling into the other microphones in the pit.

The Sitzprobe

We may have a Sitzprobe, where we bring the performers and musicians together for the first time. This may also happen at the end of the band call. On larger shows, the Sitzprobe may happen away from the theatre, which can be useful to hear each performer's unamplified singing voice, so we know what we are working towards as regards getting their amplified voice to sound like. Doing the Sitzprobe onstage can be helpful, not just for us, but in giving the performers and musicians a chance to familiarize themselves with listening to each other, and hearing themselves in the space

in a non-pressurized environment, which will give them more confidence for the tech – and far fewer requests for foldback. For some Sitzprobes we may provide some SM58 microphones on stands for people to go up and sing into.

'Virtual Sound Checking'

For the technical rehearsal it is likely you will only have the MD playing a keyboard, though sometimes you'll have the drummer too, in order to save money. You may see this referred to as a piano-tech, or in opera you'll see that only the 'répétiteur'

This band room is upstage centre, with a semi-transparent front. The MD plays the keyboards, has an Aviom feeding a Genelec speaker, and another pair of speakers to hear his own keyboard. The bassist is seated just out of shot on the left, with an array of pedals on the floor. The kit is to the right, and some acoustic foam has been added to marginally dampen the acoustics of the structure.

is called. It's helpful to record the microphones from each instrument to a multi-track recorder during the sound check so that you can carry on experimenting with the mix, or the individual sound of each instrument, once the band have gone. This 'virtual sound checking' lets us keep improving the sound of the band in their absence – though of course we will be missing the acoustic sound of the band, which can be a significant part of how it all sounds. The next time you see the band may be the dress rehearsal.

You will encounter performers with different levels of experience working on your shows. I sound check the musical pieces with the most experienced performers first, as they will be best able to communicate any needs they may have regarding the general foldback levels and what they can hear. Inexperienced performers may just ask for more of everything, including themselves, without knowing what they need.

It's tempting to stand next to the sound desk, or in the auditorium, during the Sitzprobe or sound check, because there you'll hear how it is going to sound to the audience. However, the best place to stand is onstage, with the performers. This gives you simple, direct communication with them, and you can hear what they hear, and pre-empt their foldback requests before they ask for them, and solve them in a manner that is most beneficial for us. You can hear for yourself if the foldback sounds bad, or something is missing that they need to hear. It means you can have a conversation with them at a normal conversation level, rather than having to shout to each other across the length of the auditorium. This alone immediately reduces many tensions that might arise. Likewise, during the tech, keep visiting them onstage. Establishing and maintaining a level of trust with the performers is invaluable, and you can't do that from the back of the auditorium.

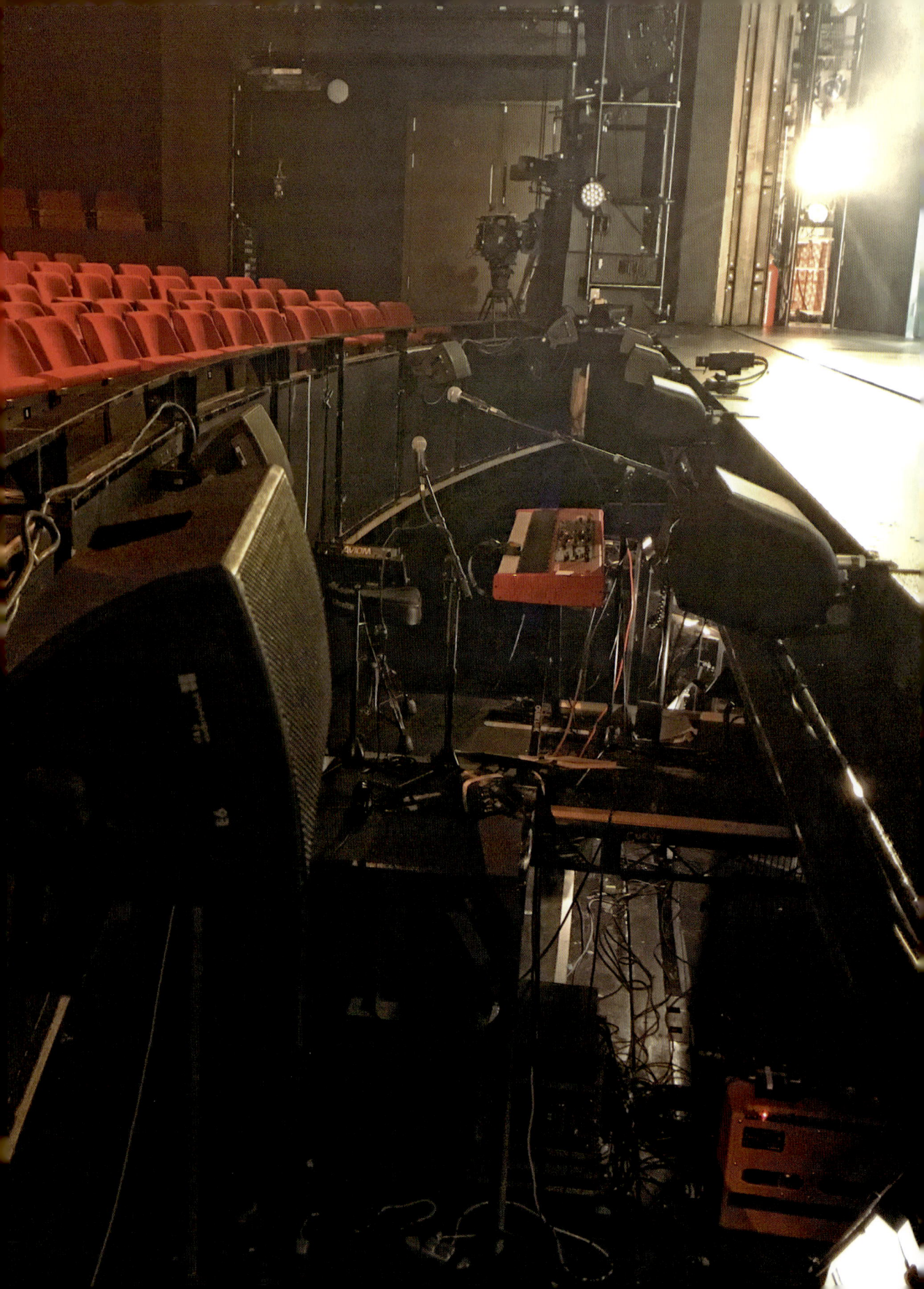

12
FOLDBACK

STAGE FOLDBACK

What elements of the music do the performers need to hear onstage to do their job? Mostly, they need to be able to hear rhythm and pitch. We will often send the kick drum, snare and hi hat to the stage foldback to give them the rhythm. Most often we will also send them the piano, or any other lead instrument, to give them something to pitch to. We rarely send them the whole mix, as it's more difficult for them to pick out what they need, and it also makes it harder for them to be able to hear themselves. It's important to set the right volume for what they hear – not too loud, not too quiet – and this level will vary from song to song.

Get up onstage to set the foldback – you can't get that level right without actually getting up on stage and listening to it. The sound in the auditorium you can deal with later, or the person on the sound desk can be working on that – deal with the foldback first so you can concentrate on the rest of the sound later.

It is important to design a stage foldback system that covers the entire stage and into the wings. If you have an orchestra in the pit, then often anyone downstage will be able to hear most of that acoustic sound perfectly well, though not necessarily what they need to hear. As soon as they start moving upstage, the acoustic sound will fall away rapidly, and they'll depend entirely on our stage foldback system to hear the band. The most common solution to this is to put some speakers in the wings facing onstage, which works well on narrower stages, but the wider your stage is, the worse it will sound centre stage, which is probably where most of our principals will be.

To improve the coverage of the stage foldback system, we may have speakers in the floor of the stage, firing upwards through grilles; we may have a grid of speakers in the grid facing straight down;

OPPOSITE: Speakers can be mounted along the front edge of the stage to provide better foldback to actors in the downstage area. Often known as 'reverse front fills' because they are pointing in the opposite direction to the audience front fills.

The band foldback system allows the cast to hear important rhythmic, pitch and melodic information. By having a number of smaller speakers, we can keep the overall volume out of each speaker quieter, so our performers' microphones will pick up less of the foldback, and at a more consistent level across the stage. Additional foldback may also be needed for offstage areas, such as the wings or booths.

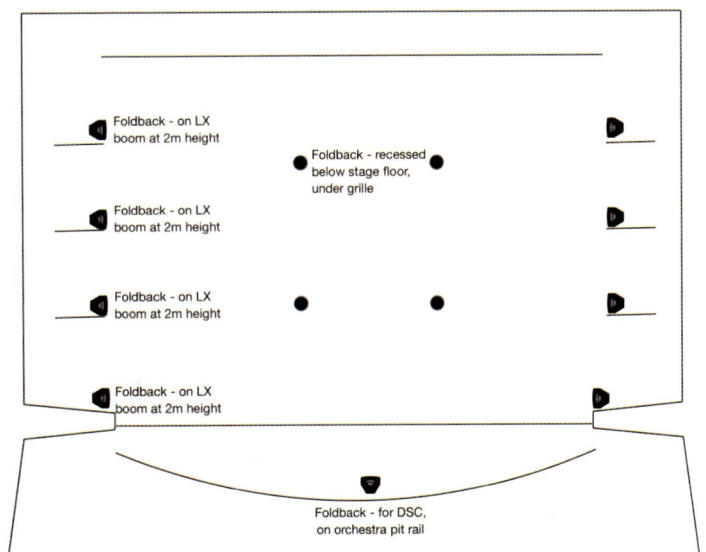

Foldback - on LX boom at 2m height

Foldback - recessed below stage floor, under grille

Foldback - on LX boom at 2m height

Foldback - on LX boom at 2m height

Foldback - on LX boom at 2m height

Foldback - for DSC, on orchestra pit rail

WHAT IS FEEDBACK? WHAT IS FOLDBACK?

These are different things, but the names are often confused.

Feedback is that horrible howling sound you get when a microphone starts picking up and amplifying the sound from a speaker, which is being fed by the microphone. It can often start off at a low volume before getting louder and louder. Once it starts, the only way to break the cycle is to temporarily turn off, or pull down the volume of the microphone or the speaker, to break the feedback loop.

The frequency and pitch of the howling sound varies from room to room, and is usually whatever frequency of sound is most dominant through the mic and speaker, or the frequency of sound the system is most sensitive to. It is often a low-mid frequency. A common trick to reduce the possibility of feedback is to deliberately drive a microphone into feedback and use a real time analyser (RTA) either built into the sound desk, or as an app on your phone, to identify which is the most problematic frequency. You can then use the EQ on that channel, with a narrow Q setting, to reduce sound at that specific frequency. This will change the tonality of the microphone, but will avoid that frequency kicking off feedback. You might repeat this to discover other problematic frequencies to EQ out. This process is known as 'ringing out' the system.

Foldback is our term for a monitoring system for the musicians or performers, so they can hear what each other, or themselves are doing, either in the pit, onstage or in the wings.

we might have a row of small speakers on the downstage edge of the stage facing upstage; and of course, our performers might wear an in-ear monitor system (IEM).

The more speakers you have for your stage foldback system, the more control you have, and the lower the volume that each of those speakers needs to run at. It is important that your stage foldback system isn't so loud that it is louder than the main amplification system for the audience. You don't want the front rows of the audience to be blasted with the stage foldback system. It can be useful to have a master fader for the stage foldback system, so you can make it louder or quieter for louder or quieter numbers, or for sections of numbers – this is often something you can automate.

VOCAL FOLDBACK

Vocal foldback is common in live music, where the singer is standing right over a wedge monitor singing into an SM58, or has an earpiece, and hears their own voice coming back to them through their wedge or earpiece. It is common in studio sound, too, where the singer may be wearing headphones.

In theatre, the situation is more complex. Typically, there aren't wedges in a set design, so foldback speakers are often further away. A common radio microphone placement is in the hairline or behind the ear, which means we are not getting as much level from the performer compared to singing into a handheld mic. For a performer to hear themselves back via foldback, that foldback has to be arriving at their ears at a volume that is louder than their own voice (and louder than any other sound sources on stage). Straightaway their microphone is picking up as much of the foldback as it is of the singer's voice. This means we are right on the edge of creating feedback, which is bad enough in itself, but we are also using that mic to feed the sound system for the audience, so we are also compromising what they hear.

For many years, theatre sound designers have rarely provided performers with vocal foldback. Experienced musical theatre performers are generally well used to performing without it, however performers who start off in other disciplines will be used to it, and will use it for vocal control, to check their pitch, and to avoid over-reaching vocally. So how do we deal with a desire for vocal foldback, on the one hand, and the detrimental effect it can have on the sound of the show, on the other?

Some sound designers have a strict 'no vocal foldback' policy. They will work hard to keep the band foldback stripped back, and the onstage levels quiet enough that they can hear themselves. That works fine until you come up against a star performer who just won't accept 'no' for an answer. Nothing will inflame a conversation with a performer about this subject more than saying it's not possible, or that no one else does it – because it's not true.

Dealing with a Request for Vocal Foldback

Whether they are a star or not, we should always engage with a request for vocal foldback, rather than dismissing it immediately. As soon as you make it clear you're not interested in their needs and desires you will lose their goodwill, and from that a litany of problems will ensue.

How can we more constructively engage with this request? Well, the request often comes soon after a performer first walks onstage. They may be feeling nervous, disconcerted, or tense. For those inexperienced in theatre it can seem very lonely up onstage, and the band can seem very disconnected. The request for vocal foldback can have many origins: it can be something they're used to having, or have had before; it can be something they've heard other people ask for; and often it can be because they're not happy with what they're hearing, and don't know the language to ask for anything else.

Before you offer any reply, the first thing you should do is to go up onstage and listen to what *they* are hearing, to find out where the request is coming from, and whether we can offer alternative solutions: is the band foldback too loud? Are they hearing more instruments than they need? Are they too far away from any band foldback so that it sounds as if they are on a big, empty, echoey stage? Can we get the band foldback system closer to them? Is there some other problem at work? Are they lacking self-confidence, or feeling vulnerable? Is someone watching their performance who is making them nervous? It's useful to ask why they need it, in a caring, sensitive-to-their-needs way, not in a 'you're-trying-to-make-my-sound-design-sound-awful' way. Often reducing or adjusting the mix of the band foldback can give them what they need whilst improving the sound out front.

Assuming we've exhausted all those options, simply sending their microphone into foldback isn't our only option to let them get a sense of themselves singing. If we send exactly what we're receiving from the microphone back to them, they will struggle to hear it until it is louder than their own acoustic voice, which is what causes issues for us.

When a performer is onstage they can often hear something of themselves coming through the sound system and reflecting back off the auditorium walls, particularly the circle front, and back on to the stage. Some performers find that slapback echo of themselves helpful: they know their mic is working, they can hear a sense of themselves occupying the auditorium. However, not all venues have this, as really it's a sort of acoustic flaw.

We can simulate the confidence-inspiring effect of slap-back by sending their vocal to the foldback but with a small delay added to it. It means they can hear that their microphone is on, and because it is slightly late, it is not competing directly with their own voice, so it can be quieter, making it less of an issue for us.

We can do a similar thing by sending some reverb of their voice to the foldback monitor. Again, they can hear the effect of their voice, without causing so much of an issue for us.

We may often combine multiple strategies to give the performer what they need.

There are scenarios where vocal foldback might not cause us major problems, for instance if the cast are singing into handhelds or headset microphones, if we can isolate the foldback just to go to speakers really close to the performer, or if our FOH level is reasonably loud anyway. There may also be scenarios where our performers can wear an IEM (in-ear monitor) earpiece, perhaps hidden in a wig or hairpiece to make it visually less obtrusive.

Despite your best efforts, sometimes performers will just demand vocal foldback. But *you* can demand things, such as they must wear a headset mic or have a handheld mic so as not to compromise the sound for the audience. If I anticipate that vocal foldback is likely to be requested, I will push towards styles of mic-ing that will better enable me to deliver it. If I know there will be a short schedule to get a show on, there'll be less time to balance the sound system carefully for each musical number, so I'll push towards

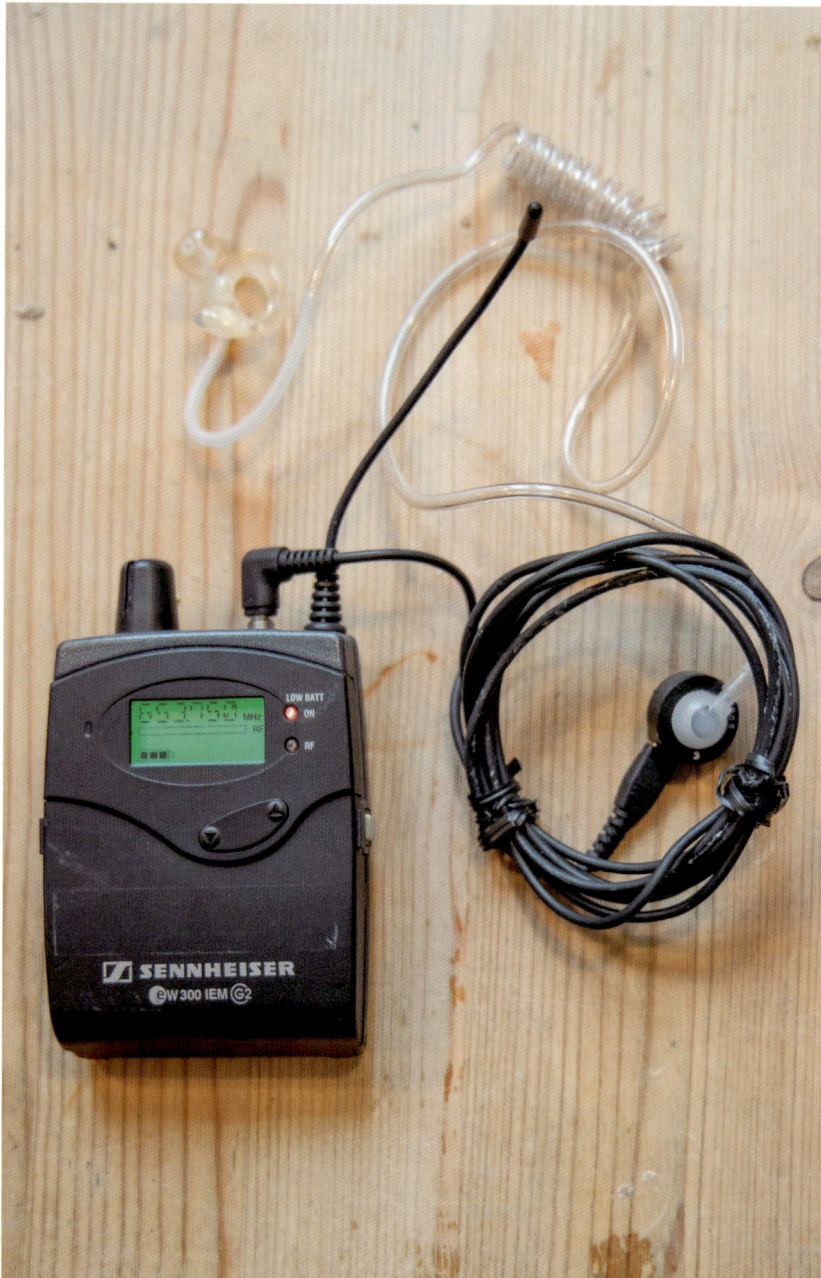

An 'in ear' monitor system. Whilst any normal headphone can be used, an acoustic tube earpiece is pictured here.

having headset microphones. Headset mics are becoming increasingly common in theatre. They enable vocal foldback to be delivered, and the higher gain they deliver before feedback means they can be used in more acoustically challenging environments.

There are other issues to consider when providing a lot of foldback on a show: for example, how do we handle the transition from song to dialogue? This is often a tricky junction at the best of times, depending on how sung-through your show is, but if we are potentially turning the vocal foldback system on and off too, it gets trickier still. There is no rule to dealing with this, as it depends on the genre, the length of gap between songs, and what happens in the scene. It can be disconcerting for a performer to have their vocal foldback suddenly drop away at the end of a song as they move into a dialogue sequence. They can feel nervous, as if their microphone has stopped working, or it can feel like a sudden plummet in energy.

If you feel you can't provide foldback, take the time to explain the problem to them, perhaps even to demonstrate the issue. Explain that you'd love to be able to provide it for them, but that in giving them what they want it is making them sound bad to the audience. Most performers don't want to sound bad, especially if they will sound worse than someone else. Above all, keep them involved in the process – it makes them feel empowered, it makes them know you're working to support them, and it shows professional respect.

13

TECHNICAL REHEARSALS

The tech is an exciting and scary part of the process. Rarely do you have enough time to look in detail at everything you'd like to. Rarely is everyone as prepared for the start of tech as they'd like to be. Rarely does everything that you've planned for weeks or months work the way you imagined. This is the moment when everyone's ideas coalesce into reality, for better or worse.

Everyone reacts differently to the pressure that a public performance is now within sight. Some deal with it well, others fall apart. Some shout and scream, seeking to blame anyone or everyone for whatever is wrong. Some plough ahead in utter denial that anything is wrong.

Whilst we will spend a lot of time in the technical rehearsal working out how to make our show sound good, most of the time we have to be aware of the psychological pressures that everyone, including ourselves, is under, and deal effectively with these.

The first rule of tech rehearsal is to stay calm. I remember on the first day of one of my first big design jobs, physically shaking at the prospect of it. But you have to mask your feelings with a poker face. If you panic, so will those around you, whether that's your team, or the director. In this high-pressure environment, it's important to deal carefully and sensitively with people. Be aware of what people's anxieties are being triggered by, and avoid triggering them. This is where your time earning the trust of the director will pay off the most.

We've probably spent a large proportion of the rehearsals collaborating with the actors, the director and the DSM. That carries on in the tech, but we

OPPOSITE: *As You Like It* at Regent's Park Theatre. Directed by Max Webster, designed by Naomi Dawson, lighting design by Lee Curran.

also add in other people too, with our most frequent collaborations being with the lighting and video designers. Our sound department, when we have one, will of course be vital in this process, and it's important to communicate to them clearly what you want to achieve, and discuss with them how best to achieve it. Ideally you will have a knowledgeable, skilled and experienced team, and it's usually far more effective to express what you want to achieve, and discuss with them how best to achieve it, taking on board their experiences and knowledge.

If we're using radio microphones for dialogue, before we start getting into anything too technical we'll get each cast member on stage, individually, in their costume, wig, hats, prosthetics or whatever they'll be wearing for the show, so we can have a quick listen to their radio microphones. We'll have balanced the system in our sound check so this is usually just making tweaks to individual microphone channels – setting a rough gain, EQ, possibly some compression for each person. Having your headshot sheet is useful for this moment. I'll ask each actor to say some lines from the show to get us started. Or I'll ask them to tell us what they had for breakfast, or to talk about their journey into work – anything to keep them talking.

Once we've got a rough EQ, I'll ask them to say their loudest line at performance energy, and their quietest, so we can check that the radio mic won't distort at the highest level, or be too noisy.

I tend to stand onstage for these sound checks – to connect with each performer, to have a close look at their mic placement, to check they are happy, to establish a line of communication. These are valuable things that will save time later, and I let my sound mixer sort out the gain and rough EQ on each mic.

BEGINNING OF THE TECH CHECKLIST

- Is your production desk set up in a useful listening position? Avoid sitting near any equipment with noisy fans. Don't be too far off to one side, but equally avoid the centre of the theatre, as these can both be unrepresentative listening positions. Be aware of which speakers you are on-axis to (in its line of sight), and which you are off-axis to (off to one side of where it's pointing). You'll need to check the on-axis levels of the speakers you are off-axis to later
- Do you have a fast network connection to transfer files from your laptop to the show computer? A USB stick is too slow to use
- Do you have space on your computer hard drive to deal with all the files you'll make, and for backups?
- Can you monitor or control every piece of equipment that you need access to? Do you have a good idea of how to use every piece of kit you'll need to use?
- Do you have a way to listen to sound off your laptop through the sound system? (I don't always find this necessary)
- Have you established between yourself and the operator, how and where files will be saved, and how backups will be made?
- Can you speak on comms to everyone you need to?
- If you don't know the names of the cast, get a headshot sheet (photos of each cast member with their names underneath) from stage management
- Is your production desk comfortable to sit at?
- Do you have a light, a script, a notepad, pen, water and snacks?

Ensure your production desk enables you to control all that you'll need to control, and to communicate with everyone.

HOW DO WE TECH A SHOW?

By the end of rehearsals we will have established where we think the sound cues that make up our sound design will go, and roughly what they will be. We will also have gone through the script with the DSM and our sound operator, so they know where those cues are, and what they do. Sometimes I will have put empty groups or folders into the cue list, as placeholders, for where

I think cues will go, but haven't made the audio for them yet.

Normally we will start a tech with the start of the show. This sounds obvious enough, but sometimes the start of the show may be the most technically complex. In some cases, it can be better to start with a simpler part of the show whilst everyone gets up to speed, fully functional, and we've established a way for the entire team to work together effectively.

How do we want to start the show? Our audience will be noisily chatting away, with the house lights on. Do we have any kind of sound or music playing whilst they are coming in? Some sort of soundscape that sets the mood or location of the first scene, or relates to the themes of the show? Are there events that have happened in the world of the story immediately prior to where our story starts? Can we use music that sets us in the period or place of the show? Is there any kind of activity onstage, is it a bare stage, or is the curtain in? In some countries and cities it is mandatory to play an announcement to the audience before the start of the show, with instructions for evacuation procedures. Do we need an announcement to get people to turn off their mobile phones and not take photos?

Whilst these have obvious functionality, they can somewhat kill the atmosphere of a buzzing audience, and make them go quiet. Do we give them time to start talking again, or do we go directly from any announcement straight into the show? Do we want something between the two as some sort of buffer between the prosaic nature of the announcement and the starting of our story? Do we want to record the preshow announcement in a way that relates to the style of our show, or in the voice of one of our characters?

If there isn't a preshow announcement, do we need to give the audience time to quieten down, to settle, to turn off their phones? Or do we want an abrupt, jarring start? Should the sound lead us in, should the lighting, or should they both go together? If there is a curtain or some form of front cloth going out, do we want a sound to accompany that movement, or is it a silent thing? How do we start the first scene, what do we want to establish? Is there some kind of scene change, some bringing on of the actors, or furniture, or some such, before the first scene actually begins?

It can be tricky to work out how to start the play until you have tech'd the first scene, because it's difficult to work out a transition before you've worked out what you are transitioning to. Sometimes it's not clear to me the best way to start the show until we've tech'd the end of it, until we've worked out our conventions of getting in and out of our world. By the time we come to tech the end of the show we will have a long-established language to draw on, of how we're telling this story. The end can inform us how to start: do the start and end mirror each other in some way, is there something clearly different at the end as a result of the plot, which we can show in its unaltered state at the beginning?

The answers to all of the above are critical in how we set up the very start of our story. There is a lot we can convey, and a lot of conventions we can establish, in those first few seconds of the show.

Examples of How to Start a Show

The classic play beginning: play a piece of music

This sometimes serves us well, especially if the music is telling us about time and place. But challenge yourself to do more than just this!

The classic musical beginning: the overture

The overture gives the audience time to settle, and latecomers to arrive and be seated, but it also serves as an important introduction to the musical themes we will hear later in the show, so our audience are familiar with them, rather them being completely strange – which is important in how we relate to music.

Brian Friel's *Dancing at Lughnasa*. Directed by Anna Mackmin

This play is a memory piece, and the narrator talks about his memory of his rural childhood home

Dancing at Lughnasa. Directed by Anna Mackmin, designed by Lez Brotherstone, lighting design by Paule Constable. MANUEL HARLAN

and music playing on the radio. I created a re-verb version (pushed through two instances of a 55-second reverb) of the music that is referenced by the narrator, to use as a preshow tone in the auditorium and as an underscoring motif through the show. I also processed the song to sound as if it was on a radio, using Audio Ease's Speak-erphone. I used the radio tuning module to have it 'tune out' into radio static. I also fed birdsong into the same module. I crossfaded the squawks we heard from an out-of-tune radio turned-in into the squawks of bird as if heard on an out-of-tune radio, before crossfading to the naturalistic sound of the birds singing. This gave us the music refer-enced in the text, an abstracted version to use as a motif, and brought us into the naturalistic world as if it had been conjured out of the same radio the narrator had conjured the music out of.

Zinnie Harris's *How to Hold your Breath*. Directed by Vicky Featherstone

Audiences will often not stop talking until they see someone walk on to the stage. This play starts with a voice-over, and we initially struggled to give the audience their cue to be quiet, so they would miss the start of the VO. To counter this, I created a 'riser' effect, using the first 'I' of the voice-over. I did this by feeding the 'I' into a 30-second reverb effect, then reversing the resulting file. So rather

than hearing something decaying, we hear it build-ing, slowly at first, before crescendoing upwards in the last 5 seconds. At which point it seamlessly went into the 'I' at the start of the VO. The riser signified to the audience that the show was start-ing, accompanied by a long fade-out of the house lights, giving people time to settle down and be quiet. The crescendo of the riser and the start of the VO was accompanied by a strong lighting ef-fect to take us fully into the world of the play.

Harold Pinter's *Mountain Language*. Directed by Katie Mitchell

This play is a study of oppression. Prisoners are being interrogated, hassled by guard dogs and tortured. It is a short play, only about 20 minutes long, so you don't have time to ramp up to the bleakness within the text. Rather than have a gen-tle fade-out of the house lights, we snapped the lights to complete black-out whilst simultaneously snapping into loud recordings of dogs barking, a helicopter buzzing overhead and the sound of sol-diers. Members of the audience screamed at this jump-shock, but it had the desired effect of cata-pulting the audience into the show, a bit dazed and confused. The prisoners in the play are equally dazed and confused by the oppression and cru-elty they are facing, so we created a sympathy be-tween the audience and the prisoners.

How to Hold your Breath, Royal Court Theatre. Directed by Vicky Featherstone, designed by Chloe Lamford, lighting design by Paule Constable. MANUEL HARLAN

Let The Right One In. Adapted by Jack Thorne. Directed by John Tiffany

The first scene starts off with a murder. A young man is walking through the woods when he is accosted and killed. Part of what we wanted to achieve with the opening was to show that this murder was of a random person, that it could have been anyone. During the preshow we had the sound of the desolate wind of the forest playing. From five minutes before the show started, our cast started to walk across the stage, each time dressed differently, often with their faces partially obscured, so we could get a sense of the community these murders were happening to, and that the victim could have been any of these people.

At the top of the show we slowly brought in a gentle piece of music, at a quiet volume, that had solo piano for the first minute of it, without any other changes to lighting or other signs that the show was beginning. The music would slowly come up in volume. Quieter audiences would notice it quickly and calm themselves. Louder audiences would carry on talking until about a minute in, when the beat started, at which point the number of cast members crossing the stage increased, becoming a movement sequence, until the music hit full volume, at which point we took the house lights out and properly shifted the audience's attention to the stage.

This sort of soft start can either lead the audience into the show gently, or disorient them because the show has started and they hadn't even realized it had. Both responses can be useful, depending on the type of story we're trying to tell.

Martin Crimp's *Attempts on Her Life*. Directed by Katie Mitchell

We decided our production of this play was set in 1997. We used pop music from that year as pre-show to help set the time period. We opened the house with the fire curtain in, obscuring the stage. To start the show, we treated the iron going out as if it were some sort of industrial shutter and played a loud, shuddering, metallic sound as it rose up, with a loud mechanical buzzer sound at the start of it. It established the curtain as a theatrical device, a very solid fourth wall, which we would use for each of our scene changes.

The Fake Audience

Audiences can vary a lot from performance to performance. They can often think the show is about to start and go completely quiet, which can be awkward if we're still a few minutes away. A matinée audience may be particularly quiet, and more prone to 'going dead' than a Saturday night crowd, who may be difficult to shut up at all! To achieve a consistent start to a show we may sometimes record a noisy audience in our theatre, and then play that back through speakers, so that if the audience goes dead, the recorded audience keeps going, and the real audience start chatting again fairly quickly. This requires some care, so the audience aren't aware of the effect.

PROGRESSING THROUGH THE TECH

The first session of technical rehearsal usually appears to be the least productive. It is where the language of the show is first established, and where we see all the design elements together for the first time. If you're working with people you've not worked with before, it's where everyone encounters how everyone else actually works, and how to communicate with each other. It's also where numerous snags are encountered, where full costumes may be worn and moved in for the first time, where the set is interacted with by the performers for the first time, and so on. It's not uncommon to get only a few pages into the script in the first session as you work out how to start the show, work out the first scene, and work out the first transition or scene change. Once you've set those conventions in place, the rest of the show will normally be easier to tech.

Don't be afraid to take time – to make everyone wait – to achieve what you need to do. Or to say 'I can't do that now; can I take that as a note and we can move on?'

As we work through the show, I will change the cue points so they work more closely with the

WORKING WITH THE LIGHTING DESIGNER

Lighting designers will often have gone through a similar script analysis process to us, and may well have determined that many of their lighting cues will tie in with the same dramaturgical events that we are tying our sound cues into. It is quite rare for lighting designers to be able to do much lighting work in the rehearsal room, so they often build up their design in the few days before the tech starts and over the course of the tech. They will also be getting their lighting cues into the prompt copy with the DSM, and we often find that they may fall on, or close to, the same cue points. It is commonplace for the lighting designer to be working with a lighting operator, who will press the 'Go' button on their lighting desk when they are told to by the DSM.

Sometimes this works fine, but sometimes the minutely different reaction times of the DSM and the sound and lighting operators can be enough to make the sound and lighting look out of sync. Instead we may synchronize the systems by sending MIDI, OSC or Timecode from the sound computer to the lighting desk. This may be in the form of MIDI Show Control (MSC) commands, MIDI program changes, or note-on messages (less common nowadays), OSC commands MIDI timecode, or SMPTE timecode. Most show-control software packages, such as QLab, are able to send these messages natively, and normally we can just have a MIDI or audio cable going from sound to lighting to be able to synchronize them. OSC uses computer network protocols, but this will involve tying the sound and lighting networks together, which can add complexity.

timings in the theatre, which can change massively from the rehearsal room. I may have had only two to six speakers in rehearsals, but I might easily have over a hundred in the theatre, with different acoustics, so levels will also change a lot.

I spend a lot of the tech experimenting with how much in the foreground or background each of the individual elements in my sound design might be. I spend a lot of time pushing elements out to the proscenium, into the surround, and back down to the upstage speakers. A piece of music may sit in the upstage speakers to underscore, but then I might want to push it out into the auditorium. It can take a lot of the tech and previews to get the right balance of where each element might be routed, and when.

I would like to reiterate here that the assertion 'Good sound design shouldn't be noticed' is nonsense. This is how we justify newspaper reviews that don't mention the sound. Good sound design *should* be noticed by those whose job it is to notice how a show is put together, just as we expect them to notice every other aspect of the show. A good sound design will often feel like an integral part of the production, and perhaps will feel so appropriate, so right and so natural that it never feels fake, it never feels forced, it never grabs the audience's attention. But there are absolutely times when the sound design *can* sit in the foreground and be noticed, when it *can* be the key driver of the show. Don't hold back from being noticed, from being in the foreground.

When I make a sound on my laptop, I will often bounce it out as a number of stems. This allows me to load up those stems into QLab, and try different mixes of each stem, with each routed to different speakers, and to the sub-bass speakers in different proportions. It provides flexibility to adjust things in QLab, both in tech, and later on in previews as minor adjustments need to be made. If I had just a single stereo file in QLab for every sound effect, every minor change would require a new mix to be bounced and transferred from my laptop, thus slowing down the tech.

If I have made most of the content in rehearsals, then most of my work in the theatre is about the transitions between scenes, which can often only be mocked up in rehearsals. The length of a transition or scene change can be affected by a number of things, both seen and unseen. There may be a very functional movement of scenery that happens, or a costume change. There may be some visible story of a passage of time, or change of location to tell in that scene change – what has happened in the world of our story between the end of this scene and the start of the next?

Sometimes the length of the scene change will be a completely fixed thing, and sometimes it may be variable. A fixed length scene change means we can provide something that has a definitive start, middle and end, which is often satisfactory – but is risky if the scene change goes wrong and takes longer than normal. A variable length scene change means we can't predict when the end will be. We may have a good idea, but we need to allow contingency time in case something goes wrong, whether by having a really long cue, or by looping parts of it.

Scene changes may be a complex dance of scenery, lighting, video and sound, something that we all create together. When working on complex sequences, I often video it so I can work on it later and fine tune what I am doing.

Is Your Concept Working?

Soon into the tech you'll get a sense of whether your concept is working or not. I've done a few shows where I've got to the end of the first tech session, or the first day, then wandered over to the director and said, 'I don't think this is working, I don't like my ideas for this'. Obviously if the ideas are theirs, I'll be more tactful than that! But if you feel that what you're doing isn't working, it's better to stop, reassess, and come up with a new plan. Don't plough ahead with something that doesn't work.

The tech may be where I discover that my taste and the directors don't really line up. Perhaps the director just wants everything louder than I do. The pressure of tech can make having conversations about differences of taste feel like wasting the precious time available. But these conversations are worth having, whether to clear up misunderstandings about what is wanted, or to discuss differences of taste. I'll wait until the next coffee or meal break to chat on a one-to-one basis with the director. The director is the boss, so you may have to compromise your desire to meet their taste, but by starting a conversation early, rather than allowing tensions to build, you can hopefully find a better middle ground.

Problems with Volume

You will at some point work with someone who just wants everything unbearably loud. They may be rather deaf due to age, or due to listening constantly to things that are unbearably loud; or they may just feel that such a high volume is necessary for what they want to create. Whatever your personal taste, as the sound designer you are responsible for protecting the hearing of the company and the audience.

If you feel that something is much too loud, then you should check your show against the local noise laws. Most countries have regulations, some just for staff, but some have them for the audience, too. They may, for example, oblige the performers to wear ear plugs onstage if the sound is above a certain volume. You should know what the laws are, and if in doubt, measure your levels.

Whilst audience members are rarely at risk – although hearing damage can be inflicted instantly – we rarely hit those sorts of volume, and most hearing damage is caused by sustained exposure over time; this means that the crew, performers and particularly the musicians are most vulnerable. I know many musicians who are reaching their later years of life and have serious hearing issues developing, putting them out of work and adversely affecting their general quality of life.

Musicians often want the volume to be loud so they can 'feel' the music. It is important to give them control over the volume they hear, by giving them personal monitor solutions or global volume controls, so they turn the volume down for when they don't need it to be loud, or as they require. However, it's still important to remind them if they've got the volume too loud for the health of their hearing.

I endeavour to keep the volume levels onstage at a reasonable level, and I ask company members to alert me if they think anything is too loud.

It's a dangerous strategy to invoke these laws if you simply have a different aesthetic to the director or producer about volume.

It can be useful to identify if any members of the company have hearing issues, which might make it difficult for them to do their job in a noisy environment. Identifying this early on can enable you to incorporate solutions into your system design at an early stage, rather than bodging something in later.

I do consider it important – as far as the system design allows – to provide audio feeds to any assistive listening systems the venue may have installed for its audience, which is often a vocal-heavy mix of the show.

LOUD SOUND EFFECT

We often find ourselves playing loud, sudden sounds through the sound system during tech rehearsals. Whenever you're about to play something loud outside the normal confines of tech'ing, warn people first. Shout: 'Loud sound effect!' as a warning. I've seen many people do this quite quietly, which is utterly worthless, as your voice needs to reach the top level of the auditorium and into the fly floor. In playing loud sounds we are potentially going to startle someone, which could result in them falling off something, or dropping something. These are serious health and safety concerns, so it is imperative we give people appropriate warning. I will also hold back from playing loud sounds if I see anyone working at any height, or if it has become really dark. Be sensitive to how your sound effects will impact the people working around you. I do also loudly apologize if I inadvertently play something really loud without warning.

Technical rehearsals can be tricky in other respects. There is an empty auditorium and no audience, which means there is no audience reaction to jokes, or other big moments – and it also means there is no audience to soak up the sound. Thus the performers will not be performing with the adrenalin of a performance and will speak more quietly, and perform more slowly than they do in an actual performance. The background noise of a tech is often quite considerable, as all the departments are talking away to each other – and all this can make it hard to get a proper sense of the appropriate volume for anything. Also, as we are tech'ing the show in small fragments it is difficult to get any sense of the arc of what we are doing.

THE QUICK FIX

There may be other design elements that we see for the first time, which give a different 'spin' on the show than we imagined. There may be some aspect of the show that we thought was going to be great, that just doesn't work in reality. There just may not be enough time to get everything as perfect as we'd like it to be. And sometimes great actors deliver poor performances.

Sound and music are the method most directors will turn to first, to make a quick fix to their show. Having a super-fast workflow to turn this around is essential.

You'll need to be quick on your feet, coming up with something that works within your concept, or finding a way to sidestep your concept to Elastoplast the part of the show that isn't working. But what if the proposed quick fix essentially kills your entire design concept? This is the moment where being an involved member of the creative team can pay off – it gives you a voice in that conversation, to discuss what is and isn't working in the whole production, why that is, how it can be fixed, and the methods we could take to fix it, whether with sound or otherwise. There are usually multiple ways to solve a problem, and they can often span many departments.

GETTING RID OF A PIECE OF MUSIC

How can we get rid of a piece of music that we have playing? Fading music out by pulling down the fader can be so boring. Here are a few other ways:

- Filter it out using a high pass filter (or a low pass filter)
- Pitch it down like a record stopping
- Snap it out with a touch of reverb on the end
- Find a bit of the music that has a stab-like quality – a sting – and use that to cover snapping out
- Crossfade to a 100 per cent wet, long reverb, then fade that out for a nice dreamy effect

When I'm making something in a hurry, I'll often put forward a few versions of the same new potential sound cue, whether that's five different types of doorbell, or something more abstract. I'll play them to the director, so we can decide what we like together – that's an important part of coming to have a shared aesthetic with the director. That said, I often play my favourite version of the cue either first, or last, which is a psychological way of pushing them towards my choices a little!

WHY DOES IT SOUND BAD?

There are many reasons why the sound may seem bad:

1. What is coming into the system sounds bad: the content, the performances (garbage in, garbage out)
2. Inconsistency of what is coming into the system
3. The amount of foldback
4. The placement of the loudspeakers
5. The relationship between the performance space, the placement of the speakers and the auditorium (for example, all the performers

come and sing downstage of the proscenium system)

6. The EQ and timing of the loudspeakers
7. The choice of loudspeakers
8. The acoustics
9. Can the person mixing hear it well enough to mix it? Are they mixing it well?
10. And of course, plain incompetence, which can manifest itself anywhere!

Each of the potential causes above requires a different solution, and different political tactics to fix it. Items one to five in the list above probably all require collaboration with the director, or MD, to fix. Item six – how it sounds – will require more sound check time. Item seven – loudspeaker choice – is either your fault or an existing venue issue, which you may or may not be able to change. Item eight – the acoustics – is often difficult to fix, so you may need a different way to achieve an improvement.

Item nine – can the person mixing hear properly? Many mix positions are right at the back of the theatre and are not ideal. A common technique is to install a speaker right in front of them to help them hear what they're mixing. Are they in a bass trap (an area where the bass frequencies rumble around, making the bass sound louder for them than us)? Are they mixing it well? Have they programmed the desk so they have everything under their fingers to be able to mix what they need to? If the desk isn't programmed well, it can feel as if they are not in control of the mix – with the mix feeling inconsistent from moment to moment. It can take the best mixer a week or two to perfect the programming of the desk for a complex show, particularly if the show is being changed a lot. Have they had time to consolidate their programming of the desk?

Item ten, incompetence: well, the solution to that will be unique in every situation.

We often feel under pressure when something sounds bad, not just because we're unhappy with our own work, but because we may feel we're losing the faith of the people we're working with.

The first step is just to take a deep breath, detach yourself from the emotion of the situation, and analyse why it is sounding bad. There will often be multiple contributing factors. What can you practically change to get the most significant improvement?

It is good to make solving the problem a public, group thing, rather than quietly trying to fix the few things that may be within your control.

One common cause in theatre for bad sound is that the locations of the speakers are often compromised for visual aesthetics. If I think that is the principal reason why the show isn't sounding good, then it's time to talk to the director. I might say, 'It's not sounding great, I know. I'm doing the best I can with the speakers where they are – I'd hoped to make them work, but they won't. Can we look with the set designer to find better positions for the speakers?'

In doing this you are involving the director in the decision about whether (a) they want it to sound bad but the speakers not to be visible, or (b) whether they can accept compromise over the visibility of the speakers to get a better sound. Thus, they can choose bad sound, accepting that they have chosen the route of bad sound, when they could have had better sound; or they can discuss solutions with the set designer that perhaps you might not have achieved if you had tried to negotiate directly with the set designer, whose first priority will be the visual aspect of the production. This is not about being sneaky or underhand: it's about emphasizing your problem, which is bad sound, to the person who can effect the change that is needed, which is better speaker positions.

The more experienced you get, the more you can pre-empt these problems and find solutions before you hit tech. But not always. Sometimes the deck is stacked against us. There have been many occasions when I've just not managed to make something sound good.

When we watch other sound designers' shows we have to bear in mind that they may have had the deck stacked against them too, and cut them some slack!

CASE STUDIES

SHOW: Kneehigh's *A Matter of Life and Death*
VENUE: Olivier Theatre, National Theatre

This 'play with music' featured a live six-piece band onstage, on a moving truck, that placed them either downstage left, upstage, or off the stage altogether. There were thirty-four pieces of music throughout the show, played by the band (a large range of acoustic and electric instruments, a full drum kit and a DJ mixer) and which were either underscoring cues, musical numbers with the cast singing, hip-hop numbers and even a DJ.

The band also sang backing vocals, with a dedicated singer who would rap for some of the hip-hop influenced numbers, using a wireless handheld microphone. The double bass, xylophone and acoustic guitar came off the band truck for a couple of numbers, so they had radio mic transmitters attached to them, with DPA 4061 microphones, except for the acoustic guitar, which used an internal pickup wired into the transmitter. Two of the cast members also played uke and accordion, but the entire cast was radio mic'd, so we picked up these instruments with their radio microphones.

The NT has a large stock of in-house microphones, so I chose which to use from those. The band all fed into a small Yamaha digital mixing desk so I could program different mixes for each song. I could also program different delay times for the different instruments according to where the band truck was, or the individual players were on stage.

The acoustic sound of most of the band was quite loud, so I lifted up some of the quieter instruments, and when the band was on the left of the stage, I fed more signal into the right-hand side of the proscenium sound system to balance out the sound. Not too much, as I wanted it to sound as if it was coming from the band, but just enough so it wasn't completely lop-sided.

For foldback the band wanted to be on headphones, so they could hear each other well regardless of what dialogue or loud sound effects were happening on stage around them. There was one mix for the drummer, and another for everyone else.

As previously mentioned, intelligibility in the Olivier is tricky, but the radio microphones and the in-house vocal system enabled us to be intelligible even with a lot of soundscape and musical underscoring present.

The show featured a lot of performer flying and other aerial stunts, and any show that has these features, or pyrotechnics or fire, reduces significantly your ability to experiment with sound during the tech – you can't have loud sound playing whilst there is a risky element of the show being sorted out.

Fortunately we'd had the full band in rehearsals, which is rare, and I'd developed most of the sound effects throughout.

The NT's three theatres are well equipped, though you have to work within the limits of the repertoire: there will normally be three shows running simultaneously in each venue, each doing a few shows per week, before there is a day off to change into one of the other shows. Often you will share elements of the sound rig with another show, so what you can do is limited by the amount of time and resources on a turnaround day. The larger two auditoriums often use radio mic's and are well supported for this. As the theatres are well-equipped, a typical show budget is actually quite low, and if you are going to do something unusual you need to plan ahead to get extra money and staff allocated to the budget early on.

SHOW: Redacted
VENUE: Redacted

This show, which we'll keep anonymous, was scored for piano and percussion, which were onstage, upstage centre. Our musicians also provided some sound effects, primarily Foley-type sounds for footsteps and the occasional crash. There was no distinction between the band area and the rest of the stage, to allow as much play to happen between the cast and music as possible.

A Matter of Life and Death, Olivier Theatre, National Theatre. Directed by Emma Rice. Set design by Bill Mitchell. Costume design by Vicki Mortimer. Lighting Design by Mark Henderson. The six-piece band played double bass, mandolin, trumpet, trombone, sax, acoustic guitar, electric guitar, banjo, mandolin, a hammer dulcimer, xylophone, a full drum kit and a DJ mixer, positioned on a truck that could be pushed around the stage. We couldn't quite squeeze the vibraphones on the truck. The band also sang backing vocals, with a dedicated singer who would rap for some of the hip-hop influenced numbers, using a wireless handheld mic. Also visible here are a couple of Meyer MSLs, one just by the vibraphone, and mirrored on the opposite side of the stage, used for sound effects and the band reinforcement.

We were on quite a small stage, so we struggled a lot with separation between the louder percussion elements and the cast, who were radio mic'd with capsules in their hairline. Also a few of them were not very strong singers, which didn't help.

In such close proximity to each other, you'd have thought that foldback wouldn't be an issue, but actually we had to put a little speaker next to the MD/pianist so he could hear the sung vocals better (as much to better conduct the singers as anything). There was click track for a couple of numbers where the cast were busy with so many physical things they didn't have the breath to sing out the number. We had another number where we used pre-recorded track to thicken out the instrumentation a little. I had a couple of speakers flanking the band, so that my often low-fi sound effects felt as if they were coming from the world of the band, too. This was effective for melding the recorded and live worlds together.

From there on in, everything else was a disaster. The theatre had a poor selection of microphones available and virtually no budget, so we used their in-house stock. During the sound check I discovered that the in-house speaker rig sounded awful: it had been pushed hard by every show that had toured in there, and as it was a cheaper system without any limiting or speaker protection on it, each speaker was knackered, but each in a slightly different way – so no matter what you did, you couldn't make the system sound good.

The theatre had decided to employ someone to mix the show who had no previous experience of theatre, though had done live music concerts before. Due to the proximity of the band to the cast, though, we needed someone who could line-crunch the mix, so we didn't pick up too much of the band on everyone's microphones.

The theatre had also decided they did not have enough money to employ a No. 2, or to have any spare microphones or transmitters. If a mic went down, it just wouldn't work from then on until the end of the show. Whilst both myself and the director flagged up these issues in rehearsals, the theatre hedged its bets that everything would be fine and they wouldn't need to pay extra, and that they could solve the problem if and when one occurred. With only eight days between the start of tech and press night, the inevitable disaster unfolded too quickly for them to respond. The inexperienced operator couldn't keep up with the amount of line crunching, so 25 per cent of the dialogue and lyrics went unamplified. Crucial plot points were inaudible. Sound cues were missed. Band levels were inconsistently plotted and recalled.

On press night, the microphones of three of the seven cast members failed in one way or another, brutally exposing the short-sightedness of the theatre's budgeting and its lack of resourcing, whilst also making both my work and the directors work look amateurish. The theatre had to source spare

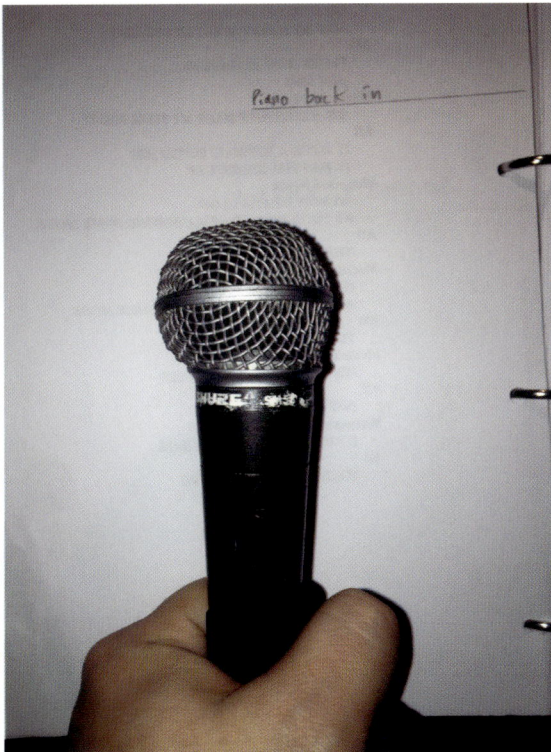

The equipment you are provided with may not always be in the best of condition.

LINE CRUNCHING

Line crunching is when the operator only turns on the microphone of the person who is speaking a line. When person A says a line, then person B says a line, then person A says a line, you will have turned microphone A on, then off, then turned mic B on, then off, then turned mic A on, then off. You only amplify the person talking, so you amplify less noise from whatever else is happening on stage and get more gain before feedback. The alternative approach, which is just to keep mic A and mic B on all the time they are onstage, can work in some scenarios, but we may hear phase issues when they are both in close proximity to each other – they'll both amplify any noise around them, and you'll have 3dB less potential gain before feedback. Line crunching gives you a really clean sound, but it can be at the expense of hearing the breathing and smaller vocal utterances and reactions of the person who isn't talking or singing. We'll identify the majority of the important reactions and turn their mic on for those.

microphones and a No. 2 – during the busiest time of the year – and bring in extra staff to help out the flailing No. 1 – but by that point the reviews had already been written.

SHOW: *CBeebies The Nutcracker*
VENUE: Sheffield Crucible
This show was a 35-minute musical made simultaneously for a theatre audience and for television broadcast. It had a principal cast of twelve, plus others in non-speaking roles, and a seven-piece band, who roved around the stage playing their instruments and singing backing vocals. 'Roving' meant the band had to be on radio microphones, and along with the cast, this made for a total of thirty-eight channels, plus seven Shure IEM systems for musicians' foldback.

We had violin, flute and clarinet being played, which we were able to pick up using a DPA 4060 over the ear of each musician playing (which could then also get their backing vocals when they sang).

We had an accordion, with a DPA 4099 specialist accordion microphone; two acoustic guitars, each with a pick-up; and several percussion instruments, each with an AKG C516 clip-on microphone. These were wired into Shure UR1-M transmitters. A couple of the band had their own custom-moulded, in-ear headphones, and we provided the others with generic ear-bud headphones.

The Sheffield Crucible stage is thrust into the auditorium with audience on three sides of the stage. This can make gain before feedback an issue, as there is little acoustic separation between the stage – the area we are amplifying – and the audience – the area where we want the amplified sound to be heard. To get the maximum level out of the cast, who were all good, strong singers we used DPA 4066 headsets. Headsets are quite visually obtrusive, especially when viewed in close-up on television, but they gave us good separation between cast members and band, and lots of gain. This was good for the theatre element and enabled them to do a better mix in post-production. We chose not to double-microphone the cast as this would look really bad on television, and we were filming it multiple times so if there was a problem we could always use another take.

We used a Yamaha CL5 mixing desk and Rio stage boxes, which meant we could just give the OB (outside broadcast) truck a single Cat5 cable from our Dante system, and they could pick up every single microphone, desk input and output. As we had such a short fit-up we used the in-house speaker system, which was over twenty-five years old and had seen better days (larger shows typically bring in a sound system, but we didn't have the time to do this). We relayed some of the musical instruments into the stage foldback speakers for the cast to hear them, but they did not need much as they were so close to the band.

We had only three days to rehearse the show from scratch: one day of tech, one dress rehearsal and two performances. That sounds like a recipe for disaster, but with super professional performers, SM, creative teams, in-house sound team, and my sound team, it went flawlessly.

A number of IEM transmitters and radio microphone receivers.

SHOW: *Boy*
VENUE: Almeida

Leo Butler's play *Boy* is about a socially isolated seventeen-year-old, struggling to deal with life after school, and the cold, brutal London he lives in. Director Sacha Wares has the Boy in almost constant motion, as he makes an epic journey into the centre of town to try to find someone from his old school class.

Miriam Buether's set design is a constantly moving travellator, weaving round the theatre space, with the audience sat around, and amongst it. Various scenic elements, such as bus shelters, are attached to the floor of the travellator so they travel round the space, too. The travellator, which we had in rehearsals, was driven by a motor that has to be physically close to the track and was quite noisy.

Sacha and I were concerned about audibility. The actors are in constant motion, and always have their backs to varying sections of the audience as the travellator takes them round. Radio microphones were the obvious answer, along with a method of programming the mixing desk to pan the actors' voices around the space to match their location. This was done by measuring the time it took to move between different points, using a stopwatch, for the three speeds the travellator ran at during the show. As soon as an actor stepped on, we could predict exactly where they'd be on the stage from that point on.

We'd discussed that this production might be quite abstract in many senses. We talked more in terms of soundscape than evoking realism, of evoking the pulse of the city, reflecting the momentum of the travellator. I experimented with this, taking some time to develop different versions of what that pulse might be. I developed abstractions of realistic sounds the Boy might hear, so we could have both real and abstracted sounds, sometimes simultaneously, creating this isolating, hard-to-pin-down world for the Boy to inhabit. We experimented in rehearsals, and I found the tempo of the pulse could be timed to match the speed of the travellator, especially as it sped up or slowed down, which made the travellator motor noise feel as if it were part of the soundtrack rather than an unwanted element.

By the end of rehearsals we had a good sense of much of the sound design, and when we wanted things to happen. We were able to develop this further during rehearsals – especially during the moments when the travellator broke down!

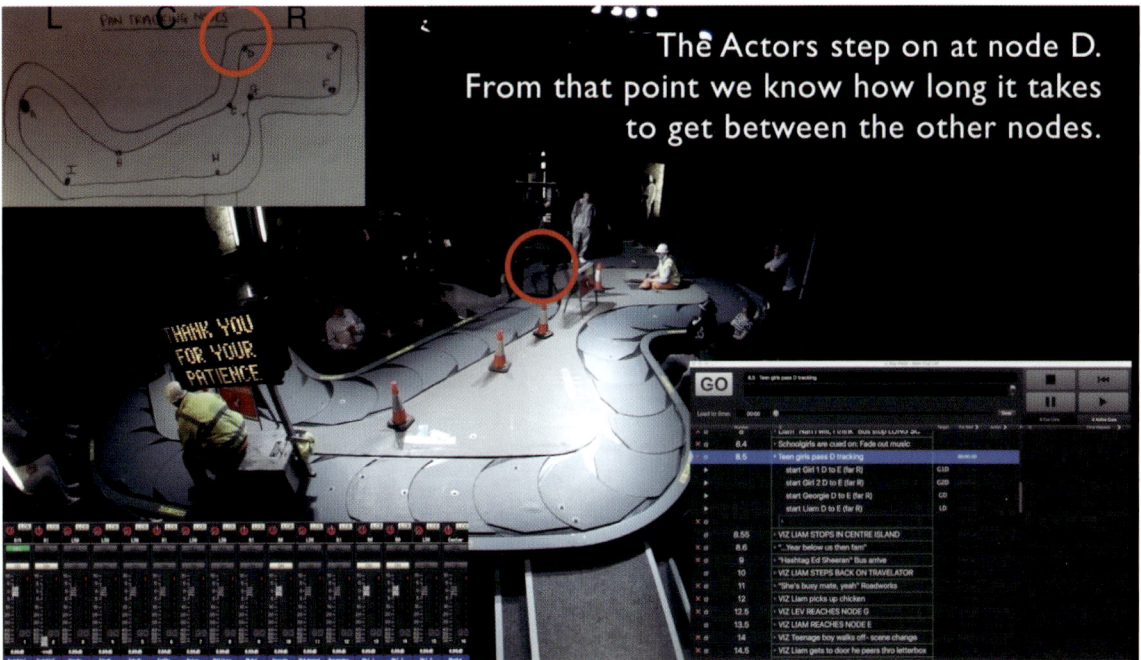

By timing the speed of the travellator between a number of points on the track, we can automatically pan the voices of our actors across our LCR loudspeaker system, by using QLab to send MIDI control changes to the pan control on the Yamaha CL5 mixing desk.

I had an associate, Ben Grant, who was in rehearsals a lot and developed much of the cue structure for the show, as well as some of the abstract elements. The Almeida's Andy Josephs was both production engineer and operator.

SHOW: *The Barbershop Chronicles*
VENUE: Dorfman, National Theatre

In Chapter 5, I described a little of how we used music in this production. In addition to the music, there was also a minimal soundtrack of London traffic versus African city soundscapes (a couple of which the director recorded on a research trip), and a couple of spot sound effects, coming from wireless speakers around the set. In many respects, from a sound perspective it started as a reasonably straightforward show.

The show opened at the NT with Dorfman HOD Sarah Weltman and her team looking after the installation of the fairly simple rig, essentially just a stereo set of speakers in the grid, replicated for each bank of seats as we were playing in-the-round, and the wireless speakers. The show was beautifully operated by in-house technician Ben Vernon, and other members of the NT sound team later on in its run. As I couldn't be around during the final previews I brought in an associate, Helen Skiera, to look after the final few shows and press night.

The show was a co-production with the NT and Fuel, who then took it to a near identical theatre at West Yorkshire Playhouse where we could recreate it for a short run. I wasn't available for this 'move', so another of my regular associates, Pete Malkin, stood in for me.

After a short break, the show returned for another run at the NT, which Helen and the NT team looked after as I was busy on another show – revivals and transfers of shows are often quite difficult to work into your schedule as they often occur at relatively short notice, clashing with other work you may have had booked in long before.

The show then toured Australia and New Zealand, playing with the audience on three sides, rather than four. This helped with the intelligibility of the show in some of the larger venues we found ourselves playing in. We toured just a QLab system and some MiniRig battery-powered speakers built into our props, using IEM systems sourced in each venue, to comply with local frequency licensing laws. For the first tour we had a sound department of one, Amir Sherhan, who would work with the sound team in each local venue to install a speaker system suitable for us, if they didn't have one already.

As the show proved popular we were keen to share it with a wider audience, so we made a version that could tour proscenium venues, which involved a substantial re-working of the show in terms of how the cast relates to the audience. For the in-the-round version, the front row of the audience were centimetres away from the cast, and there was substantial interaction with the audience preshow, which really set up the energy for the show, including a cast member live-DJ'ing on the stage.

For the proscenium version, with the audience more distant, and with us playing in larger venues, we moved to radio mic'ing the show. This was a slightly tricky process as the show hadn't been made with this in mind, and had many quick costume changes, both onstage and offstage. We toured a Yamaha QL1 mixing desk, so we could have consistency for the operator, now Laura Hammond, in each venue (which we hadn't toured previously as it was essentially playback only), and we used a member of the stage management team to supervise the costume changes.

We had to change the sound design to have a more conventional upstage, and proscenium layers of speakers to be able to use upstage for the atmospheric effects, and the proscenium for the scene change music.

In the first eighteen months of its life our production played in about twenty different venues (of which I visited only two), in three different seating configurations, without microphones and with radio microphones, with about six different sound operators, and two different associates on it. When you have this many people looking after your work, it is essential to have the relevant paperwork and photos, and to take the time to explain the intent of your design so that they can take good care of it.

The Barbershop Chronicles, the National Theatre. Directed by Bijan Sheibani, designed by Rae Smith, lighting design by Jack Knowles. MARC BRENNER

review Performa 18:15

Row: J S

Upper Centre, enter by

£0.00   Price A

Complim

14
SHOW TIME

DRESS REHEARSALS

Having finished the technical rehearsals, it is usual to do a run-through of the show. This can be a test of everyone's memory, especially if the tech has lasted a couple of weeks, and especially if we've evolved the language of the show over the course of the tech.

The first run can be a disappointing experience, as everyone staggers around trying to remember what they did. Often the language of storytelling will have evolved over the course of the tech, so the first section of the show may feel markedly different in tone from the final. We will be hearing the arc of the show for the first time, in a quieter auditorium, with closer to show energy from the performers, and it's likely the volume of everything will need adjusting.

Technical rehearsals may last anywhere from a couple of days to many weeks. The hours are long, and the pressure can mount. You will often accumulate a list of things to do, and you're unlikely to accomplish everything by the time you start the first dress. I'm often careful to set the expectations of the director appropriately, telling them if there are significant things that are work-in-progress or still to be achieved, or places to avoid sitting, so that they know it's still on my agenda.

Some shows may only have time for one dress rehearsal, some may have three. If things have gone hideously wrong you may not get any. Some may have an 'open dress rehearsal', which basically means you have an audience, so it's a show really.

Depending on the complexity of the show and the sound system, I will either stay at my production desk so I can note the input side of the sound design – whether all the microphones, music and sounds are at the right level – or, if I'm happy with that side of things, I might move around the auditorium so as to note the output side of the sound design – knowing I've got it sounding good at my production desk, is it sounding just as good everywhere else? It's difficult to note both the input and output side of your sound design simultaneously, but sometimes this is inevitable.

The dress rehearsal is where you are essentially surrendering your sound design to the show staff who will run the show. It is important to respect their jobs and to support them so they can take on that responsibility as best they can. Up until now, the sound team will largely have been working to achieve what you have asked of them, and at this point I find it useful to ask of the team what can I do for them – how can I make it easier for them to operate, to react to events? Where could it go wrong, and how can we circumvent that? What do they need?

Sometimes this might be about combining some cues that are too quick in succession. Sometimes it might be about having a chat with the director to ask the cast to be more disciplined in turning up to have their microphones fitted. I can't always accommodate every request, but it is valuable to give the sound team ownership of the design.

I always give my sound operator or No. 1 this briefing:

No one is allowed to tell you to turn anything up or down except me and the director. If anyone gives you any notes, or asks you to make any changes, say you're not allowed to without my permission, and refer them to talk to me or the director.

On larger shows there may often be a lot of producers, each of whom has their own opinions on how the show should sound. Often they tell the sound engineer their opinions, sometimes whilst they are mixing the show itself! Many others will have an opinion that they can't help but express too! It's common to hear different opinions about what a show should sound like – the composer may want the focus to be on the music, the lyricist on the lyrics, the director on the comedy, and so on.

I ensure that I am the central point of contact for all things relating to opinions, as they will often conflict and contradict each other. I can assess those opinions alongside the director's, my own, and that of any other 'stakeholders', and come up with a coherent direction to give to the sound engineer. Mixing a show is difficult enough without people walking up to you and telling you how to do it whilst you're doing it. A director wouldn't give a performer notes during a performance, and we must expect the sound engineer to be treated with the same respect.

A producer telling a sound operator that the whole show needs to be louder is a common but useless request. The overall volume of the show is a fundamental design decision that I and the director have arrived at, probably after much discussion. The 'make it louder' note is often a knee-jerk reaction when they think the show as a whole isn't working. I will try to bypass their note and find out what they think the problem with the show is. If the show feels as if it is lacking energy for a certain section, making it louder isn't the only solution, nor is it necessarily the best one. In this example, there are dozens of reasons for a lack of energy, from basic flaws in the dramaturgical flow of the show, to everyone having had too many drinks the night before.

Start by identifying the root cause, then look for possible solutions. Making it louder may be one, but often that can cause problems itself. Could a little tempo increase solve the issue? Do we have the right music choices? How are we mixing this, can we adjust the flow of the focus of the mix? If we are talking about a musical number, are the lyrics integral to the story, and if so, can we push the band louder and let the lyrics sit back in the mix a bit more? If the lyrics are integral, is the music so loud (either acoustically or amplified) that it's stamping on the lyrics?

It's easy to keep pushing something, anything, everything, louder and louder, hoping to improve it, but often this is just plain wrong, and more often it is pulling other things back in volume that will help. This is because we derive energy and excitement from dynamics. Often something that is constantly loud just becomes boring and loud. If we can find a way to vary the volume, we can create interest through a series of crescendos.

PREVIEWS

Most shows in the UK and USA will have a preview period – a number of performances where the show is performed to the public (sometimes at a reduced ticket price) and the creative team make changes to the show, sometimes minor, sometimes major, to make it work as well as possible.

Something that works well in rehearsals can fall flat in front of an audience. What seems clear to us, may be completely misunderstood by the audience. Some shows require minor script rewrites, some major. Some shows may have scenes entirely cut or re-ordered. *Spider-Man: Turn Off The Dark* famously had 182 preview performances before its opening night, to deal with performer injuries, script rewrites and a change of the creative team, including the director. It's more common to have a week or two of previews, maybe three weeks on a big show where the producers want to give themselves the opportunity to make more significant changes.

Some European theatres, following opera scheduling, may not have previews at all, instead having an open dress rehearsal followed immediately by the première. This is a highly stressful model, as you only have one show to try it in front of an audience before (a) your contract expires, and (b) the press come to review your work.

Audience members are strong acoustic absorbers, which means a full auditorium can sound vastly different from an empty auditorium, especially if there are plastic (reflective) seats rather than fabric (absorbing) seats. The reverberation time of the auditorium decreases due to this, and the sound won't travel quite as far or with as much power as it did in an empty theatre because the audience soak up the sound – known as the 'grazing' effect. We often find we have to turn everything up 3dD when the audience come in. They also laugh and clap at various moments, making some things inaudible.

Meanwhile the performers are adrenalized, and are suddenly performing louder than they ever have before. If they're using handheld microphones they'll suddenly start talking an inch closer to them than they have previously. The whole balance of sound often has to change over the first few previews to accommodate these factors.

On the first preview sit somewhere close to where you've been plotting from, so you can get a measure of how what you've been hearing in an unoccupied theatre is changed by having an audience in it.

Don't sit next to the director: they will talk to you, which isn't helpful if you are listening for things.

When you get notes from a director or anyone else, find out where they are sitting, as this gives you an idea of whether their note relates to the content in general – the inputs – or specifically to the area they are sitting in – the outputs – particularly if you've not yet had the chance to sit in that part of the auditorium. For example, in some auditoriums you get a bass trap effect under the balconies, where the bass can seem more

THE EBB AND FLOW OF PREVIEWS

The first preview is often fuelled by adrenalin. The show is fresh in everyone's mind from the tech and the dress rehearsal. By the end, everyone is relieved to have got through it in one piece.

Second previews are often a massive disappointment. The adrenalin is gone, and the tiredness from tech week is more tangible. The sparkle from the previous night will be missing, and more things will go wrong. Everyone will search for other causes of blame, but often it is simply second preview syndrome. It's perfectly normal, and the following show normally picks up. Sometimes something will go so badly wrong in the second preview that the adrenalin is forced to kick in again, but this just delays the syndrome to the following show.

The preview following a day off can also be tricky, as the day-after-day examination of the material has been broken by a day off. You'll also come in with fresh ears, and potentially question the sound choice you've made so far. A little objectivity can be useful, but also quite undermining.

present than further forwards, even if the sub-bass speakers are at the front. In some venues, the bass might not get under the balcony. If a note relates to bass levels then it might not be that the bass is too loud or too quiet in general, but that it might be too loud or too quiet in a certain part of the auditorium.

I encourage the director not to sit somewhere I haven't yet had the chance to fully balance, otherwise they're going to give me notes about one auditorium zone that may not apply elsewhere. The balcony or the rear of the auditorium are often the zones where the sound is most different from the middle of the stalls, and where it is likely I sat at my production desk.

Most production schedules mean that you have a preview every night, so the available time to make changes to the show is limited. On a typical day you may only get four or so hours onstage to work.

During previews, members of the press are invited to a photo call, to take photos and occasionally video clips, to be used alongside reviews, features and other news items. We are often asked to provide audio to video cameras for these.

Making major changes is risky when you have a preview that night, so it's always good to make sure you have a backup, or some way back to the previous version in case the new version doesn't work either. It's paramount to avoid jeopardizing that night's show. I prioritize dealing with anything that has gone seriously wrong the previous night, followed by notes from the director, followed by my notes and anyone else's.

We can all be quite sensitive and prickly after a performance if it hasn't gone to plan. Directors can be particularly prone to this – some more than others – and their notes may verge on the accusatory if the sound has, in their opinion, messed up their show. I'll often accept and concede the

note, even if I don't necessarily agree with it, rather than contradicting or challenging an emotionally charged director in the public forum of a notes session. Instead I'll say 'Yes, we can look at that', and if necessary come back the following day when the director is calmer with something like 'I've had a think overnight and I'm not sure that'll work…'. Of course, sometimes we do absolutely have to stand our ground, but pick your moments wisely.

When something does go wrong, don't start looking to cast blame. We're all in this together. Look how to fix it, and how to avoid it in the future. What can you do for the sound department to make their jobs easier so that if something goes wrong, they have some spare capacity to deal with it? When something goes wrong for your fellow creative team members, support them, rather than throwing them under the bus.

It's important to distinguish between notes and mistakes: a note is something that you'd like to be better but isn't necessarily wrong. A mistake is when something's gone wrong and the audience are aware of that. Keep perspective between the two.

When something is undeniably your fault, apologize for it. Or even if it's not directly your fault, remember *you* are ultimately responsible for the sound of the show. Don't be defensive, don't falsely blame technical issues, don't avoid the issue. These all make you appear less competent. Own the mistakes. Show you care about mistakes happening. Show some vulnerability. Apologize again, and find out how to avoid it happening again.

This is not to say you should passively accept blame for everything that goes wrong. Often when things go wrong it is as much the result of someone else's actions as our own. Some mistakes will be so big there will be consequences to them. One of the biggest disasters of my professional career was on an event where I was mixing the live sound. A large number of things went wrong with the sound, and everyone, including myself, was very unhappy about it.

Ultimately I was responsible for it sounding bad, but the post-mortem largely consisted of me explaining to many departments that whilst nine times out of ten we can make things sound good in difficult circumstances, if they were going to prioritize the needs of the sound department last in every decision they made, then sooner or later they would hit the one time out of ten when we couldn't. Of course, I had to accept culpability for not fighting harder against the compromises they made in their decisions: whilst the blame was to be shared round, the responsibility was ultimately mine.

DEALING WITH DISASTERS

Sometimes things go really wrong. Reputations can be hurt. Bad reviews can be written. People can get hurt. We do all make mistakes, and some of them can have bad repercussions. We have to learn to deal with these. Some mistakes are easy to get over. They may have affected the show but nobody got hurt. Go to the dressing rooms and apologize to all the cast concerned, explain what happened, and assure them that we'll make sure it doesn't happen again. As I've said, show your concern, that you are upset, not just that it's happened, but that it has affected them. I'll apologize to the director, the producers and anyone else.

The way others respond to your mistakes is determined not just by what went wrong, but also by how sensitively you have dealt with it afterwards and how well you have communicated with those affected. Consider how many times you've been made angrier by a minor thing someone has done, which they dealt with badly afterwards, or which they've attempted to cover up.

If we've had a big sound issue during a preview, I have on occasion asked the director if I can speak to the whole cast in the notes session the following day to apologize. If relevant, this can also be a good moment to talk about how we might all work together to stop it happening again – for example, by being on time for microphone checks before the start of each show. The focus, though, should be on apologizing, about putting yourself out there to the cast. Show that you feel vulnerable.

DEALING WITH ANGER

In the aftermath of a show that's gone horribly wrong you may get shouted at. An adrenalized performer who has just been left high and dry onstage by you and your department may well be justifiably angry and humiliated. Or it could be a producer or director who has a lot riding on the production. Sometimes the cause of someone's anger or frustration may not be so obvious, or have anything to do with the sound. Sometimes you may just be the nearest person. Sometimes these outbursts are unintended, one-off events, and apologies may be forthcoming after the show. But sometimes these can be signs of underlying pressures that can lead to a bigger event down the line and should be addressed as soon as possible.

The more you encounter people working in stressful environments, the faster you'll start to recognize the warning signs of someone who is about to reach critical mass, and hopefully be able to head things off before that – though we're often not in control of all the factors, so sometimes we have to deal with the fallout. Outbursts may happen immediately before, during or after the show. Before and during the show are difficult moments as everyone is in the middle of a time-critical job. This can also be a difficult moment to consider an appropriate response, and often we feel the need to get through the situation as best we can until after the show – though this can, of course, be a situation that some people take advantage of.

If you find yourself the target of someone's anger, there is a range of tactics that you could try – though not every tactic will work with every personality or situation you come across.

- Listen constructively, nodding, making affirmative sounds to their concerns
- Show you empathize with their situation, and are concerned both for it, and for them
- Ask for more details to show you are listening, that they are being listened to
- Ask if they have any suggestions as to how to solve the problem, if that is appropriate
- If it's within your power, look to see if there is a way to remedy the situation, if that is appropriate. Sometimes it's not within our power, but showing that you are on their side can decrease the odds of them directing their anger at you in the future
- Don't devalue or downplay the situation or their anger, or make jokes about it. You may be able to make a quip further down the line to de-escalate the situation, but doing it too soon can do the opposite

The in-the-middle-of-the-show version is 'I'm so sorry that happened. Let's talk it through afterwards so we can make sure it doesn't happen again.' The tactic is to de-escalate the situation so we can talk about it calmly later. If we think the person is at fault, or is mistaken, it can be expedient to wait until a later time to make that point, when they are calmer, and more likely to concede the point.

If you see someone verbally abusing someone else and you need to intervene, there seem to be a few agreed tactics to de-escalate the situation – though obviously, if you feel to do so would also impact your own personal safety you should consider other solutions.

- Talk calmly to the person being verbally abusive, saying their name, and making eye contact. Slow down the speed of the conversation
- Keep your body language relaxed, open and peaceable
- Don't initially engage in the subject of the argument, so they don't change the target of their abuse to you
- Don't tell them to 'calm down' unless you like someone screaming *'I AM CALM!'* at you
- Make them aware: 'Geoff, the way you're treating this person is unacceptable.' (Don't say 'unprofessional' as that is insulting, and more likely to escalate the situation)
- Once you have taken their attention away from the person they're abusing, you can use the tactics above of listening constructively to their problem, empathizing, and listening to their solutions. The priority is to de-escalate first, and then deal with the matter in a calmer way later

Working out how to respond in the best way to such a situation requires a consideration of who they are and your existing relationship to them, their employment position in the staff hierarchy as compared to you, how rational they are being, and how severe you judge their behaviour to be.

If you feel someone is crossing the line, the company manager is usually the first point of contact, and most companies have disciplinary procedures and anti-bullying policies that can be brought to bear on this.

Being an Intermediary

It is your job, in some but not all regards, to act as an intermediary between the sound department and the director, producers, and so on. Sometimes this can be how you translate the words and thoughts of a director into a reality. Sometimes it can be helping to negotiate fair wages. Sometimes this can be protecting the sound team from a stressed director who isn't happy with how things are progressing.

'It felt as if you were more on their side than mine!' This was once said to me by a director whom I felt was being unjustly harsh on the sound team. Being harsh with people rarely gets a better performance out of them. Due to the employment hierarchy the sound department may not feel that they can push back against the director or producer. That's my job, should the need arise. Of course, if someone is not doing their job well, or deliberately not doing what is asked of them, that is a different matter.

It is important to check in with the sound team who are running backstage and dealing first hand with the performers. When things go wrong, they are often the first representative of the sound department that an angry performer will meet, and they can end up being shouted at instead. Most sound people can deal with an outburst like this as they are rarely personal. But we have to ensure that this doesn't become a regular thing – it can't become a pattern of abuse where someone thinks they can vent their fury with the world at the sound department, because they think they can get away with it. It's important to get staff to log any events that happen in case it does become a pattern.

It's rare that you will be the legal employer of the sound staff, so the actual employment hierarchy will exist aside from your relationship with the sound department. But it remains important to be looking out for your team's wellbeing and stress levels, as often their actual employer won't be in a position to monitor every part of the workplace.

Shows are often 'unavoidably' stressful, and your team will be used to, and good at, performing under stress. Look out for signs that people aren't coping with the pressures. You can't necessarily fix things, but an awareness can mean you are at least not making things worse, and at best can support them further, and if necessary can raise the matter with the appropriate parties.

Developing Resilience

When we design a show, we are making ourselves vulnerable, putting ourselves out there creatively, both within our working relationships and in the public eye/ear, to be judged, to be reviewed, to be awarded awards. Which is all lovely when it goes well. But we also have to take the bad reviews and the knocks to our reputation when things don't go well.

I have done shows that have gone so badly, or worked with people with such destructive personalities, that I've been left having anxiety dreams and self-doubt for months afterwards. It's easy for these things to get lodged in our brain. We may get ourselves locked in a loop searching for causes or blame, or rightly or wrongly, blaming ourselves. 'What if I'd done… instead? What could I have done differently? How could I have avoided that?' Sometimes these can be valid questions that can provide useful answers, and constructive ways forwards. But sometimes these can create a mental loop that we struggle to escape, that can affect our ability to work on other projects.

There are many strategies for moving past these sorts of situations and thought loops. You can find many of these by doing a web search for 'developing resilience'. I find that my industry friends and colleagues can often provide perspective, support and humour to ease the way through these times. Everyone has made really bad mistakes, and we've all had jobs go horribly, horribly wrong.

Theatre is predominantly a joyful, fun place to work, so hopefully you'll only need the information in this section on rare occasions – but it's good to know how to stop mistakes and anxieties from escalating into more serious issues.

Why Does it Sound Different Tonight?

Live theatre means that every single performance of a show is different every night, whether we want it to be or not. That can be because someone says a line differently, or there's an understudy on, or a deputy musician, or someone different is mixing the show, or because the not-silent air conditioning is on, or someone is standing in a slightly different place on stage, or it's November and the entire audience have come down with colds, or half the cast are coming down with colds, or one of a dozen other factors. All the performers, all the musicians, all the effects, they all come through the sound desk, so it is usually us who are asked 'Why does it sound different tonight?' And sometimes it really doesn't sound different, but because of people's moods or differing levels of attention on different nights, it will sound different to them. That is part of the joy of the subjectivity of sound, and something we have to embrace!

Sometimes it does sound different and it is our doing, and we have to acknowledge that. If we pretend we are perfect and flawless, no one will believe us, and their trust in us will diminish. Own up to mistakes, or acknowledge that you have changed something (to make it sound better, or for whatever reason you've changed it), explain what you've done in a non-patronizing way, and

show that the action you're taking is to improve the show, because you love the show.

'I'm sorry if it sounds different to you onstage, but it sounds so much better out front. Is it worse onstage, or just different? Do you think you can get used to it?'

Sometimes it sounds different because of the audience. A full house will soak up a lot of the sound, and less will slap-back on to the stage, eliciting 'Was my mic turned on?' comments. A half-full auditorium will sound echoey, with more slap-back, and we'll be closer to feeding back. A Wednesday matinée audience will be quieter, less responsive than a Saturday night audience – and audience response is often a factor in how performers judge how much energy they put into their performance, which again can change the sound.

Whilst you can choose to ignore the question, or be irritated by it, actually it is often a good opportunity to explain to the person who is asking, the complexities of what we're dealing with. That either ends up with someone being better educated about what you do, and how what they do affects the sound of the show, or someone so bored they won't bother to ask next time....

TAKING NOTES

It's important to be able to take notes about how your sound design sounds during a performance. You need to do this at speed, precisely, and in a way that you can decode the following day. You can use your thumb to keep track of the empty space in your notebook where you can write your next note. You shouldn't need a torch or any form of distracting light, as you don't need to look at the page in order to write.

Be consistent with how you phrase your notes. A useful note will likely start with a reference to who the note is for (unless it's for yourself). If I can see QLab, for example, during a dress rehearsal, I'll write down the relevant SQ number.

It's important to include a reference to when in the show the note relates – if you don't know the scene numbers, find some other unique descriptor. In the heat of the show, you may not be able to identify the source of a problem, so don't be afraid to make a note to ask the DSM or sound operator what happened.

After the show, ask if the operator has any notes for you: perhaps some cues that could be combined, or something that can be rejigged to make their job more efficient. They may well have spotted something artistically that you haven't noticed. Be open to ideas from them, or any other members of your team. They are people with sharp ears who will be listening to it differently to you.

Never give an operator bad notes within ten minutes of the end of a performance. Respect them as a performer, and treat them the way a good director would treat the performers. Give them positive feedback, and save the bad notes for a bit later. A director wouldn't tell a performer they did a bad job the second they walked off stage, and neither should you do the same to a sound operator. If you need to cool off, take a walk outside and come back in a more civil mood. The sound operator will hopefully be as engaged and adrenalized by operating a performance as one of the performers. Or, even if it is only a simple show, they should be emotionally invested in it, and in doing their job well. Even if they have done a bad job, they probably know it and are feeling plenty bad about it without you taking out your disappointment on them. Treat them with professional respect.

If a sound operator isn't getting sufficient breaks, sleep, food, time to write up their script, consolidate what you've asked them to do, or practise, then they can't do a good job. Obviously they are responsible for their own wellbeing, but your actions go a long way to getting a good performance out of them.

Mixing many microphones and instruments is a complex job and can take the best operator a couple of weeks to get the hang of. Go easy on them in the early days until they've had a chance to do their thing. Do, of course share your vision of how you want it to sound, but don't criticize them because they missed the first few words of a sentence on the first preview. Remember how the best directors are the ones who tell you what they want rather than how to do it, a good sound designer-operator relationship means you can tell them what you want to achieve, and they can work out how to achieve it.

I don't tend to note sound ops on dropped lines unless the same ones happen repeatedly, or I think they're distracted by something else happening. Most sound ops know more about the mistakes they made than I do. There's no point driving something home they already know about.

We're all human, we all make mistakes. I have made some huge mistakes in my time as an operator, whether by accident (I accidentally kicked the power off to the mixing desk with my foot mid-show) or incompetence (I wasn't paying attention to the show, and didn't notice a mic had started feeding back into a low continuous howl for a good minute… on press night… of a show in the West End). The more pressure you put on someone, the more mistakes they're likely to make. It's fine to make a mistake. What we don't want is for them to make a second and third mistake because they're worrying about the first mistake they made.

The following day, when I'm executing my notes, I tick off the ones I've actioned. I'll maintain a list of cues to check later if I've not had the chance to listen to them all (perhaps because rehearsals are happening on stage). I try to check important sequences, but sometimes there just isn't time. I have made mistakes and had to live with hearing them during the performance. It's always good to weigh up the risk versus the reward of making a last-minute change. Some performances, ones with critics present for example, will be riskier to make changes to than others.

BACKUPS AND CONTINGENCIES

Theatre is live and doesn't always go to plan. The best way to deal with this is to have backups and contingency plans in place. The extent of these plans will depend on how complex and integral your design is to the show. There may even be a clause in your contract that you will implement backup systems. The producers are understandably keen that when something breaks down there isn't a need to cancel the show and refund tickets.

There are three main potential problems we have to contend with: when the show goes outside what we have rehearsed in the technical period, equipment failure, and staff illness.

GOING OUTSIDE PARAMETERS

What if an actor suddenly forgets a whole lot of lines that contain sound and other cues, meaning that cues potentially need to be jumped? Or if a scene change speeds up to the point that it is much shorter than we had planned it might be? Many of these sorts of problem can be dealt with by the way we program our show, and how we brief the DSM and operators. In the middle of a show it can seem like a good idea to skip over sound cues if an actor has jumped over several lines, but often a sound cue may be doing more

than the most obvious thing it is doing. It might also be changing less noticeable elements of the underscore. If you skip the cue you may well end up missing the fade out of some infinitely looping underscore element that will then continue to play for the rest of the show. It's important to label your cues, and have your sound operator and DSM know what they do, so they can work out intelligently how to respond. Generally I say that sound cues shouldn't be skipped if in a fast-moving sequence. If there is time for the sound operator to fix things more subtly, then fine, but there rarely is.

During previews, a big scene change might take forty-five seconds to complete. I may build up a scene change that has lots of elements starting at different times to make this long scene change more interesting.

In the screenshot illustrated, the programming will work well for our forty-second version of the scene change. A month after press night, when I'm long gone, the crew might have got this scene change down to twenty seconds. But with my original programming, if the scene change takes less than thirty-five seconds, SQ48 will try to fade out 'Ambulance ride from interior POV filtered' before it has started playing and so won't do anything, then 'Ambulance ride from interior POV filtered' will start playing after we start the next scene.

In the second screenshot, the programming ensures that no matter where we are in SQ47, everything will be faded out regardless.

Number	Q		Target	Pre Wait ❯
47	▼ Scene Change			00:00.00
	Scene Change music		⬆	00:00.00
	Heart attack montage		⬆	00:05.00
	Ambulance arriving stylised v4		⬆	00:20.00
	Ambulance ride from interior POV filtered		⬆	00:35.00
48	▼ End of Scene Change			00:00.00
	fade and stop Scene Change music		Scene Change...	00:00.00
	fade and stop Ambulance ride from interior POV filtered		Ambulance rid...	00:00.00

Several elements might be added to a scene change to keep it interesting if it is running longer than we hoped.

Number	Q		Target	Pre Wait ❯
47	▼ Scene Change			00:00.00
	Scene Change music		⬆	00:00.00
	Heart attack montage		⬆	00:05.00
	Ambulance arriving stylised v4		⬆	00:20.00
	Ambulance ride from interior POV filtered		⬆	00:35.00
48	▼ End of Scene Change			00:00.00
	fade and stop Scene Change		47	00:00.00

Ensure that you program your show in a way that it will fade everything that possibly might be running, even if you don't think it will still be running.

EQUIPMENT FAILURE

Having two of everything just in case something breaks isn't financially viable, so we tend to focus on what is most likely to fail. Cables are a potential failure point, but it is reasonably easy to keep a stock of spare cables and adaptors, and to run in spare cables between certain locations so we can quickly swap to a spare.

We can safeguard against a crashing computer by running a second alongside it, with a way to switch between them. If the budget is tight, then you can produce a stereo version of the show that can play off a CD player or solid-state equivalent, though this is less satisfactory and is time-consuming to make.

It is reasonably common to 'double mic' lead performers in a show, so they wear two radio microphone transmitters and two microphone capsules. This adds extra weight and bulk to what they are wearing, but if you have a performer who is onstage for nearly the whole show, or only has short periods of time offstage, this is the only way to back up their radio microphone.

Wireless speakers commonly consist of an IEM receiver, a battery, an amplifier, a speaker and an on/off switch (in case it suddenly picks up interference and starts making horrible untuned radio-type sounds). With so many components, they are liable to failure, especially if they are being carried around in a prop, disguised as a baby.... It's common to route a backup of those sound effects to the nearest wired speaker. It won't sound great, but it may be better than not having the sound effect at all. You can patch the audio input that feeds the wireless speaker into an additional mixer input channel, add some EQ to make it sound similar, and have the channel fader turned down. The operator can just fade this additional channel up to make the backup version audible.

Some equipment will break in the course of a show from normal use, due to ageing, poor design or lack of maintenance. The most common time for a failure to occur is when an item is powered up. It's important that the sound team carry out sound system checks early enough each day that if a problem occurs they have enough time to fix it, source a spare, or implement a workaround. Having some spares onsite and some tools to do basic repairs is essential. Many hire companies provide same-day emergency delivery if their kit fails, so long as you are reasonably close to them.

It is common for touring shows to tour spare components of smaller items of critical equipment. If you are touring internationally, are you touring equipment that can be easily replaced, repaired or otherwise supported where you are going?

It is always useful to have access to a big master mute button that can mute all the amplifiers, just in case we get such a horrible equipment malfunction after the mixing desk

HOT SPARES AND COLD SPARES

A 'hot' spare is a spare piece of equipment that you keep in the rack, plugged in, turned on, configured with the current show file and ready to go. This has the advantage that you lose little time in swapping to the spare. But it does, of course, mean that it is ageing at the same rate as the equipment it is backing up, and receiving the same mains spikes and fluctuations too, which means that whatever caused your main equipment to fail, could affect the spare in the same way.

A 'cold' spare isn't plugged in. Whilst it may be virtually pristine when you come to need it, it can take longer to swap in and get working.

that there's no easy way to mute everything otherwise. This is increasingly the case in our audio-over-networking world where a single tick of a check box can inadvertently route a microphone to an amplifier, something that wasn't possible in the old era of analogue and conventional digital audio.

As we head into an ever-computerized world, where everything is connected by networking cables, having backup network switches is essential.

We also have to plan for more unexpected circumstances. I have come into a theatre on one occasion to discover that someone had stolen the mixing desk that morning. And on another occasion to discover that someone had stolen the main and backup QLab computers over the weekend. In the latter we'd considered it sufficient to back up the main computer by copying the show files to the backup computer, but fortunately we had also made a backup to one of our laptops.

It is also worth planning contingencies should another department have an equipment failure. Items of moving set, 'automation', often break down, or can only move at a reduced speed: are your scene-change cues long enough to cope with a scene change suddenly taking twice as long as normal?

If we suddenly need to stop the show for whatever reason we might need a means for a stage manager to make an announcement over the sound system, particularly if they're not able to make it onstage. When a show has to stop mid-performance, the problem that caused it can often be rectified fairly quickly. What takes more time is getting everyone ready to start again from whichever point we've nominated to resume from. This is where it's useful that your DSM and sound operator know what all the cues do – hopefully they'll be able to pick up the threads of what should be playing at that point, and get everything going.

STAFF ILLNESS

In the preview period every staff member is still working out what their role entails, and how they do it. This means that staff illness, or compassionate leave, during previews is difficult to handle, and there aren't really many ways to mitigate that because everyone is often working at full capacity just doing their normal jobs. If the operator falls ill during previews or has a family bereavement they need to attend, it's fairly common for the sound designer or associate to take over in their absence, as they are likely to be the only other person who knows what is supposed to be happening. I've done it a few times – it's terrifying.

Beyond press night, it's common for the sound department to start learning each other's roles so that when someone is absent, the show can carry on. It's important to make sure that your shows are as easy to learn as possible – that doesn't mean they need to be easy to operate, they can be as complex as you need them to be – but it does mean that everything should be programmed and labelled in a clear and understandable way.

In the West End, simpler plays may often be operated by a DSM. This is always a cost-saving measure. However, whilst it can work fine when everything is working, the DSM often lacks the skills to troubleshoot or fix things when they go wrong. Often the hire company will have a technical support number they can call to resolve simple problems. I always program the DSM and company manager's mobile phone number into my phone, so if I get a call from them between 6pm and 7pm I know something might have gone wrong and I need to answer the call.

Part of the fun of live theatre is that anything can and will happen. Whilst we can't prepare for every eventuality, we can prepare for the likely ones. We can then enjoy that 'liveness' knowing that we are ready to deal with it.

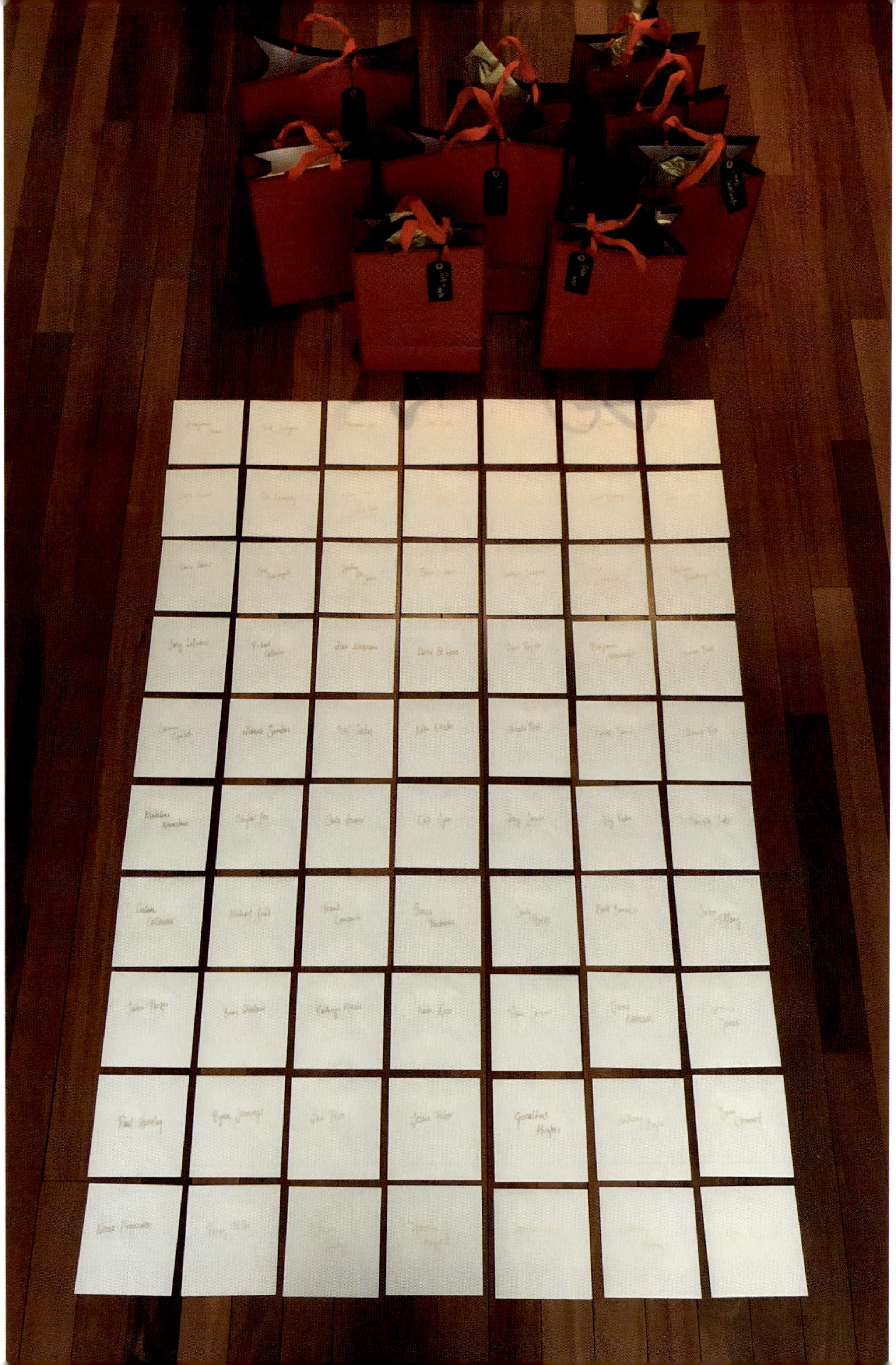

15
PRESS NIGHT AND BEYOND

PRESS NIGHT/
OPENING NIGHT

As previews progress, the show will settle closer to its final form.

Press night (UK), or opening night (US), is typically your last chance to change anything with the show. Some directors like to work up until then, some like to lock off or freeze the show before critics start arriving so the performers are stable in what they're doing.

Opening nights are always strange affairs. The audience is often not a typical 'normal' audience – they're not there because they wanted to see that particular show, but more likely because they are someone's friend or family. Press night audiences laugh in different places, and more raucously compared to a normal audience.

Press nights are traditionally a time for giving presents and cards to your team and anyone else who may have significantly contributed. You don't have to spend a fortune, but a token of your appreciation can go a long way to you being made welcome next time you work there. I'll sometimes write cards for the cast depending on how much I've interacted with them. Plan this a few days ahead so it isn't a stress on the day.

This night also typically marks the end of the sound designer's contract.

OPPOSITE: Writing out all your press-night cards can take a while if you have a large cast.

ARCHIVING, TRANSFERS
AND TOURING

Archiving your work is important for many reasons:

- It is the ultimate backup of the show, should anything happen to the copies held at the theatre
- It is your record of how you left the show at press night. Should it be adjusted by someone after you leave, with or without your approval, then this is the reference point to return to
- For future shows, you'll inevitably want to do something similar to what you've just done. Your archive can save you reinventing the wheel in the future. That said, what didn't work for this show might work in a future show
- You never know when a show might be toured, transferred or revived. *Harvest*, by Richard Bean, premièred at the Royal Court in 2005. Despite a successful run, there wasn't discussion of a future life. Then four years later, the production was revived. Fortunately I had the files, so it was easy. As we saw from *The Barbershop Chronicles*, a show can go through many incarnations and many hands, so documenting it is the only way that people down the line will know what you want

Your archive should contain the backups of every show-related file you can find. It should also contain as much paperwork as possible. Many changes may happen over fit-up and tech, so update your paperwork to incorporate these. This prevents you from repeating the same mistakes in the future, or omitting things you added after you generated the paperwork.

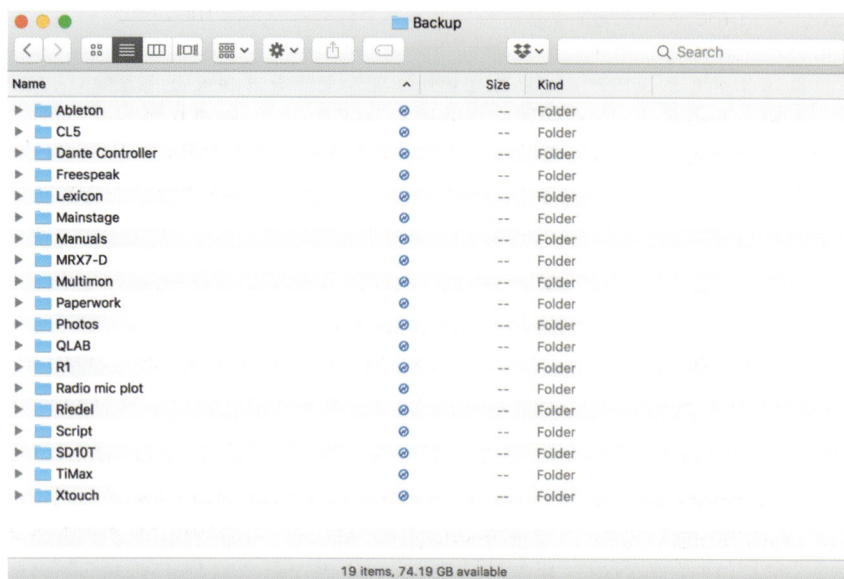

Name		Size	Kind
▶ 📁 Ableton	⊘	--	Folder
▶ 📁 CL5	⊘	--	Folder
▶ 📁 Dante Controller	⊘	--	Folder
▶ 📁 Freespeak	⊘	--	Folder
▶ 📁 Lexicon	⊘	--	Folder
▶ 📁 Mainstage	⊘	--	Folder
▶ 📁 Manuals	⊘	--	Folder
▶ 📁 MRX7-D	⊘	--	Folder
▶ 📁 Multimon	⊘	--	Folder
▶ 📁 Paperwork	⊘	--	Folder
▶ 📁 Photos	⊘	--	Folder
▶ 📁 QLAB	⊘	--	Folder
▶ 📁 R1	⊘	--	Folder
▶ 📁 Radio mic plot	⊘	--	Folder
▶ 📁 Riedel	⊘	--	Folder
▶ 📁 Script	⊘	--	Folder
▶ 📁 SD10T	⊘	--	Folder
▶ 📁 TiMax	⊘	--	Folder
▶ 📁 Xtouch	⊘	--	Folder

19 items, 74.19 GB available

Your archive should contain the backups of every single show-related file you can find. It should also contain as much paperwork about the show as possible.

I often do a post-mortem of my work: if we were to do this production again, what would I do better? What were the mistakes I made, how could I have foreseen them or circumvented them? What changes would I make to the content, system or staffing for a future revival?

Once you've archived your show, have a look through to see if you've created anything useful that could be upcycled into a future show. Maybe it's a sound file, or maybe an effects preset. What can you take from this show to make your workflow faster next time?

If you have a gap between projects, this can often be utilized to find ways to optimize your workflow, explore the features of your software and hardware, learn new skills, update your website and biog, see more shows, films and exhibitions, read more books, do your taxes, free up space on your hard drive, and so on.

ADAPTING A STAGE SOUND DESIGN FOR BROADCAST

At some point, someone will probably turn up with a video camera to make a trailer, advert or something similar. These are often referred to as 'electronic press kits' (EPKs). It is becoming increasingly common for theatre productions to be televised, broadcast to cinemas, or live-streamed. Some people take a hands-off approach to this, but I've had a few of my designs murdered in the process, so now I get involved even if I'm not paid to be, as it often reflects my work badly if I don't.

For basic press calls and EPKs, typically they just want a mono or stereo feed of 'everything'. When they ask for a mono feed, they are usually planning to have their own rifle microphone going into their other record channel to get atmospheric sounds of the theatre. Often they will want it without music so they can edit more easily – or to simplify copyright clearance.

For more complex broadcasts it is typical that there will be a television sound team, perhaps with a sound truck parked outside, who will install microphones in the auditorium to get the sound of audience responses; it is also likely that they will want to get individual microphone channels from you so they can make a broadcast mix.

A broadcast mix often sounds quite different from a theatre mix, as we often incorporate the room acoustics, the direct unamplified sound of the performers and musicians, and the way the loudspeaker system changes the sound into our mix.

Our radio microphones often have more EQ on them than a broadcast mix might have, and we might use different gain settings.

Sending a split of all the microphones used to be quite convoluted, but now is easy, and can just be a case of handing them an ethernet cable from our system.

If the show is radio mic'd, then at least we will have a decent feed of the performers' voices to send to the sound truck. Float microphones rarely provide the closeness of mic'ing that is desired for broadcast, particularly on an empty stage or in a more reverberant space. For a non-reinforced show we often need to radio mic our performers for broadcast purposes. If you're just filming a short section this can be relatively easy, but if you're doing the entire show this can be problematic to incorporate into all the physical movement and costume changes that have been tech'd without radio microphones. Some shows may be fine, others may be very difficult. If the broadcast isn't going out live, rather than the typical method of putting radio mics in the performer's hairline, we may instead have mics hidden under their costumes on their lapels, and suchlike. Whilst this position doesn't work for theatre reinforcement, they can do corrective EQ and volume automation in post-production to smooth out volume inconsistencies, and of course they don't have feedback to worry about.

The sound effects can be trickiest to translate to a stereo or 5.1 mix. Often, we will have mixed our sounds so they sound good out of the speaker they're playing out of, positioned somewhere around the stage, reaching the audience having travelled a certain distance. If we just route our sound effects straight into the mix they will often sound far too present. If I know a production is going to be broadcast I will often assign four outputs from QLab specifically for this purpose. Two of them will be a straightforward stereo mix of my design and will feature everything that can

happily route straight into that mix, and the other two will go through some FX processing to muffle the sounds (such as TDR Labs' Proximity plug-in). I'll go through the show and mix those QLab outputs over a small pair of speakers so it sounds good to me. It may often have less extremes of volume than the theatre mix. By creating this mix, rather than giving the sound truck dozens of QLab outputs, I retain more control over how I want the broadcast to sound.

A common problem I've encountered with television people mixing live theatre shows into a surround sound format is that they always add a great deal of audience ambience and room acoustic into the surround channels. Whilst this can sound fine over a 5.1 system, if that mix is broadcast on television or put online, most people will listen in stereo, and many set-top boxes will fold the surround channels into the stereo mix making the whole thing sound hideously ambient.

It's important to get into the sound truck to have a listen to their mix, or to get a copy of their first post-production pass, so that you can give them notes and steer them towards how it should sound. There are some broadcast sound teams who 'do' theatre a lot and are great at translating a theatre show into something that works on screen. However, most broadcast sound teams don't do theatre often and need guidance. I will endeavour to provide this nicely, respectfully and professionally.

FINAL IMPRESSIONS

How you terminate a project – your final impression – is as important as your first impression. To make a career out of sound design you need to get repeat work: the same directors, producers, venues or production managers need to want to employ you again, and again. It is therefore important at the end of a project to make sure the director knows that you are proud of the end product, that you've enjoyed working with them, and that you'd like to work with them again in the future – assuming all of that is true!

Technical rehearsals and preview periods can be stressful for everyone, and strains could have been put on you, and your relationship with the director. There could have been dramatic issues that the director asked you to fix, perhaps even at the expense of the concept of the design. There may have been many last minute requests, or a change in conceptual direction, any of which may have made you appear to be stressed out by what the director has asked of you. It's important to point out that you actually enjoy stress, enjoy those challenges, or at least you may have been stressed out in the moment but it hasn't deterred you from your working relationship.

It's not uncommon for designers to put on a 'poker face' when talking to a director in a stressful circumstance, maintaining a composure of calm, but consequently you might not have projected much enthusiasm either. This poker face can be useful in many circumstances, but it's important as the pressures ease off, or after the project completes, to express your enthusiasm for the show, and to be proud of what you've created together.

Leave the venue on good terms. It costs little to buy cards or small token presents for the people you've been working with, but it does make a huge difference. Be sure to thank the people who have made your design happen. The DSM may not be part of the sound team, but your design would probably be nothing without their sense of timing and acuity to the performance.

Wrap up with the producer. Send a note with your last invoice. Check in at the end of the run (or at regular intervals for a long run) to make sure that all is running smoothly.

Thank the production manager. They have a thankless task more often than not, marshalling artistic demands with practical realities, and often disappointing someone that something can't be achieved because of time, money or those irritating laws of physics. Production managers often have the most stress, with the least amount of credit and thanks.

There will be times when you aren't able to deliver a good sound design, and rather than leaving under a black cloud, find a way to acknowledge what has happened and why. If it's not your fault, make sure that that is known, but without being rude about other people. If it is your fault, be open, honest and apologetic about it. Even if things haven't gone perfectly, people may well want to work with you again if you're nice to work with.

It should go without saying, but I will say it anyway: treat everyone with respect and decency. Remember that you're in this industry for the long run. There is no excuse for taking out any of your frustrations on others. If you need further reasons for this, remember that the junior admin assistant in the producer's office today could well be the senior producer – your boss – in ten years' time. The assistant director today could some day well be the artistic director of the National Theatre. Those shouldn't be the reasons to be nice to people, but it is worth remembering.

THE END OF THE PROCESS

Sound design can be stressful. The process of creating a show, finding its language, implementing that language, finding out how to deal with moments in the show when the established language doesn't work, integrating your design with the artistic methodologies and concepts of your collaborators (and vice versa), designing and making a sound system sound good, and everything else, can be a messy and turbulent process. You may well come out of designing a project feeling quite exhausted and with some post-achievement depression. That's perfectly normal.

Well done, then, on having made it this far. You probably deserve a cup of tea. But soon it'll be time to repeat the whole process again on the next show.

CODA

I've largely discussed sound design so far within the frame of getting and designing a single show. Let's break that convention.

Your Career

You can qualify being successful as a sound designer in many ways. It may be pragmatically in terms of being able to pay for a roof over your head. It may be to enjoy your work. It may be to be artistically fulfilled. Maybe even all three!

As time goes by, you will develop your aims and goals, directors you'd like to work with, venues you'd like to work at, types of work you'd like to try, amounts of money you'd like to earn.

It's useful to pause every now and again to check how your career is going, whether you are progressing, or are stuck in some fashion. What can you do to change direction better to achieve your goals, or to find better paying work? Do you need to re-evaluate 'Brand You'? Are you getting typecast for doing a certain style of theatre? Is that a good or a bad thing? Do you need to start watching different types of theatre, and meet up for coffee with people who make different work?

Who do you know who works in those areas who could make an introduction?

Your Industry

Being a sound designer can be a lonely job at times. It is virtually unheard of for two sound designers to be employed on the same show. You may never work with another sound designer or see one at work.

On some shows you may be working with a team of other sound engineers, but there will be many times when you are the sole sound person on a show. This can be quite harmful in that you don't learn from others, their experiences, their techniques, their strategies. It's important to find ways to connect with your peers and discuss these. This can be online, or in a bar. There are trade associations you can join, which offer professional development opportunities and social events. In the UK we have the Association of Sound Designers (though it caters for all theatre sound people), and in the USA, the Theatrical Sound Designers and Composers Association. These offer great ways to improve your art and practice, as well as to build up a support and business network.

A nice cup of tea. Other tasty beverages are available.

It can be a daunting process starting out in a freelance profession, but it is important to remember that you are not in this alone. There are others out there facing the same challenges as you. You shouldn't view your peers as your competition, even though they may be striving towards the same jobs. By sharing knowledge and experiences with each other, we all make each other better, and we can support each other.

What we must not deny is that whilst being successful in this career involves ability, diplomacy and a lot of luck, being white, male and middle class is also a big factor to success in the UK and USA currently. Studies show that only one in eight sound designers are women, and they are often not working at the top of the profession; and a vastly smaller ratio still are people of colour. What is perhaps surprising, in this day and age, is that many people in the industry don't acknowledge that this is a problem, or that sexism, racism or privilege is even at play here. Obviously, these are problems that exist across our society, but our industry is lagging behind society, and we have to work to change, to improve our industry.

There are complex reasons behind many of these issues, and our industry associations have to address some of these. But there are some simple solutions, which those of us already in the industry can implement, which is simply to give (or refer) more work to women and people of colour.

Whilst sound designers don't decide who gets sound design jobs, as we get more established in the industry, we do give out opportunities for work placements, mentorships, refer people for design work when we're unavailable, and suggest people for other sound jobs.

This is a gross simplification of a complex subject, but please investigate how you can be a part of changing and improving our industry.

Theatre is a surprisingly fast-moving industry, considering it has been around for thousands of years. It tells many different kinds of stories to many different kinds of audiences. Some stories are incredibly intimate, and others are epic.

Sound design as a job description, as a skill, as an art, means different things to different people. It is a fast-evolving sector, having changed beyond recognition in the past thirty years. I've shared with you a snapshot of my process and aesthetic for my here and now. I hope it provides a useful springboard for you to find your way into the industry, develop your process, and to explore what using sound design to tell stories means to you.

I have tricks in my pocket – I have things up my sleeve – but I am the opposite of a stage magician. He gives you illusion that has the appearance of truth. I give you truth in the pleasant disguise of illusion.

The Glass Menagerie, Tennessee Williams

APPENDIX
INTERVIEWS WITH DISTINGUISHED SOUND DESIGNERS

IAN DICKINSON

Ian is a UK-based Sound Designer with extensive domestic and international credits. He is recognized for work such as Rock & Roll, The Seagull, Jerusalem *and* Angels In America, *both in London and New York. He received an Olivier Award for* The Curious Incident Of The Dog In The Night-time, *which has been critically acclaimed worldwide. Ian has been a member of the Autograph design team since 2009.*

How did you get into the industry?
It was an accident! I needed to do a work placement for my sound course, but I didn't want to do theatre – the thought of middle-class 'luvviedom' filled me with dread. But I did a placement at the Royal Exchange in Manchester. Within a week I knew it was something that I could imagine myself doing. I ended up staying all summer. After uni, I worked at the Library Theatre, and eventually became Deputy HOD at the Exchange. They were good at promoting in-house staff, and one of my first 'proper' designs was there, with an unknown Assistant Director, Marianne Elliott, who became a dear friend and who I still work with today.

Do you have a particular specialism?
I've probably become known as someone who 'only does plays', which isn't true. Most places I've been employed produced their own work, which have mostly been plays. I've just worked on my first 'proper' musical, and though it was immensely stressful I loved the whole experience. It's important to keep trying new things.

What's it like being based out of Autograph?
I love it. I've always worked at places where I've felt part of a big family. Sound design can be a lonely profession sometimes, and to know that if I have an issue – be that a design problem, an equipment failure or a crisis of confidence – there is always someone there who has my back.

Do you have any tips for anyone entering the industry?
Be personable. Be nice. It doesn't cost much yet can help immeasurably in any scenario. You might be the best sound designer on the planet, but if people don't like spending weeks locked in a dark room with you, it will count for nothing.

How do you develop a relationship with a director?

Gauge how the director wants to work with you, and how you can best achieve a result that you'll both be happy with. Be open and honest, and bring up anything that might be worrying you sooner rather than later. I'll suggest some ideas to see how they respond, which will give some indication of how they view the process. See some of their previous work so you have a point of reference.

What's the main source of the sounds you use?

It tends to be a mix of found/library recordings, and location recordings I've made myself. I love doing my own recordings as I can get exactly what I want to record. I live outside London, in a quiet location, which is very helpful.

What's the first decision you make when designing a system?

My initial thought is about the best speaker coverage, then I choose which speakers will fulfil this. Unfortunately, my next thought is usually about budget: it has to be realistic. Then I'll choose the production engineer, who will be critical to the success of my design.

What part of your job do you enjoy the most?

The satisfaction of listening to a piece of my favourite music through a well-tuned system, one I've spec'd and set up, never ceases to make me smile.

What are the issues you face most often?

There's still a lack of understanding of what we do and what we can bring to the party. Some of this is historic, and it is changing, but it leads to varied issues. We're often allocated a smaller proportion of any budgets or are quizzed about why we need so many speakers or microphones or crew! I want my shows to sound good for everyone in the auditorium.

How do you deal with stress?

I try to ensure my teams are enjoying their work, allowing them to be as involved as they want, whilst making myself available at all times to talk. We all ended up in this business because we didn't want the mundane 9-5 routine, so went looking for something more fun. It can be stressful and sometimes I find that debilitating, but I try to keep my team shielded from that. It's important to keep perspective. After all, we're just making a show; we're not saving lives. And remain polite!

DAVID MCSEVENEY

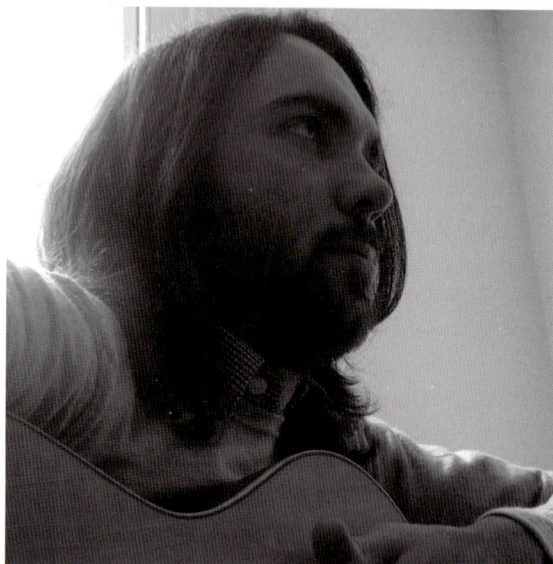

David is a London-based Sound Designer. While Head of Sound at the Royal Court Theatre he has designed over 25 productions, including premieres of plays such as Constellations, for which he was jointly nominated for an Olivier award in 2013. He has worked in West End and Broadway theatres, and for the RSC and the National Theatre. David is a founding member of the Association of Sound Designers.

How did you get into the industry?

I played music in bands as a teenager, which led into setting up PA equipment and recording demos. I also did sound for school productions & amateur companies. I moved to London and completed a theatre sound degree at Central School of Speech & Drama. Whilst there, I did a work placement that introduced me to people, eventually leading to work as an operator with a company that didn't employ sound designers at the time, so I also acted as the sound designer on three of their productions.

Do you have a specific area you like working in?

The Royal Court focuses on new writing, which is an area I enjoy very much. I'm never sure what the next play might be, or the challenges and opportunities for sound design it might bring. I often collaborate with the writer and director to evolve the show.

What's it like being based out of the Royal Court?

Working within a building means variety. I may have a design meeting in the morning, be rigging equipment for another designer in the afternoon and running sound for an event in the evening. Finding time to concentrate on a design can be a challenge, but I'm lucky to have a decent studio and lots of resources that are out of reach of many freelancers – and I get to meet lots of directors and writers. Most interesting, and quite different from being freelance, is that I work with other sound designers, which I find very inspiring.

How do you develop a relationship with a director?

I like to start a creative conversation about a new project without mentioning sound too much. Discussing style, mood, narrative arc, tone, textures, materials, and so on, allows us to find a common understanding earlier on, and makes for a broader conversation that is more useful to me going forward, to start producing demo material.

What's the main source of the sounds you use?

I create work in many different styles, so I source sounds from effects libraries, location recording, Foley, from synthesis… I also work with music and like to use musical elements in non-musical ways. I find I use material I've recorded myself across multiple projects, as I know the sounds so well. It's a great investment to build up your own collection.

What is the first decision you make when designing a system?

I start by working out what the prime reason is for the system in relation to the production. Is it likely to be a sub-heavy show? Is there a need for precise imaging to stage, or for vocal reinforcement? I'll design the rest of the system around this primary reason.

What part of your job you enjoy the most?

It's the opportunity to work on a new production, to design through the challenges of a play that has never been produced before. It's also the collaboration with other departments and disciplines.

What are the issues you face most often?

There are still outposts where sound design is mistrusted, misunderstood and undervalued, but this is getting more rare – it has improved a lot. I do regret that often a Sound Operator is a luxury, and without a sound person on site the ongoing care of a show can suffer.

How do you deal with stress?

Stick to being professional. Theatre can, and should be, an emotive field to work in, but ultimately we all have a professional role to deliver. Equally, make time for other people as humans, not just colleagues.

GARETH OWEN

Gareth has designed over 300 different musicals with an estimated audience approaching fifty million people. He is the recipient of multiple awards and nominations, including Olivier, Tony and Outer Critics awards, and is the winner of the prestigious Pro Sound 'Sound Engineer of the Year' award. His company, Gareth Owen Sound, has offices in London, New York, and Amsterdam. He is married and has two children.

How did you get into the industry?

I did work experience at SSE, who do a lot of live concert tours, and worked my way up to sound engineering, mixing for some really big bands. A friend needed cover mixing *Blues Brothers* in the West End. I didn't know what I was letting myself in for, but moved to London to live in a tent in someone's garden, whilst I learnt on-the-job how to mix a West End show! I got on well with people and was asked to design/engineer *Godspell*. I got a good mention in a review, which led to more work (and got my parents off my back). I worked for Orbital for a while, a theatre hire company, before I went freelance.

Do you have a specialism?

I tend to do commercial musicals where there's a real focus on the music element of the show – a recent example being *Bat Out of Hell*, though they're not all rock 'n' roll shows. The strongest collaborations I've built have been with musical supervisors and composers, and they often ask for me to work on their shows. Music has always been my passion.

You work out of a company, Gareth Owen Sound. What benefits does that offer?

Commercial musicals often have long lives and are replicated across the world. That requires a team of people. I focus on creating new shows that command my complete attention, working with my team for months to create the original version of the show. For future versions, I rely on my Associate team to remount them around the world, and I attend the critical moments in each one's life: the sound check, the early previews and, whenever possible, the opening night party!

Do you have any tips for anyone entering the industry?

Have a unique selling point. I'm unapologetic about amplifying shows. Even older shows can benefit from a modern sound design approach. Build relationships. If you're nice enough to work with, people will give you latitude as you're developing, learning how to do your job. Over time you become better, to the point where people consider you invaluable, and may even refuse to work on a show unless you're onboard with them.

How do you build those relationships?

It's important to acknowledge other people's perspectives. The composer or musical supervisor often know exactly how they want the show to sound, so take their opinion on board. Build a two-way relationship because the music and sound are interrelated. If you finish a show in bad graces with the music department then you've done something wrong – there should always be mutual respect there.

What's the main source of the sounds you use?

I have a well-catalogued sound effects library, and I work a lot with live sources. I'll take those ingredients and extensively process, edit and mix them. *Bat Out of Hell* has a huge soundscape in it. I avoid putting sound effects in rehearsals: it rarely does justice to the end product. Instead, I supply 'filler' sounds, something generic that people won't get attached to, which I'll replace later.

What's your approach to sound system design?

Part of how we can roll out multiple productions worldwide is to use similar equipment configured in a similar way. I, or any of the team, can walk up to any mixing desk and know the drum layout, or how to change the delay times. That familiarity allows us to more easily sculpt the sound so that even with similar equipment, each show sounds uniquely different.

What are your favourite, and least favourite, moments in a show?

The greatest moments are always about the music, and the most frustrating moments are often about the music, too! I get to work with great orchestrations, but bad orchestrations can be a real challenge because there's often no room for the vocals – you have to power them over the music to make them audible – and the end result is never pretty.

Making theatre can be stressful. How do you deal with that?

I always thought I didn't get stressed, and it took a long time to realize the headaches I got were because of stress rather than environmental circumstances. I try to avoid being rude when I'm under stress; it never helps. Everyone reacts differently to stress: some cope well, others don't. It's important to choose your moments carefully – if someone is super stressed, they might not be able to take on board anything you might say. Instead be supportive and available, and pick your moments to try and be helpful.

MELANIE WILSON

Melanie Wilson is an award-winning, multi-disciplinary performance maker. Her work is founded on the contemporary interplay between sound art, experimental forms of composition, language and live performance, and is underpinned by political interest.

How did you get into the industry?

I started in devised theatre, performing, but I was always interested in curating the music, or creating

Photograph courtesy of ALEXANDER BRATTEL

soundscapes, for us to work with. I developed my first designs that way, alongside work I was writing and performing. For about six years I was collaborating with others, and being asked by them to compose and design for them, but I didn't call myself a sound designer or get credited for it. Increasingly that led to being asked to work more formally as a sound designer.

What sort of work do you enjoy?

I'm drawn to work where sound has a strong presence, in a narrative sense, and where there's a blurring between what is music and what is sound, and so I gravitate towards contemporary forms of theatre-making. I like the authorship of composing and designing the whole soundtrack.

How do you find being freelance?

I enjoy being in rehearsals a lot, being part of that process, but that places a financial strain. I'm strategic about the work I do, choosing a few pieces each year to commit time to. There are other pieces I can start later into the process. It's important to be honest with yourself about the pragmatic realities of bills.

Do you have any tips for anyone entering the industry?

Meeting people and building relationships is key. Students write to me to ask if they can sit in rehearsals and I love getting those requests. It's important to go out and see work you like, to listen to how others are integrating sound. Peer-to-peer friendships are important too. Since joining the ASD I feel more part of a community, and that other people are in similar positions to me facing similar problems.

How do you develop a relationship with a director?

I worked with a director for the first time recently, and we sent each other lots of film clips and music. She told me what she liked and what she *really* hated! We were able to triangulate each other's tastes in advance of rehearsals. If you can translate your sound design – for example, your desire to use processed reversed lawnmower sounds – into terms of narrative, or character, or emotion, then the director will more immediately be able to understand what you're aiming for.

What drives how you create the sounds in your show?

It's usually the script. I'm designing a new play at the National Theatre currently, an adaptation of a novel from 1740. I found a Bach piece written the same year with an interesting harmonic progression. I transcribed it and broke it apart to create the underscoring. It's difficult to begin to make a piece of work as there are so many directions to go, and that gave me something to hook into.

What's your approach to sound system design?

Early on I bought eight Genelec monitors, and they've been useful to experiment with ideas for complex, spatialized sound. That idea will be translated to a larger sound system in the theatre. I really like multi-channel, spatialized sound: I can work almost subliminally, creating an immersive environment where the audience has a more primal, emotive reaction to sound.

What part of your job do you enjoy the most?

There's something special about augmenting, or elevating, the work that the writer and performers are doing. It can be really special when you add something that takes the piece to another place. I enjoy the discovery of the first moments of playing my sounds over the theatre sound system, being able to hear and sculpt them, and to share that impact with an audience.

How do you deal with stress?

When someone is in a heightened state, it's often more effective to listen, to not react in the moment, and to wait until later to have a conversation. It can be quite harmful to get drawn into a high-temperature moment, so it's as much for self-preservation. It's important to share when and why you're stressed with the people you're working with – it's not about making it their problem, but it can be helpful to talk. And it's only art – there are other things in the world that are truly tricky. Meal breaks and fresh air are important; do look after yourself.

INDEX